OX-BIP

Department of Trade and Industry

Company Law Reform

**Presented to Parliament by the
Secretary of State for Trade and Industry
by Command of Her Majesty
March 2005**

Cm 6456   £36.25

The Department of Trade and Industry invites comments, by **10 June 2005**, on the issues set out in this consultative document.

You are invited to send comments, together with any supporting evidence on any part of this consultation, preferably by email to:

companylawreform@dti.gsi.gov.uk

or by letter to:

Patrick Barry
Corporate Law and Governance Directorate
Department of Trade and Industry
5th Floor
1 Victoria Street
London
SE1H 0ET
Telephone: 020 7215 6576

The document may be viewed from the Department's website at www.dti.gov.uk/cld/review.htm

Further printed copies of the document can be obtained from The Stationery Office: telephone 0870 600 5522 or email book.orders@tso.co.uk

Open Government: Under the Code of Practice on Access to Government Information comments may be made publicly available unless consultees state otherwise. Consultees should therefore indicate specifically if their responses should be treated as confidential (standard disclaimers will be disregarded for this purpose). A summary of all responses received will be prepared and circulated to all consultees who respond to this consultative document and anyone else who requests one. It will also be posted on the DTI website. The summary will not identify respondents.

We will handle any personal data which is provided in accordance with the requirements of the Data Protection Act 1998.

Contents

Foreword

A fair, modern, and effective framework of company law is crucial to our performance as an economy, and as a society. Britain was among the first nations to establish rules for the operation of companies, and our law remains a model for many nations overseas.

But over time the law can become outdated, and risks presenting obstacles to the ways companies want and need to do business in today's world. We are determined to avoid this. That is why we established the Company Law Review, to consider in detail how our law can best be modernised.

The Review has been universally recognised as providing a thorough and authoritative assessment of the sorts of changes which need to be made, and it provides the essential blueprint for the reforms we now propose. I am enormously grateful to all those who have participated in its work. We have continued to explore every opportunity for reform which will bring the law more into line with today's business needs, and remove unnecessary burdens, particularly from the smaller firms which are so critical to our economic health.

This White Paper sets out a range of measures for the proposed Company Law Reform Bill. They have been designed to further four crucial objectives:

- to enhance shareholder engagement and a long term investment culture;

- to ensure better regulation and a "Think Small First" approach;

- to make it easier to set up and run a company; and

- to provide flexibility for the future.

Taken together, I believe these measures represent a huge step forward in ensuring that our law remains up to date, flexible, and accessible for all those who use it. They are essential if we are to maintain our internationally competitive position, and I look forward to your comments.

The Rt Hon Patricia Hewitt MP
Secretary of State for Trade and Industry,
Minister for Women and e-Minister in Cabinet

1 Summary

This White Paper builds closely on the work of the Company Law Review (CLR), and of the Government's subsequent White Paper of 2002. The CLR itself conducted a series of public consultations before publishing its final report, and the Government has taken full account of that process, of responses to the White Paper, and of subsequent consultations, both formal and informal, in determining the policy measures now set out in this document. Draft clauses are included for a number of the areas.

Company law can be very complex, and there will be some interested parties (perhaps particularly smaller firms and their advisors) who will want to gain some understanding of the central measures proposed, but who may not wish to investigate the technical minutiae of how they will be delivered in legislation. Set out below, therefore, is a list of the key legislative changes. A separate small business summary has also been prepared, highlighting the measures likely to be of most interest to smaller firms and their advisors.

Summary of Legislative Changes

Enhancing shareholder engagement and a long-term investment culture

Shareholders are the lifeblood of a company, whatever its size. We want to promote wide participation of shareholders, ensuring that they are informed and involved, as they should be. And we want decisions to be made based on the longer-term view and not just immediate return. We will:

- embed in statute the concept of Enlightened Shareholder Value by making clear that directors must promote the success of the company for the benefit of its shareholders, and this can only be achieved by taking due account of both the long-term and short-term, and wider factors such as employees, effects on the environment, suppliers and customers;

- introduce a statutory statement of directors' duties to clarify their responsibilities and improve the law regulating directors' conflicts of interest;

- relax the prohibition on provisions which prevent auditors from limiting their liability, while delivering further improvements in the quality of the audit;

- enhance the rights of proxies and make it easier for companies to enfranchise indirect owners of shares;

- remove the requirement for paper share certificates and facilitate the use by companies of e-communications where their shareholders want this;

- implement the Takeovers Directive that will facilitate takeover activity in the EU through improved shareholder protection and access to capital markets.

Ensuring better regulation and a "Think Small First" approach

Although the vast majority of UK companies are small, company law has been written traditionally with the large company in mind. We want to reset the balance and make the law easier for all to understand and use. We will:

- provide separate and better-adapted default articles (the current "Table A") for private companies;

- simplify decision-making for private companies, for example by making it easier for decisions to be taken by written resolution, and making Annual General Meetings (AGMs) opt-in rather than opt-out;

- abolish the requirement for private companies to have a company secretary;

- update company financial and narrative reports;

- simplify the rules about company share capital in particular for private companies;

- implement some aspects of the European Transparency Directive;

- introduce a power to allow the law to be restated where necessary in future to make it accessible.

In addition to the changes in the law itself, the Government will be ensuring that there is appropriate advice and guidance available to users of company law, particularly smaller firms and their advisors, so that all can understand the options available to them and the requirements placed upon them.

Making it easier to set up and run a company

We want to remove unnecessary burdens to directors and preserve Britain's reputation as a favoured country in which to incorporate. We will:

- remove the requirement on most directors to disclose publicly their home address;

- abolish the requirement for a company to have authorised share capital;

- enable a single person to form a public company;

- streamline the rules on company names and trading disclosures;

- make deregulatory changes to the register of past and present members which companies are obliged to maintain.

Providing flexibility for the future

- Company law is not static. We intend to introduce a new reform power to allow updating and amendment as circumstances dictate, subject to rigorous safeguards for full consultation and appropriate Parliamentary scrutiny.

Benefits to business

The Government believes that the measures above, by making company law better fitted to today's realities, should create improved performance across the economy as whole, as well as reducing direct compliance costs for business and producing cost savings which could amount to some £250m a year.

How to respond

The Government would welcome views on any aspects of the proposals. Responses should be sent, by **10 June 2005**, by email to:

companylawreform@dti.gsi.gov.uk

or by letter to:

Patrick Barry
Company Law Reform Bill
5th Floor
1 Victoria Street
London SW1H 0ET

Additional copies of this document are available from The Stationery Office: telephone 0870 600 5522 or email book.orders@tso.co.uk

An electronic version is available on the DTI website at www.dti.gov.uk/cld/review.htm

2 Setting the Scene

The Government is committed to ensuring that the legal and regulatory framework within which business operates promotes enterprise, growth and the right conditions for investment and employment.

Our system of company law and corporate governance is a critical part of this framework. It sets out the legal basis on which companies are formed, operated and managed. It provides the corporate vehicle which enables people to collaborate in business, and the legal structure through which companies are financed, ultimately by millions of savers and pensioners. It sets the rules for company boards and shareholders and for the exercise of decisions on business growth and investment. And it is the means by which people are held to account for the exercise of corporate economic power.

For these reasons, an effective framework of company law and corporate governance is a key building block of a modern economy. A genuinely modern and effective framework can promote enterprise, enhance competitiveness and stimulate investment. Conversely, an ineffective or outmoded framework can inhibit productivity and growth and undermine investment confidence. The high profile corporate collapses of recent years – including Enron, Worldcom and Parmalat – have demonstrated the critical importance to the modern global economy of robust frameworks for corporate activity, and the far-reaching economic consequences when these fail.

Our objectives

That is why we are committed to creating a modern, enabling and robust framework for our companies. We are determined to ensure that our system of company law and corporate governance is one which:

*   facilitates enterprise by making it easy to set up and grow a business;

*   encourages the efficient allocation of capital by giving confidence to investors;

*   promotes long-term company performance through shareholder engagement and effective dialogue between business and investors; and

*   maintains the UK's position as one of the most attractive places in the world to set up and run a business.

Global challenge

This last point is critical. Our framework must reflect the challenges of modern capital markets in which business and investment decisions are increasingly determined by global conditions. More and more companies are operating internationally. Increasingly, businesses can make choices as to where to incorporate, and recent legal judgments are tending to make such cross-border incorporations easier. Similarly, investors can choose where to put their money – around a third of stock in listed UK companies is now held by overseas owners, more than twice the level in 1993.

This increasingly global marketplace is reflected in changes in regulatory conditions – for example the move towards global convergence of accounting standards, so that ultimately companies should be able to prepare their accounts on the same basis, wherever in the world they are listed. It is also reflected in developments at European level, where there is already a large body of European law and where the Commission's Company Law and Corporate Governance Action Plan is focused on fostering the global efficiency and competitiveness of EU businesses, strengthening shareholders' rights and third party protection and rebuilding the confidence of investors.

The Government supports the Action Plan as a platform for action to remove barriers to the efficient operation of markets, make it easier for companies to set up cross-border operations, extend investment opportunities for investors and improve access to, and the availability of, capital across Europe. As in the UK, it believes that EU action should be facilitative and enable enterprise and entrepreneurship to flourish. The aim must be to promote growth, competitiveness and jobs, not put new barriers in the way of economic activity.

The recent Sarbanes-Oxley legislation in the US, enacted in response to the Enron and Worldcom collapses, has also had important consequences for companies and investors around the world.

UK response

In Britain, we have acted decisively to recognise and anticipate these challenges. In 1998, the Government commissioned the Company Law Review (CLR), an independent group of experts, practitioners and business people, to take a long-term and fundamental look at our underpinning system of company law, to see how it could be brought up to date. Many of the proposals for legislative change contained in this White Paper are a result of that Review.

The CLR is part of a wider programme of action to facilitate enterprise, encourage investment, promote long-term company performance and ensure that Britain remains one of the best places in the world to set up and run a business:

- we have brought forward the **Companies (Audit, Investigations and Community Enterprise) Act 2004 (the C(AICE) Act)** to ensure better oversight and stronger regulation of the accounting and audit profession, to increase investor confidence in company reporting and enforcement, and to strengthen powers to investigate companies. The Act has been widely welcomed as a robust but measured response to recent corporate scandals which strikes the right balance between strengthening market confidence and avoiding unnecessarily prescriptive and burdensome regulation. In addition, it encourages the development of the social enterprise sector by making it possible to form a new type of company, the "community interest company", whose profits and assets must be used for the benefit of the community;

- we have laid draft regulations which will require all quoted companies to produce an **Operating and Financial Review (OFR)**. The OFR is a new form of narrative report in which companies will need to describe future strategies, resources, risks and uncertainties, including policies in relation to employees and the environment where these are relevant to future strategy and performance. The requirement to produce an OFR represents a further major step forward in improving company reporting and transparency and in promoting effective dialogue on the key drivers of long-term company performance. It also recognises that in a modern economy, those who run successful companies need to develop relationships with employees, customers, suppliers and others which support long-term value creation;

- we have introduced the **Directors' Remuneration Report Regulations 2002**, which require quoted companies to disclose and seek shareholder approval for their executive remuneration policies, and to disclose how remuneration relates to performance. Recently-published research by Deloittes has demonstrated that these Regulations have led to substantial and direct improvements in the transparency of executive remuneration. More fundamentally, the Regulations have acted as a catalyst for increasing company accountability and effective shareholder engagement; and

- we have raised the **audit thresholds** for turnover and balance sheet totals to £5.6m and £2.8m respectively, taking some 69,000 companies out of the requirement to have their accounts professionally audited.

The Government's approach has not relied on legislation alone. One of the key strengths of our framework for corporate activity is that it has been developed in close partnership with market participants. This is reflected in the way we have worked alongside businesses, professionals and investors in driving reform and modernisation:

- the **Financial Reporting Council's** powers of oversight and enforcement have been substantially increased and extended by the C(AICE) Act. But it remains a light-touch, market-led regulator, which derives its funding equally from listed companies, the accountancy profession and Government and which, through its Council and Board, operates with the full cooperation and involvement of companies, investors and the profession;

- under the aegis of the Financial Reporting Council, a new **Combined Code on Corporate Governance** was published in July 2003 which incorporates many of the changes recommended in an independent review by Sir Derek Higgs, aimed at strengthening the independence and effectiveness of non-executive directors;

- to promote more active **shareholder engagement**, particularly where shareholders have concerns about management, strategy or performance, the Government welcomed the Institutional Shareholders' Committee principles in October 2002, and the commitment to reflect these principles in fund management contracts and insurance fund practice. The ISC is assessing the effectiveness of the principles in achieving change and the Government will take this into consideration when reviewing their impact on engagement;

- UK institutional investors manage almost half of UK equities, investing much of the long-term wealth of British savers and exercising indirect control and significant influence over much of British industry. This ownership is intermediated through an **investment chain** of relationships connecting ultimate owners with their investment in companies. Ensuring this chain works efficiently is of vital economic importance for productivity and long term growth, because the chain is a critical mechanism for ensuring that investment is efficiently allocated. The Government has systematically investigated how well the investment chain works, notably through the Myners, Sandler and Higgs reviews, and in the light of the analyses and recommendations of these reviews, has undertaken a comprehensive reform programme;

- a separate report by Paul Myners to the Shareholder Voting Working Group focused on the practical steps which market participants must take to improve the **effectiveness of the voting process** and has been well received. DTI has agreed to implement the report's legislative recommendations;

- in order to ensure that company accounts are subjected to **high-quality and independent audit**, the new Combined Code also strengthens the role of the audit committee in the light of the report from Sir Robert Smith. Audit firms have introduced more frequent rotation of audit partners and longer cooling-off periods before an auditor can be recruited by a client; and

- we have worked alongside business to take forward the recommendations of Sir Derek Higgs and Laura Tyson aimed at extending the **diversity and effectiveness of company boards**. Proposals for further action are set out in "Better Boards", published in December 2004.

Further reform and the Company Law Review

All these developments have contributed to our objective of creating a modern, enabling framework which facilitates enterprise and market confidence. But the role played by the underlying law governing the day-to-day operation of companies remains critical to business competitiveness.

Our company law reform programme is focused on four key objectives:

- Enhancing shareholder engagement and a long-term investment culture

- Ensuring better regulation and a "Think Small First" approach

- Making it easier to set up and run a company

- Providing flexibility for the future.

Enhancing shareholder engagement and a long-term investment culture

Companies work best where there is a good understanding and effective engagement between those who own companies, and those who run them on their behalf. In order to achieve this, roles and responsibilities need to be clearly defined, and there needs to be efficient and transparent mechanisms for ensuring that views are heard and decisions taken. Measures in the Bill will provide better guidance for directors on their responsibilities and duties, ensure more effective and efficient communication with shareholders, and make it easier for shareholders, including indirect investors, to exercise their rights of ownership. These changes are aimed at ensuring that directors and shareholders can work together in a way which promotes long-term company performance and value creation.

Ensuring better regulation and a "Think Small First" approach

Our company law was originally designed for large companies with numerous public investors. The current companies legislation generally works by offering smaller private companies exemptions from a fundamental framework which was designed for larger companies. But today the vast majority of companies are smaller – often owner-managed – and have different needs, with over 90% of companies having five shareholders or fewer.

For these companies, laws designed to regulate larger companies with a publicly-traded share ownership are burdensome and impose unnecessary costs. Wherever possible, the Government wants the new law to recognise smaller private companies not as the exception, but as the rule. We will therefore remove unnecessary burdens on small firms and present the provisions they use most often in a more accessible way. We will also ensure that small companies and their advisors can readily access guidance on what they need to know about the law.

Making it easier to set up and run a company

Compared with many other countries, it is relatively easy and cheap to set up a company here. The Government believes this is an important benefit to Britain – start-ups are one of the crucial motors of our economic growth, and more and more companies from overseas are seeking to incorporate here. But there are still some procedural requirements that can complicate both the setting up of a company, and its initial operation – for example, the default requirement for all companies, even the smallest, to hold an Annual General Meeting, and the requirement to appoint a company secretary. Where these obstacles can sensibly be removed, the Bill will remove them.

Providing flexibility for the future

The measures in this Bill demonstrate that law which was appropriate at one time may become an obstacle when times change. The Government believes it is crucial that there should be some measure of flexibility built into the company law framework to ensure that it can be kept up-to-date in future, subject to appropriate processes of public consultation and Parliamentary scrutiny. The Bill will provide this.

The way ahead

The CLR consulted widely with legal experts, business and practitioners in drawing up its recommendations. As a result the work of the CLR has been universally recognised as providing an authoritative assessment of the changes needed to ensure that our framework of company law remains at the forefront of international competitiveness. For this reason, the CLR's principles (and the vast majority of its specific recommendations) are firmly reflected in the Government's reform proposals.

In addition the Government has continued to take account of market developments and to discuss both the general approach to reform, and where appropriate specific proposals, with the business and legal communities and wider stakeholder interests. We intend to continue to work in partnership with these interests in keeping our law responsive and flexible. In particular, we have consulted extensively on ideas for deregulatory change, with a view to ensuring that unnecessary burdens are removed wherever practicable. Our assessment suggests that the proposals for reform set out in this White Paper will produce savings for business of around £250m a year. We would welcome any responses to this document which suggest additional areas for removing unnecessary burdens.

Approach to legislation

The Company Law Reform Bill will include amended and restated provisions of particular importance to small companies in their day-to-day operations. The Bill will set out the revised provisions in a new, more logical and easily accessible way. These areas will include such core policy areas as formation, and meetings and resolutions. It is also intended that the provisions on reports and accounts should be restated in a more accessible way. Some clauses which show the approach proposed for the content of small company reports and accounts are included in this document.

The Bill will also include new provisions setting out the duties of directors.

In other areas, the new Bill will introduce specific amendments to the Companies Act 1985. However, the scale of these changes and the nature of the provisions being amended will mean that it will not be necessary or appropriate always to restate entire areas of that Act in a new form. These are largely the more technical areas, of greater interest to larger companies, and the effect of the provisions will be to amend the 1985 Act.

This document provides a description of the policy so that all those with an interest in the area can understand what is intended. For many areas, draft clauses are included. (The draft clauses will not necessarily appear in the Bill in the order given here). In some areas, detailed clauses are still being worked on and drafts are not included. Some draft regulations which will be brought forward in parallel are also included. The DTI website provides a more detailed commentary on the key clauses (www.dti.gov.uk/cld/review.htm).

The Government welcomes all comments on what is proposed.

3 Enhancing Shareholder Engagement and a Long-Term Investment Culture

The Government believes that companies work best where the respective roles and responsibilities of directors and members or shareholders are clearly understood, where there is effective communication and engagement between directors and shareholders, and where there are efficient mechanisms for taking decisions critical to the running of the company.

The Government's proposals in this area, which are based upon the CLR's analysis, therefore aim to ensure greater transparency and accountability within the company's operations, and greater opportunity for all shareholders to play an informed part in company business.

As part of this, the Bill will provide greater clarity on what is expected of directors, making it easier for all to understand what those duties are. In particular the Bill will make clear that, while directors must promote the success of the company for the benefit of its members, this can only be achieved by taking due account of longer term performance and wider interests, such as the interest of its employees and the impact of the company's operations on the community and on the environment.

3.1   Improving shareholder dialogue

Shareholders have a key role to play in driving long-term company performance and economic prosperity. Informed, engaged shareholders – or those acting on their behalf – are the means by which the directors are held to account for business strategy and performance and by which investment decisions are taken which reflect the most efficient allocation of capital. However the investment chain has become increasingly complex, with the result that communication up and down the chain and the exercise of ownership rights and responsibilities have become more difficult.

For this reason, the Government has already taken a number of steps to increase effective shareholder engagement and the efficient working of the investment chain, including action to require all quoted companies to seek shareholder approval for the directors' remuneration report and to produce an Operating and Financial Review, as well as action in response to the Myners,

Sandler and Higgs reviews. We intend to build on these reforms by introducing a number of measures in this Bill aimed at improving communication with shareholders and indirect investors and encouraging the exercise of ownership rights.

Access to timely, transparent company information

It is important that shareholders have access to clear and meaningful information to enable them to have a constructive dialogue and increase their engagement with the company in which they hold shares. The Bill will introduce a number of measures to enhance the timeliness and transparency of company information and proceedings:

- The holding of the Annual General Meeting (AGM) will be linked to the reporting cycle to ensure shareholders have a timely opportunity to hold the directors to account. The current law requires companies to hold an AGM once a year and there can be as long a gap as 15 months between AGMs. The Bill will require public companies to hold their AGM within 6 months of the end of the financial year.

- Quoted companies will be required to put on their website the preliminary announcements of their annual results and their full accounts and reports. This information must be made available to all members of the public and not just to members.

- Shareholders of quoted companies will have a right within a 15-day holding period after the accounts become available to propose a resolution to be moved at the general meeting where the accounts are laid (usually the AGM). Such resolutions would be circulated at the company's expense.

- Quoted companies will also be required to disclose on their websites the results of polls at general meetings. This will ensure increased transparency for shareholders, whether as registered members of the company or as indirect investors, of decisions taken at general meetings.

- Shareholders of quoted companies will also have a new right, if a certain specified minority so request, to require an independent scrutiny of any polled vote. The Bill will also provide that the scrutiny report of any poll must be disclosed on the company's website.

The Government believes that there is a good case for improving voting disclosure and wants to see effective accountability by institutional investors. This will improve transparency and lead to better engagement with companies by institutional investors. In line with this approach, the Government will continue to explore the proposal that institutional investors should be required to disclose how their voting rights have been exercised. The practicalities of this approach need to be examined against alternatives such as operating through a statement of principles, such as those issued by the Institutional Shareholder Committee.

Facilitating e-communications

The use of new information and communications technologies has grown rapidly over recent years, which presents great opportunities to reduce costs and enhance the immediacy and transparency of dialogue between companies and shareholders. These developments were not anticipated at the time that the majority of the provisions in existing company law were first put in place decades ago. Existing provisions of company law impose a number of requirements about the use of paper communications, which can prevent both companies and shareholders from enjoying all the cost-savings and other benefits that sensible use of new communications technology can bring. For example, at present the Companies Act requires companies to send every shareholder the full annual report and accounts or a summary version. Unless the shareholder positively opts for electronic communication this must be in paper. In practice, while many shareholders do not need or want to receive a paper copy, very few have taken up the electronic option. The resulting costs of printing and sending paper copies of the annual report can be considerable, particularly for a large quoted company with tens of thousands or even a million or more shareholders.

The Government therefore intends to allow all companies, subject to shareholder approval, to be able to use electronic communications with shareholders as the default position, permitting (but not requiring) companies to use websites and e-mail to communicate with their registered members. Of course, electronic communication will not suit everyone. Individuals will be able to request continued communication on paper if they wish. Nonetheless, the overall reduction in paper circulation expected could produce very significant cost savings, particularly for companies with large numbers of registered members.

3.2   Enfranchising indirect investors

When investors – whether major institutional investors or retail investors – buy shares in a listed company, they are increasingly likely to hold their shares through an intermediary or a chain of intermediaries.

The use of intermediaries makes electronic trading of shares easier and cheaper, but it can also be a regulatory requirement for example in relation to shares held as part of ISAs. However, as it is the intermediary's name that appears on the company's register of members, indirect investors risk losing their governance rights. There is no automatic basis in company law for a direct relationship between a company and these indirect investors. Instead the indirect investors may have to rely on contractual arrangements with the intermediaries to pass on at least some basic information and dividends from the company and to act on their instructions.

The Bill will therefore enhance the ability of indirect investors – those not holding legal title to the shares of the company in which they invest – to play a fuller role in company proceedings.

- *Exercising rights through proxy*. The Bill will ensure that the registered shareholder can nominate a proxy or proxies who can, on their behalf, attend and speak at meetings, demand a poll, and vote on a show of hands or on a poll. This will enable those indirect investors acting as proxies to the registered shareholder to exercise all the participation rights which would otherwise rest with the registered shareholder alone.

- *Exercise of governance rights*. The Bill will make it easier for indirect investors to exercise governance rights. Some companies already make their own provisions through their articles to recognise and enfranchise their indirect investors, but the present best practice can involve considerable detailed bespoke legal advice and drafting to set out complex provisions in a company's articles. This is expensive and time consuming. In future where a company makes provisions in its articles to enfranchise indirect investors, then to the extent provided in the company articles, reference to registered members and their rights in primary legislation should be extended to include those designated by the registered member. The end result will be greater parity of treatment in law for registered members and indirect investors for the exercise of governance rights as specified in the company's articles.

- *Right to information power*. In addition, the Bill will include a reserve power for the Secretary of State to compel some or all public companies to provide information – electronically – to persons having an interest in shares if the registered member requests. At present the intermediary, as the registered member, is only entitled to one set of information and, if this is all it receives, it cannot currently pass this on to all the indirect investors. Some companies are happy to provide more copies, but others have been reluctant because of the cost involved. Some intermediaries also have not wanted to incur the costs involved in mailing the information out to the indirect investors. However, it is now increasingly reasonable to assume that indirect shareholders will have access to the internet. Electronic delivery avoids most of the costs of paper, is much quicker and more practical particularly when forwarding through a chain of intermediaries. It is anticipated that the Secretary of State's power will only be exercised if the market does not develop appropriate solutions to ensure that indirect investors have access to information they require to engage in the governance of the companies in which they invest.

3.3 Directors

Directors' duties

The general duties which directors owe to the company are at the moment found in case law – i.e. decisions in individual court cases over the years – rather than in the Companies Act. As a result, those who become company directors may do so without understanding their obligations under the law. Those obligations may also not be understood by the members of the companies, in whose interests the directors should be acting. Both the CLR and the Law Commissions believed that there was a need to make the law in this area more consistent, certain, accessible and comprehensible, and recommended that there should be a statutory statement of directors' general duties. The Government agrees that directors' duties are fundamental to company law, and that it is very important that the duties are widely known and understood. The Bill will therefore introduce a statutory statement of directors' general duties.

- The statutory statement of duties will replace existing common law and equitable rules. The duties will be owed to the company, and – as now – only the company will be able to enforce them. (In certain circumstances, the shareholders may be able to bring a derivative action, albeit essentially for the company's benefit.)

- The statement of duties will be drafted in a way which reflects modern business needs and wider expectations of responsible business behaviour. The CLR proposed that the basic goal for directors should be the success of the company for the benefit of its members as a whole; but that, to reach this goal, directors would need to take a properly balanced view of the implications of decisions over time and foster effective relationships with employees, customers and suppliers, and in the community more widely. The Government strongly agrees that this approach, which the CLR called "enlightened shareholder value", is most likely to drive long-term company performance and maximise overall competitiveness and wealth and welfare for all. It will therefore be reflected in the statement of directors' duties, and in new reporting arrangements for quoted companies under the Operating and Financial Review Regulations.

- The statement will address circumstances where there is a conflict between a director's duties to the company and his or her personal interests or duties to others. It is important however that the duties do not impose impractical and onerous requirements which stifle entrepreneurial activity. The CLR recognised that this might happen in circumstances where a director wished to exploit a business opportunity which might also be exploited by the company. Normally at the moment directors have to obtain the members' agreement, even if the company does not wish to exploit the opportunity or has already decided to abandon the opportunity. The statutory statement will implement the CLR's recommendation that the company's rights might be waived by the board, acting independently of any conflicted director.

- At present, there are a number of remedies for breaches of the duties, including the payment of damages by way of compensation where the director's action is considered negligent and the restoration of company property where assets have been misappropriated. The statement of duties will not change this.

- The statutory duties will apply to all persons acting as director. They will also apply to shadow directors, although there will be aspects of the duties that must apply differently to shadow directors.

- It is important that the statement of duties enables the law to respond to changing business circumstances and needs. It will therefore leave scope for the courts to interpret and develop its provisions in a way that reflects the nature and effect of the principles they reflect.

- The statement of duties should be widely accessible and understood. The Government will therefore publish plain language guidance explaining the statutory duties.

Regulating directors' conflicts of interest

Part 10 of the Companies Act 1985 contains a variety of provisions designed to deal with situations in which a director has a conflict of interest. The provisions are intended to clarify the director's general duties to the company in areas where conflicts of interest commonly arise, such as the making of loans by a company to a director.

The present mixture of regulation in Part 10 has grown up piecemeal, without any attempt to look at directors' transactions with their company in the round. As a result, the provisions of Part 10 are widely regarded as excessively complex and fragmented. The Government does not favour repeal of these provisions: as respondents to the CLR and the Law Commissions made clear, codification of the general duties will not in itself prevent the abuses which caused these provisions to be enacted. We have also been mindful of the argument that directors may find better guidance in clear statutory rules than in general principles. At the same time, it is clear that Part 10 is in need of major reform, and the Bill will restate, as well as amend, the current requirements. We have had five main aims in our reform of Part 10:

- the Bill will simplify the overall structure, so that the provisions are more accessible to directors and other users. In particular, types of transaction requiring shareholder approval – including property transactions; loans, quasi-loans and credit transactions; and *ex gratia* payments for loss of office – have been brought together; and, where appropriate, the clauses have been drafted so as to facilitate comparison between the requirements in these areas;

- the Bill will deregulate where the existing provisions are unnecessary or excessive. In particular, companies will be able to make loans to directors with the consent of shareholders. This is a significant reform which will provide a simple and, in many cases, readily applicable method of ensuring compliance;

- the Bill will remove existing loopholes e.g. by requiring directors to disclose the interests of connected persons if they would have to be disclosed if they were the director's interests, and by broadening the definition of a director's service contract in relation to the requirement that they be open to inspection by shareholders;

- the Bill will reflect modern business behaviour e.g. by requiring disclosure of interests to other directors as soon as is reasonably practicable, and by giving shareholders the right to receive copies of directors' service contracts on payment of a fee; and

- the Bill will clarify the law where the existing provisions are unclear or incomplete e.g. by making it clear that the rules relating to *ex gratia* payments for loss of office do not extend to payments that a company is bound to pay to a director on his retirement or other loss of office because it has a legally binding obligation to do so.

Disclosure requirements can play an important role in the regulation of directors' conflicts of interest, but it is important that such requirements are proportionate and not excessively complex. Parts 2 and 3 of Schedule 6 to the Companies Act 1985 currently set out the information about loans and other dealings in favour of directors which must be provided in the notes to a company's annual accounts. The information required is extensive and the provisions not properly understood by many directors and users of accounts. The Government is therefore considering whether the requirements relating to disclosure of transactions in which directors are interested might be simplified without any loss of necessary protection to shareholders.

Directors' liability

The law on directors' liability needs to strike a careful balance: on the one hand, the law must be firm and robust to deal fairly with cases where something has gone wrong, as a result of either negligence or of dishonesty; on the other, Britain needs a diverse pool of high-quality individuals willing to assume the role of company director, and a willingness by directors to take informed and rational risks.

The Government consulted on these issues in December 2003. In the light of the responses, it introduced two important reforms through the C(AICE) Act 2004. These are the most significant changes to the law on directors' liability for nearly 80 years. As a result from 6 April 2005 companies may:

- indemnify directors against most liabilities to third parties; and

- pay directors' legal costs upfront, provided that the director repays if he or she is convicted in any criminal proceedings or judgement is given against him or her in any civil proceedings brought by the company or an associated company.

The response to these reforms has been very positive, and we believe that they address the most important issues raised by respondents to the consultation.

Some consultees also favoured further reform of the law to permit companies to limit directors' liability to the company for breach of the duty of care, skill and diligence. The Government explained in Parliament that this would need to be considered alongside the statement of directors' duties now set out in draft in this White Paper. It would for example be possible to permit shareholders if they wished to agree some limit on directors' liability for negligence without permitting them to limit the liability of any directors who put personal interests before their duty to the company. The Government will continue to consider whether concerns about potential liability for negligence are affecting director recruitment and behaviour, and, if so, whether such concerns justify a further change in the law.

Who can be a director?

One of the flexibilities of British company law is that it allows all legal persons (for example, other companies) to be company directors in the same way as if they were individuals. This flexibility can sometimes be abused by those who wish to conceal who is controlling a company (for example those intending to commit fraud may use a company with corporate directors to help obscure the identity of the individuals involved), and the Government considered the option of banning corporate directors. Equally however, an outright ban might harm those companies who make use of the current flexibilities for entirely legitimate reasons.

We therefore propose that the Bill should include a requirement that at least one director be a natural person. This provision is intended to ensure that every company will have at least one individual who can, if necessary, be held to account for the company's actions. It is also consistent with the increased thrust being placed in the Bill on the importance of directors understanding their statutory duties.

Each company can set its own rules for who appoints its directors. It is for the company to ensure that it appoints persons who not only understand their duties but also take full responsibility for their actions and omissions. The Bill will therefore remove the restrictions on directors over 70 years old, at the same time as providing that 16 will be the minimum age for a director. This prohibition of child directors will need transitional provisions. In particular, any child under 16 appointed after publication of this White Paper will not be entitled to financial compensation in respect of early termination from office resulting from the introduction of the prohibition.

3.4   Minority shareholder rights

Derivative actions are the route by which shareholders, usually minority shareholders, are able to enforce the company's rights where directors have breached their duties, (since in these circumstances it is unlikely that the directors, who usually act on behalf of the company, will want to take action). They are therefore an important mechanism by which shareholders can hold directors to account for the proper exercise of their duties in pursuit of their company's short and long-term interests. Derivative actions are currently available to shareholders in certain circumstances as a matter of common law, not statute.

The Bill will therefore put derivative actions on a statutory footing. This proposal has been recommended by the Law Commission and endorsed by the CLR. The Bill will also clarify the complex provisions on alteration of class rights, and extend them to companies without share capital.

3.5   Auditor liability and audit quality

The Government is keen to encourage confidence in the statutory audit and to ensure a strong, competitive and high quality audit market. To help in this, over the course of the past two years the Government has promoted debate to identify further ways by which these goals can be achieved.

In the aftermath of a company failure, those who have suffered losses may look to the auditors as having the "deepest pockets" of all of those they can pursue for compensation. Consequently, the auditor may bear 100% of the compensation even though the auditors' "share" of the blame (when compared to other culpable parties) may be less. Theoretically, this makes audit firms vulnerable to very large claims where they are held to have been negligent in their conduct of an audit. In practice, however, most claims are settled out of court.

In December 2003, the Government launched a public consultation on director and auditor liability. This showed clear support for changes to the law on directors' liability, and appropriate provisions were included in the Companies (Audit Investigations and Community Enterprise) Act 2004. These come into force next month. The responses on auditor liability were more mixed and the Government concluded that it would be inappropriate to permit the capping of auditors' liability to a predetermined amount. However, it invited auditors, their clients and investors to work together to consider other approaches by which liability might be limited, and in parallel to identify ways to improve audit quality and enhance competition. The Government is grateful for the helpful and constructive approach adopted by all contributors.

In the light of that work, the Government is now persuaded of the benefits of change. The reforms will have three key parts – firstly, legislating to allow shareholders to agree limitations to the liability of auditors; secondly, some specific improvements to the quality of the audit process; and, thirdly, the establishment of an on-going process by which further enhancements to quality and competition can be identified and then implemented. The Government sees these three parts making up a balanced package of measures to improve the audit market, and believes it is important that all of these go forward together.

The Government believes that it would be inappropriate to change the law on who can sue the auditors in the civil courts. However, given the wider importance of audited financial statements, the Government proposes to make it a criminal offence knowingly or recklessly to give an incorrect audit opinion.

Proportionate liability by contract

The Government proposes that shareholders should be able to agree a limit to the auditor's liability for damage incurred by a company, to such an amount that is determined by the Courts to be just and equitable, having regard to the relative extent of responsibility of the auditor for the damage incurred.

Specifically, the Government proposes that:

- such a limitation would apply in situations where damage to the company has been caused through the (mis)conduct of an audit, to the extent the Court considers just and equitable in the circumstances of the case;

- the company would be left to recover, as part of a separate action, the loss suffered for which some other defendant (e.g. another professional advisor) was responsible;

- the auditor would continue to be fully liable for any fraud to which he or she was party;

- the company could not agree in advance a monetary limit to the auditor's liability. This means there would be no scope for maxima set as cash sums, or expressed in accordance with a quantifiable formula (for example, as a multiple of the audit fee); and

- only those causes of action arising after the commencement of the legislation would be subject to the proposed provisions.

In practical terms this would mean that, as now, with the authority of the shareholders, the directors of the company would negotiate the scope, terms and cost of the audit contract. The directors would decide how much weight should be given to factors which might influence the terms of the audit, such as the cost and availability of insurance, the attitudes to risk of the directors, shareholders and auditors and the directors' perception of the level of competition between audit firms. In addition, if the shareholders had given explicit agreement, the contract with the auditors could include a limitation of the auditor liability as set out above. The Government proposes that shareholder agreement to such limitation should be required each year and in advance of each year's audit.

The Government also proposes that the existence of any limitation of liability would be shown in the company's annual financial statements. The auditor should also provide a list of all companies with which it has agreed a limitation of liability in its own annual financial statements.

Improvements in audit quality and value

The Government welcomes the four specific proposals from auditors, their clients and investors for improvements in audit transparency and to support shareholder involvement in the audit process.

These initiatives are:

- *Publication of audit engagement letters:* there is widespread support for publicly disclosing the content of audit engagement letters. This will increase transparency and enable third parties to understand better the scope of the audit and the terms on which it has been undertaken.

- *Shareholders rights to question auditors:* it has been proposed that shareholders be able to question auditors about the audit. The Government is considering proposals that, building on recent changes in Australia, might involve enabling shareholders to question the auditor in advance of AGMs, or by writing to the auditor, via the company, with reasonable questions. All queries must relate to the auditors' report or to the conduct of the audit.

- *Publication of auditor resignation statements:* there is widespread support for fuller disclosure of information in auditors' resignation letters, to enable investors to understand the reasons for the resignation. The law currently requires an auditor either to state that there are no circumstances connected with his or her resignation that need be brought to the attention of members or creditors of the company, or else to set out the circumstances for the company to circulate. Experience suggests that the risks of legal action may be inhibiting the frankness of such statements, and all concerned are keen to improve transparency.

- *Audit lead partner's signature on audit reports:* finally, it has been recommended that the lead audit partner on an audit should be required to sign and print his or her own name on the audit report, in addition to the name of the audit company undertaking the audit. It is expected that this will serve to improve audit standards by encouraging further personal responsibility for the actions taken by the audit team.

The Government welcomes in principle these initiatives and the Financial Reporting Council and the Department of Trade and Industry are taking them forward. It is intended that any necessary changes to the law will be included in the Bill, alongside the provisions on auditor liability.

Longer-term reform

The Government is grateful to the Institute of Chartered Accountants in England & Wales (ICAEW) for helping establish a "quality forum". The Government believes that this advisory body, made up of representatives of auditors, investors, business and regulatory bodies, is playing a valuable role in facilitating communication between business, auditors and investors, and generating practical ideas to improve audit quality.

The Government and the Financial Reporting Council will be working with stakeholders to continue to identify further ways in which quality and competition in the audit market can be enhanced.

3.6 Company Takeovers

The Takeovers Directive – which completed the European legislative process in April 2004 – lays down minimum standards for takeover regulation across the Community, and applies many of the core values of the UK system at the EU level. It will also reduce barriers to takeovers in the Community through improved shareholder protection and access to capital markets.

Takeover regulation in the UK has been overseen by the Takeover Panel, essentially on a non-statutory basis, for the past 36 years. Implementation of the Takeovers Directive requires the introduction of a statutory framework but the intention is to preserve the independence and authority of the Takeover Panel and its capacity to make and enforce rules regulating takeover activity. The Department published a consultative document – available at www.dti.gov.uk/cld/current.htm – on 20 January 2005, setting out proposals for implementing the Directive. The consultation period is open until 15 April 2005.

The Bill will include provisions to implement the Takeovers Directive and place the Takeover Panel on a statutory footing. The precise nature of these provisions will be determined in the light of the responses to consultation.

4 Ensuring better regulation and a "Think Small First" approach

4.1 Improving accessibility

Clearer structure and language

Although the vast majority of UK companies are small, company law has been written traditionally with the large company in mind. The provisions that apply to private companies are frequently expressed as a tailpiece to the provisions applying to public companies. Examples of this include the frequently consulted current Part 7 of the Act (Accounts and Audit), which many users find hard to follow, and the provisions on meetings and resolutions, which are currently structured largely on the basis of the needs of larger (public) companies, with smaller (private) companies covered by way of additional provisions or exceptions.

The Government intends that the Bill should reset the balance and make the law easier for all to understand and use. The Bill will therefore be structured in such a way that the provisions which apply to small companies are very much easier to find. Where the law is hard to understand, there are significant costs, uncertainty and risks and compliance is reduced. The Bill therefore seeks to achieve much greater simplicity and clarity of language.

This policy runs as a thread through the drafting of all the provisions of the new Bill and, wherever possible, it is intended that the new law should be presented in an accessible and user-friendly fashion. In particular, where the Bill is making substantive changes with the effect of replacing entire portions of the existing Act, the opportunities for presenting the new law in a simpler and more coherent way are great and have been fully taken up. The Government believes that these areas, in particular those relating to company formation, and to meetings and decision-taking, are now more clearly and logically drafted. Reporting requirements for small companies have also been set out in a much clearer way. Consultation has confirmed that these areas are also those which smaller firms, in particular, find most important in their day-to-day operations, and the benefits of achieving more accessible law should be correspondingly significant.

Better guidance

Many parts of company law are nevertheless inherently complex and if we are to make it easier to understand for both companies and their advisors it is important that it is supplemented by clear and comprehensive guidance. Companies House already provides extensive and well respected plain English guidance both in booklet form and increasingly through their website. We intend to increase the coverage of this guidance. It will in future include aspects of company law that go beyond a company's responsibilities in relation to Companies House, for example, we will publish clear new guidance on the important area of directors' duties. Guidance will also follow the principles of "Think Small First." The great majority of companies are small and we will write the guidance to meet their needs so that they can easily identify the basic day-to-day requirements that apply to them.

Improved website

Since its introduction in 1997, the Companies House website has been used by a growing number of customers and is now accessed by 4 million customers monthly. Companies House are committed to further improvements to their website, including a wider range of web-based guidance, better links to related websites and on-line access to up to date companies legislation. Companies House will be offering web incorporation during 2007 and this will be supported by easier access to relevant material, for example, the new simplified private company articles of association.

4.2   Resolutions and meetings

Much of company law still assumes that the general meeting is the forum by which shareholder decisions are taken. The law is also written from the perspective of the public company with derogations for the small, private company. The Bill will include measures to streamline company decision-making processes and to bring them more into line with the realities of modern business life. Provisions relating to decision-taking will be restated in a form that should make it easier for the small, private company to understand the basic definitions and requirements for passing a resolution, with additional requirements for public and then quoted companies holding general meetings following on.

Annual General Meetings

Company law requires all companies to hold an AGM at least once a year and other meetings as required. Private companies may opt to dispense with AGMs, but only if all their members agree.

The CLR discussed the possibility of also enabling public companies to opt out of the requirement for AGMs, providing their members were unanimously agreed. In practice, further consultation suggests that there are unlikely to be many, if any, public companies in a position where not one single member wished to hold an AGM. There is thus likely to be very little to be gained by creating necessarily complex rules as to how a company might opt out of the requirement. The Government therefore proposes that AGMs should remain a statutory requirement for all public companies, as now.

However, it is clear that for many private companies, particularly smaller ones with very limited shareholdings, any obligation to hold an AGM is redundant and potentially burdensome. The CLR recognised this, and suggested that, as a default, private companies should not be required to hold AGMs, but that there should be a mechanism for opting into a statutory regime. Further consultation has indicated that it will be simpler, and equally effective, not to include any opting in or out mechanism for private companies. It follows that private companies will not be required to lay their accounts or to appoint an auditor, if they have one, at an AGM. No special statutory provision is needed for those companies which wish to continue to hold AGMs, to lay their accounts and appoint an auditor, if they have one, at the AGM. They will be able to incorporate the necessary provisions into their constitution voluntarily if they so wish.

Written resolutions

The Bill will make it easier for private companies to take decisions by written resolution. It will provide that in future, a simple or 75% majority of those eligible to vote will be required for a written ordinary or written special resolution to be passed, rather than unanimity. This reform should enable most small private companies to take decisions more quickly and efficiently and, together with the proposal to remove the requirement for private companies to hold AGMs, should relieve many small private companies from the burden of having to hold formal general meetings.

It should be noted however that shareholders will still have the right to call a general meeting if they wish. The 2002 White Paper sought views on whether a single member should be allowed to require an AGM, the laying of accounts and reappointment of an auditor. In light of the consultation and concerns that such a power might undermine the deregulatory purpose of these core reforms, the Bill proposes only to retain the existing provision whereby members holding 10% of the vote will be able to requisition a general meeting.

Simplification of notice periods and short notice requirements

At present, a minimum of 21 days' notice must be given for an AGM and 14 days for an Extraordinary General Meeting (except in the case of an unlimited company). The Bill will equalise the minimum notice period for all company meetings to 14 days. Companies may set a longer notice period if they wish and it is anticipated that listed companies subject to the Listing Rules will observe the Combined Code requirements on minimum notice periods for meetings.

As now, companies can also hold meetings at shorter notice if holders of a sufficient majority of shares or voting rights agree. This majority is currently set at 95%, though private companies may elect to reduce the majority required to 90%. The Bill will make this figure the default for private companies, so that members holding 90% of voting rights should be able to agree to a meeting being held at short notice.

Unanimous consent

The Bill will not codify the principle of "unanimous consent". This common law principle provides that any decision taken (however informally) by all of a company's shareholders together constitutes a decision of the company. Unanimous consent is fundamental to our company law, and it has not been proposed that any alterations should be made to the substance. The CLR did suggest that it would be helpful to codify the principle in statute but, as discussed in the 2002 White Paper, work has suggested that the attempt to do so would risk constraining the flexibilities which the principle currently provides.

Dispersed meetings

The CLR also suggested that there was a case for clarifying in law what constitutes a "meeting" and that it should make clear that companies can use more dispersed forms of "meeting" involving real-time, two-way communication between all participants. However, common law already allows a valid general meeting to be held using overflow rooms with audio-visual links to enable participants to see and hear what is going on in the other rooms and to be seen and heard by those in other rooms. It is likely that, as new technologies allow, market practice on how general meetings are held will continue to develop, and case law will continue to develop. While it is clearly important that companies should be able to make use of new technologies where appropriate, there does not seem to be a need for new legislative provision in this area.

4.3   Company constitutions

A feature of GB company law is that the members are free, subject to certain legal constraints, to make their own rules about the internal affairs of their company. These rules are a key part of a company's constitution and can generally be found in a company's articles of association ("articles").

Although companies have considerable freedom to include whatever rules they see fit in their articles, in practice the articles tend to contain provisions on a relatively restricted range of matters, for example rules on decision taking by the members and directors and various matters connected with shares (such as the payment of dividends).

Since 1856, model articles have been provided for certain types of companies by law, for example, Companies Act 1985 Table A ("Table A") provides model articles for companies limited by shares. Table A operates as a "default" set of articles for all such companies: that is, the articles of a company limited by shares will be set out in Table A if the company does not register articles at Companies House, or to the extent that any articles which it does register do not exclude or modify the provisions of Table A.

Table A – reasons why this is no longer an appropriate form of model articles

Table A has been revised several times over the past 150 years or so, but it remains a product of the mid-19th Century both in terms of the language that it uses and in substance. It is drafted with what we would today think of as "public" rather than "private" companies in mind and successive revisions to Table A have tended to include increasingly elaborate provisions, designed to cover every conceivable event or set of circumstances that a company may find itself in (however unlikely it is that the majority of companies who are using Table A would ever find themselves in those circumstances).

The result is that the vast majority of the provisions in Table A are irrelevant to the vast majority of companies who are using Table A as their articles. In addition, whilst many new provisions have been added to Table A over the years, redundant provisions have rarely, if ever, been removed.

We are left with a "one size fits all" approach to the model articles, which has a number of problems:

• Table A is user-unfriendly, poorly laid out and often unintelligible to non-specialists;

- much of Table A is taken up with matters which are remote from the concerns of smaller companies (so that it is not unusual for private companies to have articles which are completely irrelevant to the owners and managers of such companies);

- Table A does not take account of relatively recent changes in the law, for example, the introduction of single member companies, and will need also to reflect further changes which are proposed in this White Paper.

Following the recommendations of the CLR, the Government considers that reform of Table A is an important part of making our company law fit for purpose in the modern economy. The Government proposes that in future there should be:

- a radically simplified set of model articles for private companies limited by shares, reflecting the way that small companies operate;

- a separate set of model articles for public companies limited by shares (similar in scope to the current Table A, but with clearer layout and drafting);

- (for the first time) a full set of model articles for private companies limited by guarantee; and

- comprehensive, clear and concise guidance for small companies who are using, or thinking of using, model articles.

For companies set up under the new legislation, the new sets of model articles will operate as default provisions for the types of company for which they are prescribed, in the same way as Table A now does. Existing companies will be able to replace their current articles (whether or not these are as set out in Table A) with the new model articles, if their members pass a special resolution to do so.

The private company articles

The Bill will contain a power for the Secretary of State to prescribe, by secondary legislation, stand alone model articles for public companies, private companies limited by shares and private companies limited by guarantee. Draft model articles for private companies limited by shares (the "private company articles") are set out in the White Paper.

The private company articles will replace Table A for those private companies limited by shares which are in future formed under the new Act and will play an important role in the simplification of the law for small companies. Like Table A the private company articles will apply by default where a company does not register its own articles at Companies House (to the extent that the company in question has not specifically excluded or modified the model articles). Table A will continue to provide the model articles for companies formed before the new model articles come into force.

The text of the private company articles follows the principles set out in the CLR's Final Report, for example, archaic and legalistic language has been avoided. In the interests of producing a "leaner" set of model articles and making the model articles more accessible to the directors and shareholders of small companies, we have omitted model articles on areas of law for which there are already procedural rules in the Companies Act (for example, the draft model articles do not contain any provisions on decision-taking by shareholders – see below).

Will the private company articles be suitable for all private companies?

The private company articles contain the minimum number of rules which it is envisaged that a typical private company limited by shares will need and which the shareholders will want to have. (There is little point having a default rule if the majority of companies will want to disapply it). They are primarily aimed at small, owner-managed companies.

Some or all of these rules may be suitable for less typical private companies, but if they are not, it will be open to any private company limited by shares which is using, or intends to use, the private company articles to add to, amend, or delete rules from the model articles as they see fit (as is the case with Table A), or to adopt completely different "bespoke" articles of their own.

Articles on decision-taking by members

The private company articles do not include equivalent articles to the Table A provisions on general meetings. It is envisaged that the majority of private companies will want to take advantage of the new written resolution procedure and as such the majority of private companies limited by shares are unlikely to need detailed rules on the procedure for calling, and the conduct of, meetings of the company's members.

If the members of a private company want or need to have a meeting (for example, the written resolution procedure cannot be used for resolutions to remove auditors or directors), all of the provisions necessary for the conduct of such meetings will be in the Act (although it should be noted that the provisions in the Act will be different from the current default position in Table A in a number of respects).

The public company articles will make detailed provision for meetings and private companies will be able to incorporate these provisions into their articles if they find them useful.

Draft guidance notes on the private company articles

By the time that the private company articles come into force, guidance on the new model articles (and other linked areas, for example, conflicts of interest and special resolutions) will be available from Companies House. An illustration of the types of things that will be set out in the guidance on the model articles is at Annex B.

The draft guidance has been drafted with the benefit of informal consultation with Companies House and small firms advisory bodies. In line with feedback received from consultees the draft guidance seeks to explain, in plain English, what articles of association are and how the private company articles work (rather than giving a detailed commentary on each of the individual model articles – which are written in plain English and are intended to be self-explanatory).

The public company articles

Separate model articles will be provided for public companies (the "public company articles"). In terms of content, these will be similar to the existing Table A (that is, the public company articles will include more detailed rules to cater for more complex circumstances), but will be drafted in plainer English and updated to reflect changes in the law. Private companies which find that the new private company articles fail to address their needs will be able to import provisions from the public company model on a voluntary basis.

4.4   Dematerialising share certificates

It has been possible since 1996 for quoted company shares to be held in secure electronic form, and shares representing around 85% of the value of the UK equity market are now held this way. However, around ten million retail shareholders continue to hold their shares in paper form. An industry working group has suggested that there would be long term cost savings for everyone

– including retail shareholders – if all quoted company shares were held electronically, and that such a move would help to maintain London's pre-eminence as a European financial centre. The Government therefore wishes to make sure that company law requirements do not stand in the way of a move towards a fully dematerialised securities market, and has invited all interested parties to develop the ideas further. The Government would be willing in principle to include provisions in the Bill which would permit companies to stop issuing paper share certificates. Such legislation would not prevent retail shareholders from continuing to hold their shares directly, with their names on the company's register of members.

4.5   Company secretaries

The Government agrees with the CLR's recommendation that it should no longer be a requirement for private companies to appoint a company secretary. Shareholders will of course continue to be able to require that a company secretary be appointed, if they so wish, or they may choose to let their directors decide. However, for the vast majority of companies (particularly those which only have one shareholder), a company secretary is almost certainly unnecessary.

4.6   Offences

The approach to sanctions in the Bill will follow closely the suggestions made by the CLR for a clearer, more accessible, and more consistent approach across the legislation. Key elements of the proposed approach include refinements to the "officer in default" framework, to make it clear which individuals in which circumstances may be liable for a breach, and a shift towards the removal of criminal liability from the company itself in certain circumstances.

The approach to the overarching "in default" framework – in other words, the question of which individuals should generally be liable for breaches of legal requirements in which circumstances – is very much in line with the CLR and the previous White Paper.

Officer in default

In essence *directors* should normally be liable where they authorise, participate in, permit, or fail to take active steps to prevent (including monitoring failures where appropriate) a default. *De facto* directors will be covered on the same basis.

Secretaries should be liable, if directors have properly charged them with the relevant function (or if the function has been conferred on them by the articles), where they authorise, participate in, permit, or fail to take active steps to prevent the default.

The CLR recognised the importance of ensuring that those whom they termed *managers* (a further category of company officer, beyond directors and secretaries) did not escape potential liability. In simple terms, these should be those who a) are relatively senior employees, with a policy and decision-making role which can affect the enterprise substantially and b) have responsibility for the function which is the subject of the breach. The draft clauses give effect to this policy by using the term "senior executive" which it is felt more accurately describes the category of person envisaged. This category of senior executive will generally cover senior employees within the company, but not (on the whole) external third-parties.

The CLR also suggested that a further category, *delegates*, should have liability on a case by case basis. By delegates is meant individuals to whom a particular function has properly been delegated, by or under the authority of the directors or secretary. Consultation suggested that the previous White Paper drafting may not have been sufficiently clear on the circumstances in which a delegate might be liable. The new draft clauses are designed to make clear that, for delegation to be "proper", it must be reasonable in all the circumstances.

It is also important to be clear that delegation will not be the same as assignment. In other words, even a "proper" act of delegation will not remove potential liability from those delegating, albeit they would be able to adduce the delegation as evidence of their having taking reasonable steps to secure compliance. Decisions on whether delegates should be targeted in a particular offence can only be decided on a case by case basis. For example, if a statutory function is one which many companies often and reasonably outsource to informed third-parties, it may well be appropriate that those third parties should be brought within the frame of liability for breach. Offences where it is suggested that delegates should potentially be liable are noted in Annex D.

Liability of the company

The CLR also suggested that there should be a presumption against liability falling on the company itself where (for certain types of offences) the criminal act was capable of seriously damaging the company, and liability on the responsible individual would provide a sufficient deterrent; or where meaningful and effective alternative sanctions exist. This would ensure that liability was better targeted, and would avoid imposing a penalty on the company, and thus the shareholders, where the fault was entirely that of specific company officers. Offences for which it is suggested that the company itself (as opposed to its officers) should no longer be liable are also noted at Annex D.

Enforcement

Targeting sanctions on a company's officers will make it essential that every company complies with the requirements to have officers, and the new requirement that at least one director be a natural person. Every week, Companies House writes to over 800 companies that do not meet the present requirements. In most cases, either the company is defunct and is subsequently struck-off the register or the company rectifies the omission. But there is a continuing problem with companies that continue to carry on business despite having no director, or at least none notified to Companies House. The Government proposes to give the Registrar of Companies power to issue a notice requiring a company to comply with the requirement within a specified period. There will be a criminal sanction, falling on the company, for failure to comply with the notice.

Other sanctions changes

As recommended by the CLR, the Secretary of State's power to bring proceedings on a company's behalf (Companies Act 1985 Section 438) will be repealed, and the penalty for fraudulent trading (Section 458) will be increased from seven to ten years.

4.7 Register of members

Companies' registers of members are an integral part of their constitutional apparatus. They are necessary to ensure that the members can be contacted, whether by the company, by other members, or by others such as those wishing to make a takeover bid or otherwise wishing to influence the members in their exercise of their rights as members. Company law therefore requires companies both to maintain registers with essential contact details and, for companies with share capital, information about size of holdings, and also to make these registers publicly available. The Bill will make some deregulatory changes to the requirements to make it easier for companies to maintain their registers without affecting their usefulness.

The Bill will keep the public right both to inspect and to obtain a copy of a company's register of members, supported both by the ability to apply for a court order if the company refuses. There have been instances where these rights have been abused, for example using intimidation of shareholders to force a company to withdraw from a contract. The Serious Organised Crime and Police Bill includes measures to address such intimidation directly.

Companies' registers of members are also on the public record as their Annual Return to Companies House must include either the current register or, if a register has been returned in one of the 2 preceding years, the changes to it since the last return. The CLR recommended that for public companies this requirement should be reduced to details of only those members with significant holdings: this will be implemented through the existing power to make Regulations changing the content of the Annual Return.

Information about past members is of great importance to the people concerned. Therefore the register of members will continue to be prima facie evidence of the information it contains. At present, companies have statutory immunity from claims relating to entries after 20 years; the CLR recommended this period be reduced. The Bill will provide that the period be 10 years in keeping with the Law Commissions recommendation on the statute of limitation.

It also makes the same reduction to the period for which companies are required to keep past members' details, while making clear that this old information may be kept separate from information on current members.

4.8   Capital maintenance and share provisions

Companies limited by shares have traditionally been seen as a mechanism by which the owners of such companies (the shareholders) limit how much of their money is at risk (generally speaking, if a company is insolvent and unable to pay its debts the creditors have no claim against the shareholders). But a company is also a way of protecting creditors and the rights of minority shareholders, in so far as money paid into the company by its shareholders (the company's capital) belongs to the company and can only be paid back to the shareholders in certain circumstances. This makes life easier for creditors (and shareholders who do not have a controlling interest in the company). The rules that give effect to these general principles are sometimes referred to as the capital maintenance rules.

Whilst it is obviously important to protect the interests of a company's creditors, the current provisions give rise to some of the most complex and technically challenging provisions of the current Act – 94 sections of detailed rules in total. These are capable of catching a number of potentially beneficial or at least innocuous transactions and as a result companies, and their advisors, can spend disproportionate amounts of time and money ensuring that they do not inadvertently fall foul of the rules.

Deregulation for private companies

Capital maintenance is largely irrelevant to the vast majority of private companies and their creditors. This is recognised by the current Act, which carves out a number of exceptions to the capital maintenance rules for private companies only. However because the provisions which are of most interest to private companies are drafted as exceptions, private companies have first to understand all of the rules and then identify that an exception applies to them, and if so how it works. Moreover the exceptions, while useful, do not simplify the law as much as is possible.

The Bill will therefore introduce a number of deregulatory measures targeting requirements that now appear unnecessary and burdensome for private companies.

Abolition of financial assistance provisions for private companies

The provisions on financial assistance are designed to protect creditors and shareholders against the misuse and depletion of a company's assets. The CLR concluded that it was inappropriate for private companies to continue to carry the cost of complying with the rules on financial assistance as abusive transactions could be controlled in other ways, e.g. through the provisions on directors duties which will be included in the Bill, or through the wrongful trading and market abuse provisions that have come into force since the Companies Act 1985. Private companies will therefore no longer be prevented from providing financial assistance for the purchase of their own shares.

Capital reductions by private companies

The current Act provides a means by which both private and public companies limited by shares may reduce their share capital (which includes share premium and any capital redemption reserve). The procedure can be time consuming and expensive as it involves confirmation by the court.

The Bill will introduce a new and simpler mechanism for capital reductions for private companies. This will be available as an alternative to the current court approval procedure. The new procedure will require a special resolution of the company's members, based on a solvency statement made by the directors. The solvency statement will require the directors to confirm that the company is solvent and will be able to pay its debts at all times within a year of the capital reduction. It will be a criminal offence for a director to make a solvency statement without having reasonable grounds for the opinion expressed in it. The introduction of the solvency statement procedure for capital reductions will render the private company rules on the purchase of the company's own shares out of capital redundant. The Bill will repeal these rules.

The CLR had proposed that the solvency statement procedure for capital reductions should equally be available for public companies, but the response to this proposal in the 2002 White Paper was mixed. Whilst many respondents were in favour of simplifying the procedure for capital reductions, concern was expressed that the proposed additional safeguards built into the procedure for public companies – to meet unavoidable EU requirements – meant that few public companies would use the solvency statement procedure in practice. The Government therefore does not propose to introduce this change at present for public companies.

Distributions and intra-group transfers of assets

So as to protect the interests of the creditors of a company, company law contains restrictions on when companies can pay dividends. The current Act lays down technical rules which determine what is a lawful distribution by a company to its members. These statutory provisions operate alongside the common law which is expressly retained and which remains an essential component in the regulation of improper distributions.

The 1989 decision in the case of *Aveling Barford v. Perion Ltd* (which was decided by reference to common law rules on distributions and maintenance of capital rather than the statutory rules) is widely considered to have cast doubt on the validity of intra-group asset transfers conducted by reference to book value rather than by reference to market value. It is understood that such transactions are often carried out by reference to book value rather than market value for a variety of business, administrative or tax reasons. The Bill will make clear that where the transferring company has distributable profits, its assets can be transferred at book value. This will remove any uncertainty about the current law, and also avoid the need for companies to carry out complex asset revaluations requiring significant professional advice and fees to advisors.

Application of share premium account

Amounts transferred to the share premium account where shares are issued at a premium (i.e. for an amount more than the shares' nominal value) can only be used in specific, limited circumstances. In line with the CLR's recommendations, the Bill will provide that the share premium account can no longer be used to write off a company's preliminary expenses (i.e. on formation).

Further capital maintenance reform

The Government believes that it would be beneficial to introduce greater flexibility into the capital maintenance regime for public companies. However, in advance of significant amendments to the EU legislation it would not be possible to make major changes to our capital maintenance regime in respect of public companies at this stage. Thus, for example, the financial assistance rules will continue to apply to public companies. While the CLR recommended a number of further technical changes to these rules, the Government is seeking to give priority to the CLR's overarching recommendation for fundamental reform of the capital maintenance regime through reform of the 2nd Company Law Directive. The Government very much welcomes the proposals in the Company Law Action Plan for a review of the 2nd Directive and is committed to working with the Commission and other Member States to take this forward as rapidly as possible. The proposed company law reform powers will provide a mechanism for effecting reform for all classes of British company as and when appropriate.

Miscellaneous provisions on shares

At the moment all companies with shares are required to have a limit on the maximum amount of shares they can allot– called the authorised share capital. This limit can be raised with shareholder agreement. In practice it is normally set at a level that is much higher than it is anticipated the company will need.

This means that authorised share capital normally serves no useful purpose. As recommended by the CLR, the Government proposes to remove the requirement on the basis that it is an unnecessary piece of regulation. It will of course continue to be possible for shareholders to include provisions with a similar effect in a company's articles if the special circumstances of that company make such restrictions important to the shareholders.

Linked to this, for private companies, will be the removal of the requirement for shareholder approval of allotments of shares (except where the company has or will, as a result of the allotment, have more than one class of shares); and the removal of the requirement for authorisation in the articles to issue redeemable shares.

Both public and private companies will be free to issue redeemable shares without the need to specify the terms and manner of redemption of those shares in their articles. Shareholders will therefore be able to approve an allotment of redeemable shares on terms that the directors determine. The terms and manner of redemption will need to be provided to the Registrar of Companies in the return of allotments. This return will in future contain a statement of the company's total allotted share capital.

The Bill will permit the direct issue of warrants to bearer in respect of fully paid shares (that is, there will be no need for the shares to first be issued in registered form and then converted to bearer form).

Trustees in bankruptcy and personal representatives of deceased members will have the right to be registered as a shareholder notwithstanding any contrary provision in the articles. In addition, where a company has refused to register the transfer of a share, the directors must provide the transferee with such information about the reasons for the refusal as the transferee may reasonably request.

Redenomination of share capital

At the moment a company may issue new shares in any denomination it wants (e.g. euros, dollars, sterling or other). What it cannot do is convert its existing share capital into another currency without cancelling or buying back its existing shares (the shares it wants to redenominate) and issuing a fresh batch of shares in another currency.

This is cumbersome and unnecessary and we are introducing a simplified procedure to enable companies, if they wish, to easily convert their share capital from one currency to another, and to renominalise their shares, after conversion, to achieve round share values (i.e. avoid having shares with a value expressed in fractions of a currency after conversion).

Notice period for pre-emption rights

In line with the CLR's recommendations on pre-emption rights, and as supported by Paul Myner's recent review of pre-emption rights, the present statutory minimum period of 21 days for acceptance of rights offers will be retained, but we will take a power, in the Bill, to vary this period (upwards as well as down but to no less than 14 days). This power will require an affirmative resolution of both Houses of Parliament.

4.9 Companies House

A number of changes will be made to ensure that the system for companies to file information with Companies House is kept efficient and business-friendly. Many of these will focus on encouraging and exploiting new forms of e-communication, and the Registrar (i.e. Companies House) will have greater powers to specify the form and manner in which companies must submit information.

There will also be measures to help ensure the accuracy and timeliness of information on the public register. These will include:

- the law will state with greater clarity what information will appear on the register, and what will not;

- the ability for Companies House simply to telephone companies who have provided incomplete information, so that they can easily obtain the missing element without having formally to reject the incoming form;

- the ability to remove items from the public register which have been erroneously placed there or which are "surplus" and unnecessary;

- where information has been properly placed on the register, but subsequently proves to be inaccurate or misleading, there will be a new and simple court-based procedure for ensuring that it can be removed.

These measures will be coupled with a new offence, making it unlawful knowingly or recklessly to deliver to the Registrar material which is misleading, false or deceptive in a material particular.

Company strike-off and restoration

At present, only private companies are able to request voluntary strike-off from the register. This will be extended to public companies.

Other measures will make it easier to restore companies to the register where they should not in fact have been removed. Companies House will be able to do this by administrative means (in more straightforward cases), and simplifications will be introduced to current statutory court procedures to cater for other cases.

4.10 Reports and accounts

The Government's plans for a modernised company reporting and accounting system include a number of important changes which have already been effected. These include the raising of the audit thresholds for turnover and balance sheet totals to £5.6m and £2.8m respectively, taking some 69,000 companies out of the requirement to have accounts professionally audited; and the introduction of the OFR for all quoted companies, a key plank in promoting more effective dialogue between companies and investors and helping to maintain trust and confidence in capital markets.

Simplification of Part 7

The accounting, auditing and reporting sections of the current law (Part 7 of the Companies Act) are amongst the most relevant of all provisions in that Act to companies in the normal course of their business. A number of consultees, particularly smaller firms and their advisors, have said that it is hard for them to find and understand the requirements which relate to them because in the interests of brevity the approach has been to express some provisions as modifications of those which apply to larger companies.

The Government has therefore looked very carefully at possible ways in which the provisions could be restated in a more coherent way, making it clearer to users which provisions affect which categories of company. One approach is to set out sequentially a separate, comprehensive "code" for each of the different sizes of company, starting with small, private companies, which can be read independently. The indicative clauses published in this document are drafted on this basis. However, this approach has disadvantages in terms of length and there may be some scope for setting out separately the limited number of provisions that are common to companies of whatever size.

Time limits

The bill reduces the time limit for private companies to file their annual reporting documents at Companies House after the year end from 10 months to 7 months and for public companies from 7 months to 6 months. These changes, recommended by the CLR following external consultation, reflect improvements in technology and the increased rate at which information becomes out of date, as well as filing times in other countries which tend to be less generous than in the UK.

Abbreviated accounts

Small and medium sized companies can currently file abbreviated accounts at Companies House. This enables them to keep some information confidential (for example on profit margins). The CLR recommended that the option be abolished in the interests of greater transparency and that instead companies should file their full statutory accounts. Consultation showed that there were both proponents and opponents of abolition of this option. The Government has decided that the option, which is currently popular with a great many companies, should be retained, but that both small and medium sized companies should be required to disclose the amount of turnover for the relevant financial year.

Disclosures in the directors' report

It was a recommendation of the CLR that once the OFR was in place the DTI should consider what current directors' report requirements remained necessary, both for companies required to produce OFRs and for others, and remove those that were no longer required. The Government agrees that it is in the interests of more effective company reporting to remove ineffective or otiose disclosure requirements, whilst maintaining any requirements for which there is a clear public policy interest.

Following review on this basis, its proposed to remove requirements for disclosures in respect of **the employment of disabled persons, and employee involvement**. The requirement for companies with over 250 employees to state their policy on the employment of disabled persons has been completely overtaken by substantive requirements under the Disability Discrimination Act. Retention of the requirement is effectively doing no more than asking companies to state that they are complying with the law, and is therefore uninformative. The requirement for companies with over 250 employees to state action taken to inform and consult employees has been overtaken by more substantive requirements under the European Works Council Directive and, from March 2005, the Information and Consultation Directive.

It is also proposed to amend, but not remove entirely, the requirement to disclose political and charitable donations. Companies of all sizes are required to make a disclosure relating to political donations and charitable donations if aggregate donations in either case exceed £200. In the case of political donations, the recipient must be named and the total amount given to that recipient disclosed; and prior shareholder authorisation is required for donations which in aggregate exceed £5,000 in the course of the year. It has long been recognised that a director may face a conflict of interest when the company makes a political or charitable donation, and it would be wrong to remove this important disclosure requirement entirely. However, the £200 threshold for disclosure now appears very low, and it is proposed to raise it in both cases to £2,000.

Disclosure of criminal convictions

The CLR also suggested that companies should in addition be required to disclose any criminal convictions in their annual report and accounts, and the 2002 White Paper discussed options for implementing this underlying idea.

Responses to the White Paper on this point were divided, with little evidence provided that publicising convictions (beyond what already happens in, for example, the local press) would encourage compliance. Proposed options appeared to be either very difficult to enforce (if the law were to require directors to admit guilt in their published report and accounts) or disproportionately expensive (if, say, Companies House were to be required to maintain a web-based register, as mooted in the 2002 White Paper). The Government therefore does not propose to proceed with this suggestion.

4.11 Public/private split

The Government wishes to ensure that a private company (defined as any company that is not a public company):

- is prohibited from offering its shares or debentures to the public, or colluding in any such offer made by another person; and

- is required to re-register as a public company if it does anything that facilitates the transfer of its shares or debentures, by any person, to persons other than those to whom the company, as a private company, would be allowed by law to offer such securities.

The first of the limbs set out above is not novel. Section 81 of the Companies Act 1985 currently prohibits private companies from offering their shares and debentures to the public. However, the second limb will be new, and will be enforceable by a power for various persons (including the Secretary of State) to apply to the court for an order that the company must re-register as a public company.

These proposals will take forward, so far as is feasible, the CLR recommendations that:

- company law should continue to prohibit private companies from offering their shares to the public;

- the meaning of offer to the public for the purposes of that prohibition (and in particular the related exemptions) should be aligned as far as possible with the exemptions which apply in relation to an offer to the public for the purposes of securities regulation; and

- private companies should be prohibited from admitting their shares to trading on a prescribed investment exchange, or from assisting in any way an application for admission of their shares to trading made by any other person.

4.12 Jurisdictional migration

The Government's proposals regarding jurisdictional migration encompass two conceptually distinct provisions:

- to enable a company registered in Great Britain to transfer its registered office between England and Wales, and Scotland;

- to enable:

    i) a company registered in Great Britain either to migrate to a jurisdiction other than Great Britain (including another EEA State, or a third country); and

(ii) a company formed under the law of a jurisdiction other than Great
      Britain to migrate to Great Britain

without, in either case, forming a new company in the 'incoming'
jurisdiction.

Since the publication of the CLR's *Final Report*, the European Commission has
consulted on outline proposals for a company law directive on the cross-
border transfer of the registered office of a limited company. A formal proposal
for such a Directive is expected shortly from the Commission.

The provisions of the directive would, of course, supersede the CLR
recommendations in respect of the migration of companies between England,
Wales and Scotland and other EEA States. The CLR recognised this in their
report, and, in line with spirit of their thinking, the Government does not
propose to pre-judge the outcome of the EU negotiations by seeking express
provision at this stage enabling migration between Great Britain and other
EEA States.

The Government would envisage exploring the possibility of using regulations
to implement the directive and to extend the directive regime, insofar as its
further intention is that the Bill should contain a power for the Secretary of
State to make the necessary provision for migration between Great Britain and
non-EEA jurisdictions. It also wishes to make provision, by secondary
legislation, to enable companies registered in Great Britain to transfer their
registered office between England and Wales, and Scotland.

4.13   Overseas Companies

Changes will be made to the current framework in respect of overseas
companies, in line with the substance of the recommendations of the CLR.
Under the current Act, there are in effect two parallel regimes, one applying
where a company is incorporated outside the UK and Gibraltar, but has set up
a branch in Great Britain; the other where a company is incorporated outside
GB and establishes a place of business in GB. The Bill will enable a single
regime to apply to all overseas companies, i.e. all companies which are
incorporated outside GB and which establish *a place of business* in GB. This
regime will, as the CLR recommended, be based on the requirements of the
11th Directive, in other words it will generally reflect the existing provisions
applying to non-UK companies setting up branches in GB.

The provisions relating to overseas companies appear a good candidate for removal from primary legislation and placing into subordinate legislation because of their relatively self-contained nature, and because it seems largely possible to ensure that all necessary provisions can be set out in one place.

4.14 Arrangements and reconstructions

The Bill will make a number of generally technical changes, generally in line with CLR recommendations, to ensure that, on application by the company or other proposer of the scheme, the courts will be able to determine what constitutes a "class" of creditors or members; and to ensure that, even where a class is wrongly constituted, court approval should stand where the court is satisfied there was no effect on the outcome. The courts will also be able, on request, to direct the manner in which meetings should be called, held and conducted.

The CLR had suggested that there might be a case for the introduction of a non-court based statutory merger procedure. However, in the light of the other changes being made as noted above, and in the absence of any clear business demand emerging from previous rounds of consultation, the Government does not propose to take these ideas forward.

4.15 Authorisation of political donations

The Political Parties, Elections and Referendums Act 2000, which implemented the Committee on Standards in Public Life's recommendations on the funding of political parties in the UK, introduced a requirement for prior shareholder authorisation of political donations by companies above an annual threshold of £5,000. This recent reform appears to have been widely supported, and no substantive changes are proposed. However, certain technical changes are proposed to the current requirements in order to remove unnecessary burdens and make them more business friendly. These are:

- to make it clear that certain non-contentious "donations" (e.g. paid time-off for elected local councillors, or the provision of a meeting room for trade union officials) are not caught by the requirement for shareholder approval; and

- to allow companies greater procedural freedom in obtaining the necessary shareholder authorisation, in particular by permitting them to seek separate authorisation for donations to political parties and donations to other political organisations.

In addition, as noted in 4.10, the threshold for disclosure of political donations will be raised to £2,000.

4.16 Company charges

Many companies use their assets as security for loans. The Companies Act provides that these transactions are invalid in the event of the company's insolvency unless they have been properly registered. Under the Act, the system of registration is based on transactions that have already been completed. The CLR consulted over changes to improve the present system; they also sought views on whether it should be replaced with a different system.

Following this consultation, the CLR were concerned lest the provision that a charge is invalid if not registered (i.e. the sanction of invalidity) contravened the European Convention on Human Rights. This sanction underpins the present system. As about half of their respondents had favoured developing a system of notice-filing, they recommended that the Law Commissions be asked to make recommendations for reform to both company law and security over property other than land in both England and Wales and in Scotland. Because of the fundamental differences between Scots law and English law with regard to the law of property and of rights in security, the Government made separate requests to the two Commissions.

In its Report on Registration of Rights in Security by Companies (Scot Law Com No 197) the Scottish Law Commission recommended that the validity of rights in security granted by companies should cease to be dependent on particulars of the right in security having been registered in the Register of Charges at Companies House. As respects floating charges in Scotland, the principal recommendation of the Scottish Law Commission was that registration of the floating charge in a new Register of Floating Charges, to be kept by the Keeper of the Registers of Scotland, should be the means whereby the floating charge would be created or constituted, with priority being dependent on the date of registration. The Scottish Law Commission also suggested that the annual return submitted by a company should contain short details of outstanding rights in security granted by the company and that, on payment of a prescribed fee being made to it by an inquirer, a company should be under a statutory duty to meet a request for the same details respecting any rights in security granted since the date of the last annual return. The current requirement to maintain a register of charges at the company's registered office would cease. These recommendations span both matters devolved to the Scottish Executive and also those reserved to Westminster.

The Law Commission for England and Wales, which was asked to carry out a more fundamental review (including the kinds of transaction that should be registered and the rules that govern priority), has consulted extensively over fundamental changes. The balance of informed opinion shifted considerably during this process. Therefore the Commission has not yet made its recommendations.

The Government is considering with interest the recommendations of the Scottish Law Commission, noting that those relating to devolved matters are for the Scottish Executive. It looks forward to receiving the recommendations of the Law Commission for England and Wales.

4.17 Transparency Directive

Transparency Directive Implementation

The Transparency Directive[1] is an important part of the Financial Services Action Plan. The Financial Services Action Plan has been the European legislative framework for developing the Single Market in financial services. The purpose of the Transparency Directive is to enhance transparency in EU capital markets. It does this by establishing rules on periodic financial reports and disclosure of major shareholdings for issuers whose securities are admitted to trading on a regulated market in the EU. The Directive completed the European legislative process on 15 December 2004 and must be implemented into national law by all Member States no later than 20 January 2007.

Most of the requirements of the Transparency Directive can be implemented by secondary legislation using powers under Section 2(2) of the European Communities Act 1972. The Treasury will consult on proposed regulations to be made under the European Communities Act in due course. However, the proposed approach for those parts of the Transparency Directive relating to the disclosure of shareholdings – historically part of company law – requires primary legislation. The Government therefore proposes to include the necessary provisions in the Bill.

Disclosure of shareholdings

The Directive requires Member States to impose obligations on:

- *issuers* of securities, which are traded on a regulated market in the Member State, to disclose certain information; and

---

[1] Directive 2004/109/EC of the European Parliament and of the Council of 15 December 2004.

- *shareholders*, and certain parties able to exercise control of voting rights, to disclose certain information to the issuer of the shares in question.

Member States also have to appoint a competent authority to supervise these obligations. In the UK this will be the Financial Services Authority (FSA). For the majority of the Directive's provisions, the FSA already has sufficient powers under the Financial Services and Markets Act 2000 (FSMA) to permit implementation by way of regulations made under the European Communities Act 1972. However, the FSA currently has no powers under FSMA to make rules in respect of disclosure of shareholdings and hence the requirement for primary legislation to implement the Directive's provisions in this area.

The existing requirements for shareholders to disclose substantial shareholdings are set out in Part 6 of the Companies Act 1985. In order to bring together supervision of all Transparency Directive obligations under one competent authority, the Government proposes to transfer this responsibility to the FSA. Part 6 of the Companies Act 1985 will be repealed in so far as it relates to a shareholder's continuing disclosure obligations.

Scope of the new FSA disclosure regime

In relation to mandatory disclosure of interests in shares, the Bill will establish the scope of the new disclosure regime and give the FSA powers to make rules with regard to shareholder notification. Before the FSA can make rules, it must, under the provisions of FSMA, undertake extensive consultation with stakeholders and publish a cost-benefit analysis of its proposals for public comment.

It is proposed that the scope of the FSA regime would be broadly similar to the scope of the regime under Part 6 of the Companies Act 1985, which imposes disclosure obligations in relation to an "interest in shares". However, in order to reduce burdens, the Government is proposing to make a number of deregulatory changes to the current disclosure regime.

- **Basis of disclosure obligation.** The obligation of disclosure under Part 6 of the Companies Act 1985 relates to "interests in shares". The obligation of disclosure under the Directive relates to "major holdings in issuers". In broad terms, this is best understood as a holding of voting rights. The holding of voting rights is currently only one of the "interests in shares" whose acquisition or disposal is required to be disclosed under the present Part 6. The Government considers that it would be less burdensome to investors if a disclosable interest were redefined in terms of the "control of exercisable voting rights". This change was favoured by the large majority of respondents to a consultation on company law reform undertaken by the DTI in 1995.

- **Issuers subject to the regime.** The current notification regime applies to interests in all public companies as defined by the Companies Act 1985. The Transparency Directive requires disclosure in relation to holdings of shares of an issuer, including those incorporated outside the UK, whose shares are admitted to trading on a regulated market and to which voting rights are attached (Article 9). The Government believes that it is desirable, in the interests of market transparency and the investing public, to retain a slightly wider scope in UK legislation than that required by the Transparency Directive. This would allow the FSA, following consultation, to apply disclosure requirements to those with control of exercisable voting rights in shares of particular issuers. At a minimum, this would include those with control of exercisable voting rights in shares of issuers whose shares are *admitted to trading on a regulated market in the UK*. At a maximum, this could also include those with control of exercisable voting rights in shares of all issuers whose shares are *admitted to trading on other markets in the UK*. The FSA is committed to only going beyond the minimum requirements of European legislation if extensive consultation with stakeholders shows that the benefits exceed the costs. In either event, public limited companies whose shares are not traded on a market in the UK would be excluded from the scope of the disclosure regime.

- **Sanctions for breach of notification obligations.** Part 6 of the Companies Act 1985 imposes criminal liability on shareholders in breach of the notification rules. The Government has concluded that it would be appropriate and proportionate to repeal the criminal sanctions and to give the FSA equivalent powers to those it has to deal with breaches of rules under FSMA.

The Government proposes to maintain the flexibility of the current regime in respect of the **disclosure of holdings of financial instruments**. The Directive requires disclosure in respect of holdings of a particular class of financial instruments: financial instruments that result in an entitlement to acquire shares with voting rights "under a formal agreement" and "on such holder's own initiative alone" (Article 13). Under Section 210A(1) of the Companies Act 1985, the Secretary of State has the power to amend by regulation the provisions as to what is taken to be an interest in shares. In order to retain the ability to require wider disclosure, where appropriate, the Government proposes to maintain the scope of the current regime and give the FSA equivalent powers to require disclosures in respect of holdings of financial instruments.

Part 6 of the Companies Act 1985 also provides, under section 212 and related provisions, for certain companies to require disclosure of information about interests in their shares. The Government is considering whether or not these provisions should remain in legislation, and if so whether it should be possible for all companies with shares to use them.

5 Making it easier to set up and run a company

5.1 Company formation

The law on the formation of companies is necessarily one of the most frequently used parts of the Companies Act. Evidence suggests that the GB formation process it is not, by international standards, particularly cumbersome for those who wish to form companies. Nonetheless, there have been suggestions for changes of substance to make the process smoother and more efficient, and the CLR was also concerned that improvements could be made to the drafting of the provisions to make them simpler and more readily comprehensible.

The drafting set out in the White Paper is designed to focus on the practicalities, for example the key requirements for a company to have a registered office and how that office can be changed. The draft clauses implement and reflect the CLR's key proposals, namely:

- one person should be able to form any sort of company;

- the key rules on the internal workings of the company should be in one document (the "articles");

- there should be separate model articles for private companies limited by shares and public companies;

- unless a company positively chooses to restrict its objects neither the company's capacity, nor the authority of the directors to bind the company, should be limited by them;

- members should be able to choose to entrench elements of the company's articles (making certain provisions harder to amend subsequently than would otherwise be the case); and

- companies should be able to migrate between different parts of GB. (Provision will be made elsewhere for migration into and out of Great Britain).

The clauses also adopt the CLR's proposed replacement of the statutory declaration required on formation with a statement of compliance. The Government is looking at whether current requirements elsewhere in the Act for statutory declarations (legally-attested signatures) can generally be removed or replaced with less onerous and costly requirements.

Company types

The Bill will not make changes to the types of company which are available to be formed, namely: private and public companies limited by shares; private companies limited by guarantee; and unlimited companies. (The C(AICE) Act 2004 has also provided for new community interest companies).

All existing possibilities for re-registration between company types will also be retained and a public company will be able to re-register as an unlimited private company without first having to re-register as a private company limited by shares. However, no new provision will be introduced to allow for re-registration between a private company limited by shares and a private company limited by guarantee, and vice versa. The CLR had suggested that this option should be explored, but given the inherent difficulties in converting an economic interest in a company (a share) into a liability (the guarantee) and the likely low level of demand for re-registrations of this sort, it is not felt that the development of a new procedure is worthwhile.

5.2   Company names and trading disclosures

It is important that anyone can use a company's registered name to trace the company's record at Companies House and so find information about it easily and reliably. The Bill will provide for Regulations to specify the trivial differences between names which will be ignored when deciding whether two names are effectively the same. They will also specify circumstances in which a name would be accepted notwithstanding that it would otherwise be considered the "same as" another: it is intended to use this power so that, for example, a parent company and its subsidiary may have names that differ by abbreviations such as "UK" or "GB".

The Bill will also implement the CLR recommendation that it be possible to require a company to change its registered name if it was chosen to exploit another's reputation or goodwill.

In addition, the Bill will change the interface between the Companies Act and the Business Names Act. At present, the Business Names Act applies when a company trades under a name other than on the register at Companies House. In particular, in future:

- the prohibition of names that are so misleading as to be likely to cause harm to the public will apply to all business names rather than, as present, only company names; and

- there will be a single set of requirements, set out in Regulations, for the company name to be included in correspondence and signs at premises – at present, the two Acts have different requirements.

5.3 Directors' home addresses

Every company director will in future be given the option of providing a service address for the public record with the home address being kept on a separate record to which access will be restricted (though this will not be retrospective). This will replace the present system under which only directors at serious risk of violence and intimidation can have their home addresses kept off the public record. While this system is satisfactory for the tiny minority of directors who can show they are at serious risk, it has some weaknesses. For example, experienced directors may be unwilling to take directorships in controversial companies as their home addresses will already be on the public record; companies whose directors have addresses on the public record may be unwilling to do business with controversial companies; and it does not protect directors of companies whose customers or suppliers become controversial. The general effect of the current law appears to be to deter some people from becoming directors.

At the same time, it is important that the service address functions effectively, and the law will be tightened to increase the obligation on directors to keep the record up-to-date, and ensure that the address on the public record is fully effective for the service of documents.

6 Flexibility for the Future

6.1 Powers

The Government published a consultation document "Flexibility and Accessibility" in May 2004, which sought views on specific proposals to introduce new legislative powers as part of the Bill. The CLR had suggested that many areas of company law, particularly those where provisions were most likely to require updating over time, should be moved from primary into secondary legislation. However, as the Government's consultation document explained, it is not in practice easy to establish a clear dividing line between "core" provisions (which could remain in primary legislation) and "detail" (which could sit in regulations), and such a line might risk separating one subject into two places. The Government's proposal was therefore that changes to company law in future could be made by a special form of secondary legislation (rather than by primary legislation), to produce both *reform and restatement* of the law. This would further the fundamental objectives which the CLR identified, by helping company law remain flexible for the future and accessible to all of those who use it, particularly smaller firms.

The introduction of powers of this type is not intended to take the place of making any necessary substantive reforms now, in the Bill; nor is it intended to take the place of any restatement of the law in more accessible fashion where that can be accomplished in the Bill itself.

The consultation exercise revealed substantial support for powers both to reform and to restate. The point was made that company law, unlike many other forms of "regulation", is the provision of a legal form which is to some extent mobile over time, and which can only work if it successfully balances various potentially conflicting interests, since otherwise people will use an alternative business vehicle (or the company form from a different jurisdiction). It is in a sense self-regulating, and reform by secondary legislation may therefore be more appropriate than for some other areas of law.

The Government therefore intends to proceed with its proposals. Several consultees did however stress that simplification of the drafting of the law is not easy; needs to be handled with care if it is to avoid inadvertent consequences; and is only one element in making the law accessible to business users, with other forms of support and guidance potentially just as helpful. The Government intends to take full account of these important points in going forward.

Consultation also suggested that, while there was general support for the need for some form of broad criteria delimiting the exercise of the powers (reflecting the principles established for the reform of company law by the CLR), it would be important that the criteria did not function as excessively strict vires constraints, as this might introduce an element of uncertainty and potential challenge to orders made under the powers. Consultees were also keen that the requirement for consultation be as full and open as possible in all circumstances. Again, the Government is reflecting these important points in taking the policy forward.

Finally, consultees agreed with the Government's proposals that there should be very strict requirements both for public consultation and for Parliamentary scrutiny. These will be based very much on the procedures currently in place for Regulatory Reform Orders under the Regulatory Reform Act.

6.2   Institutional arrangements

The CLR proposed the creation of various bodies which would be responsible for reviewing the law and/or for formulating detailed rules in specific areas. The Government's White Paper of 2002 discussed the idea of the proposed new statutory bodies – the *Company Law and Reporting Commission*, and the *Private Companies Committee* – which would have had a continuing remit to review company law as a whole and recommend changes, and rejected these ideas on the basis that they risked entrenching in statute arrangements which might over time themselves become unnecessarily inflexible. The Government does however intend to continue to develop any proposals for changes to company law in close consultation with those who might be affected. The proposed reform and restatement power could only be exercised after full consultation with interested parties.

The 2002 White Paper indicated that the Government saw more attraction in the idea of a *Standards Board*, which would have had responsibility for setting detailed rules on company reporting and disclosure. The Government now believes, however, that, in the light of more recent events, there is no case for the creation of a new body. The increasing importance of International Accounting Standards (IAS) is tending to limit the areas in which a purely domestic standards-setting body would have a role; and the changes already made to the Financial Reporting Council (FRC), and the responsibilities of the bodies that fall under it, are now providing some of the functions originally envisaged as the functions of the Standards Board.

6.3 Company investigations

The Government is keen to ensure that there is effective management of the large investigations undertaken by Companies Act inspectors. Administrative measures are being reviewed in order to help avoid prolonged and unduly expensive inspections. However, there is also a need for new statutory provision. A new power will be introduced to enable the Secretary of State to direct Companies Act inspectors, both at the outset of and during the life of an inspection, as to the scope, conduct, timing and certain other matters in relation to their investigation, and to discontinue an investigation.

Additionally, there will be an amendment to section 8 of the Company Directors Disqualification Act 1986 so that the Secretary of State can make a decision to apply to the Courts for the disqualification of a company director in the light of any information obtained by Companies Act inspectors, without the need for the information to be included in a report by such inspectors.

6.4 Miscellaneous repeals

The development of company law over the last 150 years means that there are many provisions in the current legislation which are no longer required. While a number of examples of these are given elsewhere in the White Paper, there are also a number of other, more miscellaneous provisions which it is planned to repeal. These are described in Annex C.

7 Draft Clauses

Company Law Reform Bill

CONTENTS

Alteration of status

Statement of company's objects

Other provisions

7 Draft Clauses

PART A1

GENERAL PROVISIONS

Companies and Companies Acts

A1   Companies

(1)   In this Act, unless the context otherwise requires —

"company" means an incorporated company formed and registered under this Act or an existing company; and

"existing company" means an incorporated company formed and registered under the former Companies Acts.

(2)   References in this Act to an existing company do not include a company registered under the Joint Stock Companies Acts, the Companies Act 1862 or the Companies (Consolidation) Act 1908 in what was then Ireland.

A2   Companies Acts

(1)   In this Act —

"the Companies Acts" means —

(a)   this Act, and

(b)   the Companies Act 1985 (c. 6) [and the Companies Consolidation (Consequential Provisions) Act 1985 (c. 9)], as amended by this Act; and

"the former Companies Acts" means —

(a)   the Joint Stock Companies Acts, the Companies Act 1862, the Companies (Consolidation) Act 1908, the Companies Act 1929 and the Companies Act 1948, and

(b)   the Companies Act 1985 [and the Companies Consolidation (Consequential Provisions) Act 1985], so far as repealed by this Act.

(2)   Except as otherwise provided —

(a)   expressions that are defined for the purposes of this Act have the same meaning in the Companies Act 1985, and

(b)   expressions that are defined for the purposes of that Act have the same meaning in this Act.

Types of company

A3   Limited and unlimited companies

(1)   A company is a "limited company" if the liability of its members is limited by its constitution.
It may be limited by shares or limited by guarantee.

(2)   If their liability is limited to the amount, if any, unpaid on the shares held by them, the company is "limited by shares".

(3)   If their liability is limited to such amount as the members undertake to contribute to the assets of the company in the event of its being wound up, the company is "limited by guarantee".

(4)   If there is no limit on the liability of its members, the company is an "unlimited company".

A4   Private and public companies

(1)   A "private company" is any company that is not a public company.

(2)   A "public company" is a company limited by shares —
    (a)   whose certificate of incorporation states that it is a public company, and
    (b)   in relation to which the requirements of the Companies Acts, or the former Companies Acts, as to registration or re-registration as a public company have been complied with on or after 22nd December 1980.

A5   Companies limited by guarantee and having share capital

(1)   A company cannot be formed as, or become, a company limited by guarantee with a share capital.
Provision to this effect has been in force since 22nd December 1980.

(2)   For the purposes of subsection (1) and any other provision of the Companies Acts relating to companies limited by guarantee, any provision in the constitution of a company that purports to divide the company's undertaking into shares or interests is a provision for a share capital.
This applies whether or not the nominal value or number of the shares or interests is specified by the provision.

A6   Community interest companies

(1)   In accordance with Part 2 of the Companies (Audit, Investigations and Community Enterprise) Act 2004 (c. 27) —
    (a)   a company limited by shares or a company limited by guarantee and not having a share capital may be formed as or become a community interest company, and
    (b)   a company limited by guarantee and having a share capital may become a community interest company.

(2)   The provisions of this Act have effect subject to that Part.

PART A2

COMPANY FORMATION

General

A7 Method of forming company

(1) A company is formed under this Act by one or more persons —

    (a) subscribing their names to a memorandum of association (see section A8), and

    (b) complying with the requirements of this Act as to registration (see sections A9 to A13).

(2) A company may not be so formed for an unlawful purpose.

A8 Memorandum of association

(1) A memorandum of association is a memorandum stating that the subscribers —

    (a) wish to form a company under this Act, and

    (b) agree to become members of the company and, in the case of a company that is to have a share capital, to take at least one share each.

(2) The memorandum must be in the prescribed form and must be authenticated by each subscriber.

Requirements for registration

A9 Documents to be sent to registrar

(1) The memorandum of association must be delivered to the registrar, together with —

    (a) an application for registration of the company, and

    (b) a statement of compliance (see section A13).

(2) The application for registration must contain —

    (a) a statement containing the following information —

        (i) the company's proposed name,

        (ii) whether the company's registered office is to be situated in England and Wales, in Wales or in Scotland,

        (iii) whether the liability of the members of the company is to be limited, and if so whether it is to be limited by shares or by guarantee,

        (iv) whether the company is to be a private or a public company;

    (b) in the case of a company that is to have a share capital, a statement of initial shareholdings and a statement of capital (see section A10);

    (c) in the case of a company that is to be limited by guarantee, a statement of guarantee (see section A11);

    (d) a statement of the company's proposed officers (see section A12);

    (e) a statement of the proposed address of the company's registered office; and

      (f)   any proposed articles of association (see Chapter 2 of Part A3).

(3)   If the application is delivered by a person as agent for the subscribers, details of his name and address must also be included.

(4)   The application must be in the prescribed form and must be authenticated by the subscribers to the memorandum.

(5)   The documents must be delivered —

      (a)   to the registrar of companies for England and Wales, if the registered office of the company is to be in England and Wales or in Wales;

      (b)   to the registrar of companies for Scotland, if the registered office of the company is to be in Scotland.

A10   Statement of initial shareholdings and share capital

(1)   The statement of initial shareholdings and statement of share capital delivered to the registrar in connection with the formation of a company that is to have a share capital must comply with this section.

(2)   The statements must be in the prescribed form.

(3)   The statements must be authenticated by, and contain the names and addresses of, the subscribers to the memorandum of association.

(4)   The statement of initial shareholdings must state with respect to each subscriber to the memorandum —

      (a)   the number and nominal value of the shares to be allotted to him on formation, and

      (b)   the amount (if any) payable in respect of each share on formation, whether on account of the nominal value or by way of a premium.

(5)   The statement of capital must state with respect to the company's share capital to be allotted on formation —

      (a)   the total number of shares of the company,

      (b)   the aggregate nominal value of those shares,

      (c)   for each class of shares —

          (i)   prescribed particulars of the rights attached to the shares,

          (ii)   the total number of shares of that class, and

          (iii)   the aggregate nominal value of shares of that class, and

      (d)   the amount paid up and the amount (if any) unpaid on each share (whether on account of the nominal value of the share or by way of premium).

(6)   For the purpose of subsection (5) shares are of one class if the rights attached to them are in all respects uniform.

A11   Statement of guarantee

(1)   The statement of guarantee delivered to the registrar in the case of a company that is to be limited by guarantee must —

      (a)   be in the prescribed form, and

      (b)   be authenticated by the subscribers to the memorandum of association.

(2)   The statement must contain the names and addresses of the subscribers to the memorandum.

(3)   The statement must state that each member undertakes that, if the company is wound up while he is a member, or within one year after he ceases to be a member, he will contribute to the assets of the company such amount as may be required for —

    (a)   payment of the debts and liabilities of the company contracted before he ceases to be a member,

    (b)   payment of the costs, charges and expenses of winding up, and

    (c)   adjustment of the rights of the contributories among themselves,

not exceeding a specified amount.

A12   Statement of proposed officers

(1)   The statement of the company's proposed officers delivered to the registrar must —

    (a)   be in the prescribed form, and

    (b)   be authenticated by the subscribers to the memorandum of association.

(2)   The statement must contain the names and other details (see [provision yet to be drafted]) of the person who is, or persons who are, to be the first director or directors of the company.

(3)   In the case of —

    (a)   a company that is to be a public company, or

    (b)   a company that is to be a private company whose articles require the appointment of a secretary or of joint secretaries,

the statement must contain the names and other details (see [provision yet to be drafted]) of the person who is or the persons who are to be the first secretary or joint secretaries of the company.

(4)   In the case of a company that is to be a private company whose articles permit but do not require the appointment of a secretary or of joint secretaries, the statement may contain the names and other details (see [provision yet to be drafted]) of a person who is or persons who are to be the first secretary or joint secretaries of the company.

(5)   The statement must contain a consent authenticated by each of the persons named as a director, as secretary or as one of joint secretaries, to act in the relevant capacity.

(6)   If all the partners in a firm are to be joint secretaries —

    (a)   it is sufficient if the statement contains the name and other details of the firm (even if it is not a legal person), and

    (b)   consent may be given by one partner on behalf of all of them.

A13   Statement of compliance

(1)   The statement of compliance required to be delivered to the registrar is a statement in the prescribed form by —

    (a)   a [lawyer] engaged in the formation of the company, or

    (b)   a person named as a director or secretary of the company in the statement delivered as to the company's proposed officers,

that the requirements of this Act as to registration have been complied with.

(2)   The statement must be authenticated by the person making it.

(3)   A person who in a statement of compliance under this section makes a false statement that he knows to be false or does not believe to be true commits an offence.

(4)   A person guilty of an offence under this section is liable—

    (a)   on conviction on indictment, to imprisonment for a term not exceeding two years or a fine (or both);

    (b)   on summary conviction—

        (i)   in England and Wales, to imprisonment for a term not exceeding twelve months or to a fine not exceeding the statutory maximum (or both);

        (ii)   in Scotland, to imprisonment for a term not exceeding six months, or to a fine not exceeding the statutory maximum (or both).

In relation to an offence committed before the commencement of section 154(1) of the Criminal Justice Act 2003 (c. 44), for "twelve months" in paragraph (b)(i) substitute "six months".

Registration and its effect

A14   Registration

(1)   If the registrar is satisfied that—

    (a)   that the company's name complies with Chapter 2 of Part 1 of the Companies Act 1985 (c. 6) (general requirements as to company names), and

    (b)   that the requirements of this Act as to registration are complied with

he shall register the documents delivered to him.

(2)   The registrar may accept the statement of compliance as sufficient evidence of compliance.

(3)   References in the Companies Acts to registration of the company are to registration under this section (or, where the context requires, under corresponding earlier provisions).

A15   Issue of certificate of incorporation

(1)   On the registration of a company, the registrar of companies shall give a certificate that the company is incorporated.

(2)   The certificate must state—

    (a)   the name and registered number of the company,

    (b)   the date of its incorporation,

    (c)   in the case of a limited company, that it is a limited company,

    (d)   in the case of a public company, that it is a public company,

    (e)   in the case of an unlimited company, that it is an unlimited company, and

    (f)   whether its registered office is situated in England and Wales, in Wales or in Scotland.

(3)   The certificate must be signed by the registrar or authenticated by his official seal.

(4) The certificate is conclusive evidence that the requirements of this Act as to registration have been complied with and that the company—

    (a) is duly registered under this Act, and

    (b) where relevant, is duly registered as a limited company or public company, as the case may be.

A16 Effect of registration

(1) The registration of a company has the following effects.

(2) The subscribers to the memorandum, together with such other persons as may from time to time become members of the company, are a body corporate by the name stated in the certificate of incorporation.

(3) That body corporate is capable of exercising all the functions of an incorporated company.

(4) The status and situation of the registered office of the company are as stated in the certificate of incorporation.

(5) If the company has a share capital it is deemed to have allotted to the subscribers to the memorandum the shares specified in the statement of initial share capital.

(6) The persons named in the statement of proposed officers as director, secretary or joint secretary of the company are deemed to have been appointed to that office.

PART A3

PROVISIONS RELATING TO COMPANY'S CONSTITUTION

CHAPTER 1

ARTICLES OF ASSOCIATION

General

A17 Articles of association

(1) A company may have articles of association prescribing regulations for the company.

(2) A company's articles of association form part of its constitution.

A18 Power of Secretary of State to prescribe model articles

(1) The Secretary of State may by regulations prescribe model articles of association for companies.

(2) Different model articles may be prescribed for different descriptions of company.

(3) A company may adopt all or any of the provisions of model articles.

(4) Any amendment of model articles by regulations under this section does not affect a company registered before the amendment takes effect.

7 Draft Clauses

8

Company Law Reform Bill
Part A3 — Provisions relating to company's constitution
Chapter 1 — Articles of association

"Amendment" here includes addition, alteration or repeal.

(5) Regulations under this section shall be made by statutory instrument subject to annulment in pursuance of a resolution of either House of Parliament.

A19 Default application of model articles to limited companies

(1) In the case of a limited company —
   (a) if articles are not registered as part of the company's constitution, or
   (b) if articles are so registered, in so far as they do not exclude or modify the relevant model articles,
   the relevant model articles (so far as applicable) form part of the company's articles in the same manner and to the same extent as if articles in the form of those articles had been duly registered.

(2) The "relevant model articles" means the model articles prescribed for a company of that description as in force at the date on which the company is first registered.

Alteration of articles

A20 Alteration of articles

(1) A company may alter its articles by special resolution.

(2) This is subject to any restriction imposed by the Companies Acts.

A21 Entrenched provisions of the articles

(1) A company's articles may provide that specified provisions of the articles —
   (a) may not be altered or repealed, or
   (b) may be altered or repealed only if conditions are met, or procedures are complied with, that are more restrictive than those applicable in the case of a special resolution.
   This is referred to below in this section as "provision for entrenchment".

(2) Provision for entrenchment may only be made —
   (a) in the company's articles on formation, or
   (b) by an amendment of the company's articles agreed to by all the members of the company.

A22 Notice to registrar in case of entrenched provisions

(1) Where —
   (a) a company's articles on formation contain provision for entrenchment, or
   (b) a company's articles are altered so as to include such provision,
   the company must give notice to the registrar in the prescribed form.

(2) Where a company whose articles contain provision for entrenchment is required to send to the registrar any document making or evidencing an alteration in the company's articles, the company must deliver with it a statement of compliance.

Company Law Reform Bill
Part A3 — Provisions relating to company's constitution
Chapter 1 — Articles of association

9

(3) The statement of compliance required to be delivered to the registrar is a statement in the prescribed form by —

    (a) a [lawyer] engaged in acting for the company, or

    (b) a director or secretary of the company,

certifying that the alteration has been made in accordance with the company's articles.

The statement must be authenticated by the person making it.

(4) The registrar may rely on the statement of compliance as sufficient evidence of the matters stated in it.

(5) A person who in a statement of compliance under this section makes a false statement that he knows to be false or does not believe to be true commits an offence.

(6) A person guilty of an offence under this section is liable —

    (a) on conviction on indictment, to imprisonment for a term not exceeding two years or a fine (or both);

    (b) on summary conviction —

        (i) in England and Wales, to imprisonment for a term not exceeding twelve months or to a fine not exceeding the statutory maximum (or both);

        (ii) in Scotland, to imprisonment for a term not exceeding six months, or to a fine not exceeding the statutory maximum (or both).

In relation to an offence committed before the commencement of section 154(1) of the Criminal Justice Act 2003 (c. 44), for "twelve months" in paragraph (b)(i) substitute "six months".

A23 Notice to registrar of removal of entrenched provisions

(1) Where a company whose articles contain provision for entrenchment alters its articles so that they no longer contain any such provision, it must give notice of that fact in the prescribed form to the registrar.

(2) The notice must be accompanied by a statement of compliance.

(3) The statement of compliance required is a statement in the prescribed form by —

    (a) a [lawyer] engaged in acting for the company, or

    (b) a director or secretary of the company,

certifying that the alteration has been made in accordance with the company's articles.

The statement must be authenticated by the person making it.

(4) The registrar may rely on the statement of compliance as sufficient evidence of the matters stated in it.

(5) A person who in a statement of compliance under this section makes a false statement that he knows to be false or does not believe to be true commits an offence.

(6) A person guilty of an offence under this section is liable —

    (a) on conviction on indictment, to imprisonment for a term not exceeding two years or a fine (or both);

7 Draft Clauses

10

Company Law Reform Bill
Part A3 — Provisions relating to company's constitution
Chapter 1 — Articles of association

  (b)   on summary conviction—
        (i)   in England and Wales, to imprisonment for a term not exceeding twelve months or to a fine not exceeding the statutory maximum (or both);
        (ii) in Scotland, to imprisonment for a term not exceeding six months, or to a fine not exceeding the statutory maximum (or both).

In relation to an offence committed before the commencement of section 154(1) of the Criminal Justice Act 2003 (c. 44), for "twelve months" in paragraph (b)(i) substitute "six months".

A24   Effect of alteration of articles on company's members

(1)   A member of a company is not bound by an alteration to its articles after the date on which he became a member, if and so far as the alteration—
      (a)   requires him to take or subscribe for more shares than the number held by him at the date on which the alteration is made, or
      (b)   in any way increases his liability as at that date to contribute to the company's share capital or otherwise to pay money to the company.

(2)   Subsection (1) does not apply in a case where the member agrees in writing, either before or after the alteration is made, to be bound by the alteration.

A25   Registrar to be sent copy of amended articles

Where a company is required to send to the registrar any document making or evidencing an alteration in the company's articles, the company must send with it a copy of the articles as altered.

Supplementary

A26   Copies of articles etc to be provided to members

(1)   A company shall, on being so required by any member, send to him a copy of the company's articles.

(2)   Where any alteration has been made in the company's articles, every copy issued after the date of the alteration must be in accordance with the alteration.

(3)   If a company makes default in complying with this section, an offence is committed by—
      (a)   every officer of the company who is in default, and
      (b)   every responsible delegate.

(4)   A person guilty of an offence under this section is liable on summary conviction to a fine not exceeding level 3 on the standard scale.

A27   Former provisions of memorandum treated as provisions of articles

Provisions that immediately before the commencement of this Act were contained in a company's memorandum but are not provisions of the kind specified in section A8 (provisions of new-style memorandum) have effect after the commencement of this Act as provisions of the company's articles.

Company Law Reform Bill
Part A3 — Provisions relating to company's constitution
Chapter 2 — Resolutions and agreements to be recorded by registrar

11

CHAPTER 2

RESOLUTIONS AND AGREEMENTS TO BE RECORDED BY REGISTRAR

A28 Resolutions and agreements to which this Chapter applies

(1) This Chapter applies to—

    (a) any special resolution;

    (b) any resolution or agreement agreed to by all the members of a company that, if not so agreed to, would not have been effective for its purpose unless passed as a special resolution;

    (c) any resolution or agreement agreed to by all the members of a class of shareholders that, if not so agreed to, would not have been effective for its purpose unless passed by some particular majority or otherwise in some particular manner;

    (d) any resolution or agreement that effectively binds all members of a class of shareholders though not agreed to by all those members;

    (e) a resolution to give, vary, revoke or renew authority for the purposes of [section 80ZB of the Companies Act 1985 (c. 6) (allotment of shares etc by directors) (see clause H5)];

    (f) a resolution of the directors of a company under section 147(2) of that Act (resolution in connection with re-registration in consequence of company acquiring its own shares);

    (g) a resolution conferring, varying, revoking or renewing authority under section 166 of that Act (market purchase of company's own shares);

    (h) a resolution for voluntary winding up passed under section 84(1)(a) of the Insolvency Act 1986 (c. 45);

    (i) a resolution of the director of an old public company under section 2(1) of the Companies Consolidation (Consequential Provisions) Act 1985 (c. 9) that the company should be re-registered as a public company;

    (j) a resolution passed by virtue of regulation 16(2) or (6) of the Uncertificated Securities Regulations 1995 (S.I. 1995/3272) (resolution allowing title to shares to be evidenced without a written instrument or preventing or reversing such a resolution).

(2) References in subsection (1) to a member of a company, or of a class of members of a company, do not include the company itself where it is such a member by virtue only of its holding shares as treasury shares.

A29 Copy to be forwarded to and recorded by registrar

(1) A copy of every resolution or agreement to which this Chapter applies, printed or in some other form approved by the registrar, must be—

    (a) forwarded to the registrar of companies within 15 days after it is passed or made, and

    (b) recorded by him.

(2) If a company fails to comply with this section, an offence is committed by—

    (a) the company, and

    (b) every officer of it who is in default.

(3) A person guilty of an offence under this section is liable on summary conviction to a fine not exceeding level 3 on the standard scale and, for

12

Company Law Reform Bill
Part A3 — Provisions relating to company's constitution
Chapter 2 — Resolutions and agreements to be recorded by registrar

continued contravention, a daily default fine not exceeding one-tenth of level 3 on the standard scale.

(4) For the purposes of this section, a liquidator of the company is treated as an officer of it.

A30 Copies to be issued or provided to members

(1) This section applies to any resolution or agreement relating to a company that has been recorded by the registrar —
   (a) under section A29, or
   (b) under section 380 of the Companies Act 1985 (c. 6) (which made provision corresponding to this Chapter),
and that is for the time being in force.

(2) A copy of every such resolution or agreement must be embodied in or annexed to every copy of the company's articles issued by the company.

(3) A company must, on request by a member, send him a copy of any such resolution or agreement.

(4) If a company fails to comply with subsection (2) or (3), an offence is committed by —
   (a) the company, and
   (b) every officer of it who is in default.

(5) A person guilty of an offence under this section is liable on summary conviction to a fine not exceeding level 3 on the standard scale for each occasion on which copies are issued or, as the case may be, requested.

(6) For the purposes of this section, a liquidator of the company is treated as an officer of it.

CHAPTER 3

MISCELLANEOUS AND SUPPLEMENTARY PROVISIONS

Change of name

A31 Change of name

(1) A company may change its name —
   (a) by special resolution;
   (b) by resolution of the directors in accordance with section 31(2) of the Companies Act 1985 (change of name in order to comply with direction of Secretary of State);
   (c) [under [provisions yet to be drafted on opportunistic registration and restoration to the register]);]
   (d) by any other means provided for by its articles.

(2) A change of name is effective only if the new name complies with the requirements of Chapter 2 of Part 1 of the Companies Act 1985 (general requirements as to company names).

Company Law Reform Bill
Part A3 — Provisions relating to company's constitution
Chapter 3 — Miscellaneous and supplementary provisions

13

A32   Change of name: procedure

(1)   A special resolution changing the name of a company is subject to Chapter 2 of this Part (resolutions and agreements to be recorded by registrar).

(2)   Where a resolution of the directors is passed in accordance with section 31(2) of the Companies Act 1985 (change of name in order to comply with direction of the Secretary of State), the company must give notice to the registrar of the change in the prescribed form.

(3)   [Procedure on change of name under provisions relating to opportunistic registration or restoration to the register.]

(4)   Where a change of name has been approved by the company by other means provided for by its articles—
    (a)   the company must give notice to the registrar in the prescribed form, and
    (b)   the notice must be accompanied by a statement of compliance.

(5)   The statement of compliance required to be delivered to the registrar is a statement in the prescribed form by—
    (a)   a [lawyer] engaged in acting for the company, or
    (b)   a director or secretary of the company,
that the change of name has been made by means provided for by the company's articles.
The statement must be authenticated by the person making it.

(6)   The registrar may rely on the statement of compliance as sufficient evidence of the matters stated in it.

(7)   A person who in a statement of compliance under this section makes a false statement that he knows to be false or does not believe to be true commits an offence.

(8)   A person guilty of an offence under this section is liable—
    (a)   on conviction on indictment, to imprisonment for a term not exceeding two years or a fine (or both);
    (b)   on summary conviction—
        (i)   in England and Wales, to imprisonment for a term not exceeding twelve months or to a fine not exceeding the statutory maximum (or both);
        (ii)   in Scotland, to imprisonment for a term not exceeding six months, or to a fine not exceeding the statutory maximum (or both).
In relation to an offence committed before the commencement of section 154(1) of the Criminal Justice Act 2003 (c. 44), for "twelve months" in paragraph (b)(i) substitute "six months".

A33   Change of name: issue of new certificate of incorporation

(1)   When a company changes its name the registrar shall—
    (a)   enter the new name on the register in place of the former name, and
    (b)   issue a certificate of incorporation altered to meet the circumstances of the case.

7 Draft Clauses

14

Company Law Reform Bill
Part A3 — Provisions relating to company's constitution
Chapter 3 — Miscellaneous and supplementary provisions

(2) The change of name has effect from the date on which the altered certificate is issued.

A34 Change of name: effect

(1) A change of name by a company does not affect any rights or obligations of the company or render defective any legal proceedings by or against it.

(2) Any legal proceedings that might have been continued or commenced against it by its former name may be continued or commenced against it by its new name.

A35 Change of name: conditional change

(1) This section applies where a change of name is conditional on the occurrence of an event.

(2) The company must when giving notice to the registrar of the change —
    (a) specify that the change is conditional, and
    (b) state whether the event has occurred.

(3) If the notice states that the event has not occurred the registrar is not required to act under section A33 (issue of new certificate of incorporation) until the company gives notice under this section.

(4) When the event has occurred —
    (a) the company must give notice to the registrar in the prescribed form, and
    (b) the notice must be accompanied by a statement of compliance.

(5) The statement of compliance required to be delivered to the registrar is a statement in the prescribed form by —
    (a) a [lawyer] engaged in acting for the company, or
    (b) a director or secretary of the company,
that the event has occurred.
The statement must be authenticated by the person making it.

(6) The registrar may rely on the statement of compliance as sufficient evidence of the matters stated in it.

(7) A person who in a statement of compliance under this section makes a false statement that he knows to be false or does not believe to be true commits an offence.

(8) A person guilty of an offence under this section is liable —
    (a) on conviction on indictment, to imprisonment for a term not exceeding two years or a fine (or both);
    (b) on summary conviction —
        (i)   in England and Wales, to imprisonment for a term not exceeding twelve months or to a fine not exceeding the statutory maximum (or both);
        (ii) in Scotland, to imprisonment for a term not exceeding six months, or to a fine not exceeding the statutory maximum (or both).

Company Law Reform Bill
Part A3 — Provisions relating to company's constitution
Chapter 3 — Miscellaneous and supplementary provisions

15

In relation to an offence committed before the commencement of section 154(1) of the Criminal Justice Act 2003 (c. 44), for "twelve months" in paragraph (b)(i) substitute "six months".

Alteration of situation of registered office

A36 Alteration of registered office: transfer to different part of Great Britain

(1) The Secretary of State may make provision by regulations enabling —
   (a) a company whose registered office is situated in England and Wales, or in Wales, to transfer its registered office to Scotland; and
   (b) a company whose registered office is situated in Scotland to transfer its registered office to England and Wales, or to Wales.

(2) The regulations may —
   (a) prescribe procedural requirements to be satisfied by a company proposing to transfer its registered office;
   (b) specify conditions or limitations on the freedom to transfer;
   (c) contain such supplementary or consequential provision as appears to the Secretary of State to be necessary (in particular, for protecting the rights of creditors and other persons);
   (d) provide that a transfer is ineffective if there is a failure to comply with specified requirements of the regulations;
   (e) impose criminal liability for breach of specified provisions of the regulations.

(3) Regulations under this section shall be made by statutory instrument.

(4) No such regulations shall be made unless a draft of them has been laid before Parliament and approved by a resolution of each House of Parliament.

A37 Alteration of registered office: Wales

(1) A company whose registered office is situated in England and Wales may, if the address of its registered office is in Wales, by special resolution alter the situation of its registered office to "Wales".

(2) A company whose registered office is situated in Wales may by special resolution alter the situation of its registered office to "England and Wales".

(3) Where a company passes a resolution under this section —
   (a) it must give notice to the registrar in the prescribed form, and
   (b) the alteration is not effective until entry of that notice on the register.

Alteration of status

A38 Alteration of status

The status of a company as limited or unlimited, or as a private or public company, may only be changed by re-registration in accordance with the provisions of Part 2 of the Companies Act 1985 (c. 6).

16

Company Law Reform Bill
Part A3 — Provisions relating to company's constitution
Chapter 3 — Miscellaneous and supplementary provisions

Statement of company's objects

A39   Statement of company's objects

(1)   Unless a company's articles specifically restrict the objects of the company, its objects are unrestricted.

(2)   If (or so far as) the objects of a company are unrestricted, neither the company's capacity nor the authority of persons to bind the company is limited by its constitution.

(3)   If (or so far as) the objects of a company are restricted, the validity of any act done by the company shall not be called into question on the ground of lack of capacity.

(4)   Where a company alters its articles so as to add, remove or alter a statement of the company's objects —

    (a)   it must give notice to the registrar in the prescribed form,

    (b)   on receipt of the notice, the registrar shall register it, and

    (c)   the alteration is not effective until entry of that notice on the register.

(5)   Any such alteration does not affect any rights or obligations of the company or render defective any legal proceedings by or against it.

Other provisions

A40   Binding effect of memorandum and articles

The provisions of a company's memorandum and articles, when registered, bind the company and its members to the same extent as if they —

    (a)   had been signed and sealed by each member, and

    (b)   contained covenants on the part of each member to observe their provisions.

A41   Character of obligation to pay money under memorandum or articles

(1)   Money payable by a member to a company under its memorandum or articles is a debt due from him to the company.

(2)   In England and Wales it is an ordinary contract debt.

A42   Right to participate in profits otherwise than as member void

In the case of a company not having a share capital any provision in the company's articles, or in any resolution of the company, purporting to give a person a right to participate in the divisible profits of the company otherwise than as member is void.

A43   Application of enactments etc to single member companies

(1)   Any enactment or rule of law applicable to companies formed by two or more persons or having two or more members applies with any necessary modification in relation to a company formed by one person or having only one person as a member.

Company Law Reform Bill
Part A3 — Provisions relating to company's constitution
Chapter 3 — Miscellaneous and supplementary provisions

17

(2)   In subsection (1) "enactment" includes —
   (a)   an enactment contained in subordinate legislation within the meaning of the Interpretation Act 1978 (c. 30), and
   (b)   an enactment contained in, or in an instrument made under, an Act of the Scottish Parliament.

7 Draft Clauses

Company Law Reform Bill

CONTENTS

CHAPTER 4

APPOINTMENT AND REMOVAL OF DIRECTORS

General

Appointment

Register of directors, etc

Removal

CHAPTER 5

SERVICE CONTRACTS

CHAPTER 6

SUPPLEMENTARY PROVISIONS

PART B

DIRECTORS

CHAPTER 1

GENERAL DUTIES

Introductory provisions

B1 **Scope and application of general duties**

(1) The general duties specified in sections B2 to B8 are owed by a director of a company to the company.

(2) The duties apply to shadow directors as they apply to directors, subject to any necessary adaptations.

(3) A person who ceases to be a director continues to be subject—
  (a) to the duty in section B6 (duty to avoid conflicts of interest) as regards the exploitation of any property, information or opportunity of which he became aware at a time when he was a director, and
  (b) to the duty in section B7 (duty not to accept benefits from third parties) as regards things done or omitted by him before he ceased to be a director.

To that extent those duties apply to a former director as to a director, subject to any necessary adaptations.

The general duties

B2 **Duty to act within powers**

As a director of a company you must—
  (a) act in accordance with the company's constitution, and
  (b) only exercise powers for the purposes for which they are conferred.

B3 **Duty to promote the success of the company for the benefit of its members**

(1) As a director of a company you must act in the way you consider, in good faith, would be most likely to promote the success of the company for the benefit of its members as a whole.

(2) Where or to the extent that the company is established for purposes other than the benefit of its members, your duty is to act in the way you consider, in good faith, would be most likely to achieve those purposes.

(3) In fulfilling the duty imposed by this section you must take account (where relevant and so far as reasonably practicable) of —

    (a) the likely consequences of any decision in both the long and the short term,

    (b) any need of the company —

        (i) to have regard to the interests of its employees,

        (ii) to foster its business relationships with suppliers, customers and others,

        (iii) to consider the impact of its operations on the community and the environment, and

        (iv) to maintain a reputation for high standards of business conduct, and

    (c) the need to act fairly as between members of the company who have different interests.

(4) The duty imposed by this section has effect subject to any enactment or rule of law requiring directors, in certain circumstances, to consider or act in the interests of creditors of the company.

B4 Duty to exercise independent judgment

(1) As a director of a company you must exercise independent judgment.

(2) This duty is not infringed by your acting —

    (a) in accordance with an agreement duly entered into by the company that restricts the future exercise of discretion by its directors, or

    (b) in a way authorised by the company's constitution.

B5 Duty to exercise reasonable care, skill and diligence

(1) As a director of a company you must exercise reasonable care, skill and diligence.

(2) This means the care, skill and diligence that would be exercised by a reasonably diligent person with —

    (a) the knowledge, skill and experience that may reasonably be expected of a director in your position, and

    (b) any additional knowledge, skill or experience that you in fact have.

B6 Duty to avoid conflicts of interest

(1) As a director of a company you must avoid a situation in which you have, or can have, a direct or indirect interest that conflicts, or possibly may conflict, with the interests of the company.

(2) This applies in particular to the exploitation of any property, information or opportunity (and it is immaterial whether the company could take advantage of the property, information or opportunity).

(3) This duty is not infringed —

    (a) if there is no real possibility of a conflict of interest;

    (b) if the conflict of interest arises in relation to a proposed transaction or arrangement with the company (but see section B8 (duty to declare interest in proposed transaction with company));

    (c)   if the conflict of interest arises in relation to a transaction or arrangement duly entered into by the company;

    (d)   if authorisation has been given by the company in accordance with subsection (4).

(4)   Authorisation by the company may be given—

    (a)   by the matter being proposed to the members of the company and authorised by them; or

    (b)   where the company is a private company and nothing in the company's constitution invalidates such authorisation, by the matter being proposed to and authorised by the directors; or

    (c)   where the company is a public company and its constitution includes provision enabling the directors to authorise the matter, by the matter being proposed to and authorised by them in accordance with the constitution.

(5)   If you or any other interested director participate in the proceedings required by subsection (4)(b) or (c), the authorisation is effective only if it would have been effectively agreed to without the participation of any interested director.

(6)   Any reference in this section to a conflict of interest includes a conflict of interest and duty and a conflict of duties.

B7   Duty not to accept benefits from third parties

(1)   As a director of a company you must not accept a benefit from a third party conferred by reason of—

    (a)   your being a director, or

    (b)   your doing (or not doing) anything as director.

(2)   A "third party" means a person other than the company, an associated company or a person acting on behalf of the company or an associated company.

(3)   Benefits received by you from a person by whom your services (as a director or otherwise) are provided to the company are not regarded as conferred by a third party.

(4)   This duty is not infringed—

    (a)   if there is no real possibility of a conflict of interest;

    (b)   if the matter has been proposed to the members of the company and authorised by them.

(5)   Any reference in this section to a conflict of interest includes a conflict of interest and duty and a conflict of duties.

B8   Duty to declare interest in proposed transaction with the company

(1)   As a director of a company you must declare the nature and extent of any interest, direct or indirect, you have in a proposed transaction or arrangement with the company.

(2)   If an earlier declaration of interest proves to be, or becomes, inaccurate or incomplete (for instance, because of subsequent changes in the matters to which it relates) you must make a further declaration.

(3) Any declaration required by this section —
  (a) may be made to the other directors or to the members of the company, and
  (b) must be made before the company enters into the transaction or arrangement.

(4) You will be regarded as failing to comply with the duty imposed by this section if you fail to make a declaration, or fail to declare fully the nature and extent of your interest, because you are unaware of matters of which you ought reasonably to be aware.

(5) In Chapter 2 (declaration of interest: further provisions) —
  sections B12 to B15 impose other requirements that you must comply with, but they are not part of the duty imposed by this section; and
  sections B16 to B19 contain supplementary provisions, including provisions about exceptions, notices and sole directors, that apply both in relation to those requirements and in relation to the duty imposed by this section.

Supplementary provisions

B9   Cases within more than one of the general duties

Except as otherwise provided, more than one of the general duties may apply in any given case and the operation of any of them is not affected by the application or otherwise of any of the others.

B10   Relationship between general duties and other rules

(1) The general duties are based on certain common law rules and equitable principles as they apply in relation to directors and have effect in place of those rules and principles as regards the duties owed to a company by a director.

(2) The general duties shall be interpreted and applied in the same way as common law rules or equitable principles, and regard shall be had to the corresponding common law rules and equitable principles in interpreting and applying the general duties.

(3) In a case where section B6 (duty to avoid conflicts of interest) or section B8 (duty to declare interest in proposed transaction or arrangement) is complied with by disclosure to or authorisation by the directors, the transaction or arrangement is not liable to be set aside by virtue of any common law rule or equitable principle requiring the consent or approval of the members of the company.
This is without prejudice to any enactment, or provision of the company's constitution, requiring such consent or approval.

(4) The application of section B8 (duty to declare interest in proposed transaction or arrangement) is not affected by the fact that the case also falls within Chapter 3 (transactions requiring shareholder approval).

(5) Where Chapter 3 applies (transactions requiring shareholder approval) and —
  (a) approval is given under that Chapter, or
  (b) the matter is one as to which it is provided that approval is not needed,

it is not necessary also to comply with section B6 (duty to avoid conflicts of interest) or section B7 (duty not to accept benefits from third parties).

(6) Except as otherwise provided, the general duties have effect notwithstanding any other enactment or rule of law or anything in the company's constitution.

B11 Civil consequences of breach of general duties

The consequences of breach (or threatened breach) of any of the general duties are the same as would apply if the corresponding common law rule or equitable principle applied.

CHAPTER 2

DECLARATION OF INTEREST: FURTHER PROVISIONS

Requirements as to declaration of interest

B12 Requirements as to declaration of interest in transaction or arrangement

(1) If a director of a company —
   (a) is in any way, directly or indirectly, interested in a proposed transaction or arrangement with the company, or
   (b) becomes in any way, directly or indirectly, interested in a transaction or arrangement entered into by the company,
   he must declare the nature and extent of that interest to the other directors.

(2) For the purposes of this section a director is regarded as having an interest in a transaction or arrangement in any case where a person connected with him has an interest.

   If in such a case the director would not otherwise be regarded as having an interest in the transaction or arrangement by virtue of the connected person's interest, the declaration required is of the nature of the director's connection with that person and the nature and extent of that person's interest in the transaction or arrangement.

(3) If an earlier declaration of interest proves to be, or becomes, inaccurate or incomplete (for instance, because of subsequent changes in the matters to which it relates), a further declaration must be made.

(4) Any declaration required by this section must be made —
   (a) at a meeting of the directors,
   (b) by notice in writing, or
   (c) by general notice (see section B17).

(5) The declaration must be made as soon as is reasonably practicable.

   Failure to comply with this requirement does not affect the underlying duty to make the declaration.

(6) A director is regarded as failing to comply with the duty imposed by this section if he fails to make a declaration, or fails to declare fully the nature and extent of his interest (or, where subsection (2) applies, the interest of a connected person) because he is unaware of matters of which he ought

B13 Relationship between requirements and other rules

(1) Compliance (or failure to comply) with the requirements of section B12 does not affect the general duties in Chapter 1.

(2) Compliance with the requirements of section B12 does not remove the need for approval required under any applicable provision of Chapter 3 (transactions requiring shareholder approval).

(3) Nothing in this Chapter prejudices the operation of any rule of law restricting directors of a company from having an interest in contracts with the company.

B14 Offence of failure to comply with requirements

(1) A director who fails to comply with any of the requirements of section B12 commits an offence.

(2) Subject to subsection (3) a person guilty of an offence under this section is liable—
    (a) on conviction on indictment, to a fine;
    (b) on summary conviction, to a fine not exceeding the statutory maximum.

(3) A person who acts dishonestly in committing an offence under this section is liable—
    (a) on conviction on indictment, to imprisonment for a term not exceeding seven years or a fine (or both);
    (b) on summary conviction—
        (i) in England and Wales, to imprisonment for a term not exceeding twelve months or to a fine not exceeding the statutory maximum (or both);
        (ii) in Scotland, to imprisonment for a term not exceeding six months, or to a fine not exceeding the statutory maximum (or both).
    In relation to an offence committed before the commencement of section 154(1) of the Criminal Justice Act 2003 (c. 44), for "twelve months" in paragraph (b)(i) substitute "six months".

(4) The references in this section to the requirements of section B12 include—
    (a) in relation to a sole director, the requirements of section B19;
    (b) in relation to a shadow director, the requirements of section B20.

B15 Civil consequences of failure to comply with requirements

Failure to comply with the requirements of section B12 does not affect the validity of the transaction or arrangement or give rise to any civil liability.

Common provisions

B16 Circumstances in which declaration not required

(1) A director need not declare an interest that cannot reasonably be regarded as giving rise to any real possibility of a conflict of interest.

(2)   A director need not declare an interest if, or to the extent that, the other directors are already aware of it.

For this purpose the other directors are treated as aware of anything of which they ought reasonably to be aware.

(3)   A director need not declare an interest in the terms of his service contract if, or to the extent that, those terms have been or are to be considered —

(a)   by a meeting of the directors, or

(b)   by a committee of the directors appointed for the purpose under the company's constitution.

B17   General notice treated as sufficient declaration

(1)   General notice in accordance with this section is a sufficient declaration of interest in relation to the matters to which it relates.

(2)   General notice is notice given to the directors of a company to the effect that the director —

(a)   has an interest (as member, officer, employee or otherwise) in a specified body corporate or firm and is to be regarded as interested in any transaction or arrangement that may, after the date of the notice, be made with that body corporate or firm, or

(b)   is connected with a specified person (other than a body corporate or firm) and is to be regarded as interested in any transaction or arrangement that may, after the date of the notice, be made with that person.

(3)   The notice must state the nature and extent of the director's interest in the body corporate or firm or, as the case may be, the nature of his connection with the person.

(4)   General notice is not effective unless —

(a)   it is given at a meeting of the directors, or

(b)   the director takes reasonable steps to secure that it is brought up and read at the next meeting of the directors after it is given.

(5)   Nothing in this section affects whether, or when, a declaration must be made.

B18   Provisions as to notice in writing

(1)   This section applies where a declaration of interest is made by notice in writing.

(2)   The director must send the notice to the other directors.

(3)   The notice may be sent [in paper form] or, if the recipient has agreed to receive it [in electronic form], in an agreed electronic form.

(4)   The notice may be sent —

(a)   by hand or by post, or

(b)   if the recipient has agreed to receive it by [electronic means], by agreed electronic means.

(5)   The form and the means adopted must be such that the recipient is able to read the text of the notice and to keep and refer to it at a later date.

(6)   Where a director declares an interest by notice in writing —

> (a) the making of the declaration is deemed to form part of the proceedings at the next meeting of the directors after the notice is given, and
>
> (b) section D60 (minutes of meetings) applies as if the declaration had been made at that meeting.

B19 Application of provisions to sole director

(1) No declaration of interest is required in the case of a sole director of a company that is not required to have more than one director.

(2) Where a declaration of interest is required of a sole director of a company that is required to have more than one director —

> (a) the declaration must be recorded in writing,
>
> (b) the making of the declaration is deemed to form part of the proceedings at the next meeting of the directors after the notice is given, and
>
> (c) section D60 (minutes of meetings) applies as if the declaration had been made at that meeting.

(3) Nothing in this section affects the operation of section 322B(1) of the Companies Act 1985 (c. 6) (contract with sole member who is also sole director: terms to be set out in writing or recorded in minutes).

Supplementary

B20 Application of provisions to shadow director

(1) The provisions of this Chapter apply to a shadow director as to a director, subject to the following adaptation.

(2) In section B12 (requirements as to declaration of interest), subsection (4)(a) (declaration at meeting of directors) does not apply.

(3) In section B17 (general notice treated as sufficient declaration), subsection (4) (notice to be given at or brought up and read at meeting of directors) does not apply.
General notice by a shadow director is not effective unless given by notice in writing in accordance with section B18.

CHAPTER 3

TRANSACTIONS REQUIRING SHAREHOLDER APPROVAL

Service contracts

B21 Directors' service contracts: provision requiring shareholder approval

(1) This section applies to provision under which the guaranteed term of a director's employment —

> (a) with the company of which he is a director, or
>
> (b) where he is the director of a holding company, within the group consisting of that company and its subsidiaries,

is, or may be, longer than five years.

(2) A company may not agree to such provision unless it has been approved —
    (a) by resolution of the members of the company, and
    (b) in the case of a director of a holding company, by resolution of the members of that company.

(3) The guaranteed term of a director's employment is —
    (a) the period (if any) during which the director's employment —
        (i) is to continue, or may be continued otherwise than at the instance of the company, and
        (ii) cannot be terminated by the company by notice, or can only be so terminated in specified circumstances, or
    (b) in the case of employment terminable by the company by notice, the period of notice required to be given,
or, in the case of employment having a period within paragraph (a) and a period within paragraph (b), the aggregate of those periods.

(4) If more than six months before the end of the guaranteed term of a director's employment the company enters into a further service contract (otherwise than in pursuance of a right conferred by or under the original contract on the other party to it), this section applies as if there were added to the guaranteed term of the new contract the unexpired period of the guaranteed term of the original contract.

(5) A resolution approving provision to which this section applies must not be passed unless a memorandum setting out the proposed contract incorporating the provision is made available to members —
    (a) in the case of a written resolution, by being sent or submitted to every eligible member at or before the time at which the proposed resolution is sent or submitted to him;
    (b) in the case of a resolution at a meeting, by being made available for inspection by members of the company both —
        (i) at the company's registered office for not less than 15 days ending with the date of the meeting, and
        (ii) at the meeting itself.

(6) No approval is required under this section on the part of —
    (a) a body corporate that is not —
        (i) a company within the meaning of [this Act], or
        (ii) a body registered under section 680 of the Companies Act 1985;
    (b) a body corporate that is a wholly-owned subsidiary of another body corporate.

(7) If a company agrees to provision in contravention of this section —
    (a) the provision is void, to the extent of the contravention, and
    (b) the contract is deemed to contain a term entitling the company to terminate it at any time by the giving of reasonable notice.

(8) In this section "employment" means any employment under a director's service contract.

Property transactions

B22 Property transactions: requirement of shareholder approval

(1) A company may not enter into a transaction under which —

    (a) a director of the company or its holding company, or a person connected with such a director, acquires from the company (directly or indirectly) a substantial non-cash asset, or

    (b) the company acquires a substantial non-cash asset (directly or indirectly) from such a director or a person so connected,

unless the transaction has been approved by a resolution of the members of the company.

For the meaning of "substantial non-cash asset" see section B23.

(2) If the director or connected person is a director of its holding company or a person connected with such a director, the transaction must also have been approved by a resolution of the members of the holding company.

(3) An agreement by a company to enter into a transaction for which approval is required under this section does not itself require approval under this section if it is expressed to be conditional on the requisite approval being obtained for the transaction.

(4) But a company shall not be subject to any liability by reason of a failure to obtain such approval.

(5) No approval is required under this section on the part of —

    (a) a body corporate that is not —

        (i) a company within the meaning of [this Act], or

        (ii) a body registered under section 680 of the Companies Act 1985;

    (b) a body corporate that is a wholly-owned subsidiary of another body corporate.

(6) For the purposes of this section —

    (a) a transaction involving more than one non-cash asset, or

    (b) a transaction that is one of a series of transactions involving non-cash assets,

shall be treated as if they involved a non-cash asset of a value equal to the aggregate value of all the non-cash assets involved in the transaction or, as the case may be, the series of transactions.

B23 Property transactions: meaning of "substantial"

(1) This section explains what is meant in section B22 (requirement of approval for substantial property transactions) by a "substantial" non-cash asset.

(2) An asset is a substantial asset in relation to a company if its value —

    (a) exceeds 10% of the company's asset value and is more than £5,000, or

    (b) exceeds £100,000.

(3) For the purposes of subsection (2)(a) a company's "asset value" at any time is —

    (a) the value of the company's net assets determined by reference to the accounts prepared and sent to members in respect of the last preceding financial year, or

(b) if accounts for the last preceding financial year have not been prepared and sent to members, the amount of the company's called-up share capital.

(4) Whether an asset is a substantial asset shall be determined as at the time the transaction is entered into or any earlier time at which the company binds itself to enter into the transaction.

B24 Property transactions: company subsequently going into insolvent liquidation

(1) This section applies where —
    (a) a director of a company or its holding company, or a person connected with such a director, acquires an asset (directly or indirectly) from the company, and
    (b) the company —
        (i) is insolvent at the time of the transaction, or
        (ii) becomes insolvent in consequence of the transaction,
    and subsequently goes into insolvent liquidation.

(2) In those circumstances a resolution passed within the period of twelve months before the onset of insolvency is effective for the purposes of section B22 (requirement of shareholder approval for substantial property transactions) only if —
    (a) the requirements of section B25 as to independent valuation were met, or
    (b) the resolution would have been validly passed —
        (i) in the case of a written resolution, if the director in question and any persons connected with him had not been eligible members in relation to the resolution;
        (ii) in the case of a resolution at a general meeting, if the director in question and any persons connected with him had not been entitled to attend and vote on the resolution.

(3) For the purposes of this section —
    (a) a company is "insolvent" if it is unable to pay its debts within the meaning of section 123 of the Insolvency Act 1986 (c. 45), and
    (b) a company "goes into insolvent liquidation" if it goes into liquidation within the meaning of section 247 of that Act at a time when its assets are insufficient for the payment of its debts and other liabilities and the expenses of the winding up.

(4) In subsection (2) "the onset of insolvency" means —
    (a) the commencement of the winding up, or
    (b) where the company goes into liquidation —
        (i) following conversion of administration into winding up by virtue of Article 37 of Council Regulation (EC) No 1346/2000, or
        (ii) at the time when the appointment of an administrator ceases to have effect,
    when the company enters administration.

(5) For this purpose a company enters administration —
    (a) in a case where an administrator is appointed by administration order, when the administration application is made;

      (b)   in a case where an administrator is appointed under paragraph 14 or 22 of Schedule B1 to the Insolvency Act 1986 (c. 45) following filing with the court of a copy of a notice of intention to appoint under that paragraph, when the copy of the notice is filed;

      (c)   in a case where an administrator is appointed otherwise than as mentioned in paragraph (a) or (b), when the appointment takes effect.

(6)   In the application of this section to Scotland a reference to filing with the court is a reference to lodging in court.

B25   Property transactions: requirements as to independent valuation

(1)   The requirements as to independent valuation are—

      (a)   the asset and the consideration to be given for it must be valued by a qualified independent person ("the valuer"),

      (b)   a report by the valuer complying with the requirements of this section must be made by him to the company, and

      (c)   the report must be available for inspection by members of the company—

            (i)   at the company's registered office for not less than 15 days ending with the date of the meeting on which the resolution is passed, and

            (ii)   at the meeting itself.

(2)   A "qualified independent person" means a person who is qualified at the time of the report to be appointed, or to continue to be, an auditor of the company.

(3)   Where it appears to the valuer to be reasonable to do so, he may arrange for the valuation or part of it to be made (or for him to accept such a valuation) by another person who—

      (a)   appears to him to have the requisite knowledge and experience to value the asset, and

      (b)   is not—

            (i)   an officer or employee of the company,

            (ii)   an officer or employee of another body corporate that is the company's subsidiary or holding company or a subsidiary of the company's holding company, or

           (iii)   a partner or employee of such an officer or employee as is mentioned in sub-paragraph (i) or (ii).

The references in paragraph (b)(i) and (ii) to an officer or employee do not include an auditor.

(4)   The valuer's report must—

      (a)   describe the asset and the consideration to be given for it,

      (b)   state the value of the asset and the amount or value of the consideration,

      (c)   describe what method of valuation was used, and

      (d)   specify the date of the valuation.

(5)   Where the asset is valued by a person other than the valuer himself, the report must state that fact and also state the person's name and what knowledge and experience he has to carry out the valuation.

(6)   The valuer's report must be accompanied by a statement by him—

    (a)   in the case of a valuation made by a person other than the valuer himself, that it appeared to the valuer reasonable to arrange for it to be so made or to accept a valuation so made;

    (b)   that the method of valuation used (whether by himself or another person) was reasonable in all the circumstances;

    (c)   that it appears to the valuer that there has been no material change in the value of the asset since the date of the valuation; and

    (d)   that on the basis of the valuation the value of the consideration to be received by the company is not less than the value of the consideration to be given by it.

B26   Property transactions: exclusion of service contracts, compensation for loss of office, etc

(1)   Section B22 (requirement of shareholder approval for substantial property transactions) does not apply to a transaction so far as it relates—

    (a)   to anything to which a director of a company is entitled under his service contract, or

    (b)   to any payment made or other benefit provided to a director—

        (i)   by way of compensation for loss of office as director,

        (ii)   by way of compensation for loss of any other office or employment with the company, or

        (iii)   as consideration for or in connection with his retirement from his office as director of the company, or from any other office or employment with the company.

(2)   For the purposes of subsection (1)(b) anything paid or provided—

    (a)   to a person connected with a director, or

    (b)   to any person at the direction of, or for the benefit of, a director or a person connected with him,

is treated as paid or provided to the director.

B27   Property transactions: exception for transactions with members or other group companies

Approval is not required under section B22 (requirement of shareholder approval for substantial property transactions)—

    (a)   for a transaction between a company and a person in his character as a member of that company, or

    (b)   for a transaction between—

        (i)   a holding company and its wholly-owned subsidiary, or

        (ii)   two wholly-owned subsidiaries of the same holding company.

B28   Property transactions: exception in case of company in winding up or administration

Approval is not required under section B22 (requirement of shareholder approval for certain property transactions) on the part of a company—

    (a)   that is being wound up (unless the winding up is a members' voluntary winding up), or

    (b)   that is in administration within the meaning of Schedule B1 to the Insolvency Act 1986 (c. 45).

B29 Property transactions: exception for transactions on recognised investment exchange

(1) Approval is not required under section B22 (requirement of shareholder approval for substantial property transactions) for a transaction on a recognised investment exchange effected by a director, or a person connected with him, through the agency of a person who in relation to the transaction acts as an independent broker.

(2) For this purpose—

   (a) "independent broker" means a person who, independently of the director or any person connected with him, selects the person with whom the transaction is to be effected; and

   (b) "recognised investment exchange" has the same meaning as in Part 18 of the Financial Services and Markets Act 2000 (c. 8)

B30 Property transactions: civil consequences of contravention

(1) This section applies where a company enters into a transaction in contravention of section B22 (requirement of shareholder approval for substantial property transactions).

This includes cases where there is a contravention of that section because a resolution subsequently proves to be ineffective by virtue of section B24 (company subsequently going into insolvent liquidation).

(2) The transaction is voidable at the instance of the company, unless—

   (a) restitution of any money or other asset that was the subject-matter of the transaction is no longer possible,

   (b) the company has been indemnified for any loss or damage resulting from the transaction, or

   (c) rights acquired in good faith, for value and without actual notice of the contravention by a person who is not a party to the transaction would be affected by the avoidance.

(3) Whether or not the transaction has been avoided, the persons specified in subsection (4) are liable—

   (a) to account to the company for any gain that he has made directly or indirectly by the transaction, and

   (b) (jointly and severally with any other person so liable under this section) to indemnify the company for any loss or damage resulting from the transaction.

(4) The persons so liable are—

   (a) the director of the company or its holding company, or the person connected with such a director, with whom the company entered into the transaction, and

   (b) any director of the company who authorised the transaction.

This is subject to subsections (5) and (6).

(5) In the case of a transaction entered into by a company with a person connected with a director of the company or its holding company, that director is not liable if he shows that he took all reasonable steps to secure the company's compliance with section B22.

(6) In any case a person so connected, or a director who authorised the transaction, is not liable if he shows that, at the time the transaction was entered into, he did not know the relevant circumstances constituting the contravention.

(7) Nothing in this section shall be read as excluding the operation of any other enactment or rule of law by virtue of which the transaction may be called in question or any liability to the company may arise.

B31 Property transactions: effect of subsequent affirmation

(1) Where a transaction is entered into by a company in contravention of section B22 (requirement of shareholder approval) but, within a reasonable period, it is affirmed —
    (a) in the case of a contravention of subsection (1) of that section, by resolution of the members of the company, and
    (b) in the case of a contravention of subsection (2) of that section, by resolution of the members of the holding company,
    the transaction may no longer be avoided under section B30.

(2) The provisions of —
    (a) section B24 (company subsequently going into insolvent liquidation: circumstances in which resolution not effective), and
    (b) section B25 (requirements as to independent valuation),
    apply in relation to a resolution under this section as they apply in relation to a resolution under section B22.

B32 Property transactions: shadow directors

For the purposes of sections B22 to B31 a shadow director is treated as a director.

Loans, quasi-loans and credit transactions

B33 Loans or quasi-loans: requirement of shareholder approval

(1) A company may not —
    (a) make a loan or quasi-loan to a director of the company or of its holding company, or to a person connected with such a director, or
    (b) give a guarantee or other security in connection with a loan or quasi-loan made by any person to such a director, or to a person connected with such a director,
    unless the transaction has been approved by a resolution of the members of the company.

(2) If the director or connected person is a director of its holding company or a person connected with such a director, the transaction must also have been approved by a resolution of the members of the holding company.

(3) A resolution approving a transaction to which this section applies must not be passed unless a memorandum setting out the matters mentioned in subsection (4) is made available to members —
    (a) in the case of a written resolution, by being sent or submitted to every eligible member at or before the time at which the proposed resolution is sent or submitted to him;

    (b)   in the case of a resolution at a meeting, by being made available for inspection by members of the company both—

        (i)   at the company's registered office for not less than 15 days ending with the date of the meeting, and

        (ii)   at the meeting itself.

(4)   The matters to be disclosed are—

    (a)   the amount of the loan or quasi-loan,

    (b)   the purpose for which the loan or quasi-loan is required, and

    (c)   the extent of the company's liability under any transaction connected with the loan or quasi-loan.

(5)   No approval is required under this section on the part of—

    (a)   a body corporate that is not—

        (i)   a company within the meaning of this Act, or

        (ii)   a body registered under section 680 of the Companies Act 1985;

    (b)   a body corporate that is a wholly-owned subsidiary of another body corporate.

B34   Meaning of "quasi-loan" and related expressions

(1)   A "quasi-loan" is a transaction under which one party ("the creditor") agrees to pay, or pays otherwise than in pursuance of an agreement, a sum for another ("the borrower") or agrees to reimburse, or reimburses otherwise than in pursuance of an agreement, expenditure incurred by another party for another ("the borrower")—

    (a)   on terms that the borrower (or a person on his behalf) will reimburse the creditor; or

    (b)   in circumstances giving rise to a liability on the borrower to reimburse the creditor.

(2)   Any reference to the person to whom a quasi-loan is made is a reference to the borrower.

(3)   The liabilities of a borrower under a quasi-loan include the liabilities of any person who has agreed to reimburse the creditor on behalf of the borrower.

B35   Credit transactions: requirement of shareholder approval

(1)   A company may not—

    (a)   enter into a credit transaction as creditor for the benefit of a director of the company or of its holding company, or a person connected with such a director, or

    (b)   give a guarantee or other security in connection with a credit transaction entered into by any person for the benefit of such a director, or a person connected with such a director,

unless the transaction has been approved by resolution of the members of the company.

(2)   If the director or connected person is a director of its holding company or a person connected with such a director, the transaction must also have been approved by a resolution of the members of the holding company.

(3) A resolution approving a transaction to which this section applies must not be passed unless a memorandum setting out the matters mentioned in subsection (4) is made available to members—

    (a) in the case of a written resolution, by being sent or submitted to every eligible member at or before the time at which the proposed resolution is sent or submitted to him;

    (b) in the case of a resolution at a meeting, by being made available for inspection by members of the company both—

        (i) at the company's registered office for not less than 15 days ending with the date of the meeting, and

        (ii) at the meeting itself.

(4) The matters to be disclosed are—

    (a) the nature of the credit transaction,

    (b) the purpose for which the land, goods or services sold or otherwise disposed of, leased, hired or supplied under the credit transaction are required, and

    (c) the extent of the company's liability under any transaction connected with the credit transaction.

(5) No approval is required under this section on the part of—

    (a) a body corporate that is not—

        (i) a company within the meaning of this Act, or

        (ii) a body registered under section 680 of the Companies Act 1985;

    (b) a body corporate that is a wholly-owned subsidiary of another body corporate.

B36 Meaning of "credit transaction"

(1) A "credit transaction" is a transaction under which one party ("the creditor")—

    (a) supplies any goods or sells any land under a hire-purchase agreement or a conditional sale agreement,

    (b) leases or hires any land or goods in return for periodical payments, or

    (c) otherwise disposes of land or supplies goods or services on the understanding that payment (whether in a lump sum or instalments or by way of periodical payments or otherwise) is to be deferred.

(2) Any reference to the person for whose benefit a credit transaction is entered into is to the person to whom goods or services are supplied, or land is sold or otherwise disposed of, under the transaction.

(3) In this section—

    "conditional sale agreement" has the same meaning as in the Consumer Credit Act 1974 (c. 39); and

    "services" means anything other than goods or land.

B37 Related arrangements: requirement of shareholder approval

(1) A company may not—

    (a) take part in an arrangement under which—

        (i) another person enters into a transaction that, if it had been entered into by the company, would have required approval under section B35 or B33, and

        (ii)   that person, in pursuance of the arrangement, obtains a benefit from the company or a company associated with it, or

    (b)   arrange for the assignment to it, or assumption by it, of any rights, obligations or liabilities under a transaction that, if it had been entered into by the company, would have required such approval,

unless the transaction has been approved by a resolution of the members of the company.

(2)   If the director or connected person for whom the transaction is entered into is a director of its holding company or a person connected with such a director, the transaction must also have been approved by a resolution of the members of the holding company.

(3)   A resolution approving a transaction to which this section applies must not be passed unless a memorandum setting out the matters mentioned in subsection (4) is made available to members —

    (a)   in the case of a written resolution, by being sent or submitted to every eligible member at or before the time at which the proposed resolution is sent or submitted to him;

    (b)   in the case of a resolution at a meeting, by being made available for inspection by members of the company both —

        (i)   at the company's registered office for not less than 15 days ending with the date of the meeting, and

        (ii)   at the meeting itself.

(4)   The matters to be disclosed are —

    (a)   the matters that would have to be disclosed if the company were seeking approval of the transaction to which the arrangement relates,

    (b)   the nature of the arrangement, and

    (c)   the extent of the company's liability under the arrangement or any transaction connected with it.

(5)   No approval is required under this section on the part of —

    (a)   a body corporate that is not —

        (i)   a company within the meaning of this Act, or

        (ii)   a body registered under section 680 of the Companies Act 1985;

    (b)   a body corporate that is a wholly-owned subsidiary of another body corporate.

(6)   In determining for the purposes of this section whether a transaction is one that would have required approval under section B35 or B33 if it had been entered into by the company, the transaction shall be treated as having been entered into on the date of the arrangement.

B38   Loans etc: exception for director's expenditure on company business

(1)   A company does not need approval under section B33 or B35 (requirement of shareholder approval for loans etc) for any thing done —

    (a)   to provide a director with funds to meet expenditure incurred or to be incurred by him —

        (i)   for the purposes of the company, or

        (ii)   for the purpose of enabling him properly to perform his duties as an officer of the company, or

    (b)   to enable a director to avoid incurring such expenditure, if it is done on the following terms.

(2) The terms are that if the loan made or other thing done has not been approved by resolution of the members of the company —

    (a) in the case of a private company, not later than 18 months after the loan is made or the liability arises, or

    (b) in the case of a public company, not later than six months after the conclusion of the next annual general meeting of the company,

the loan is to be repaid or, as the case may be, any liability of the company under any transaction connected with the thing in question is to be discharged.

(3) A resolution giving such approval must not be passed unless a memorandum setting out the matters mentioned in subsection (4) is made available to members —

    (a) in the case of a written resolution, by being sent or submitted to every eligible member at or before the time at which the proposed resolution is sent or submitted on him;

    (b) in the case of a resolution at a meeting, by being made available for inspection by members of the company both —

        (i) at the company's registered office for not less than 15 days ending with the date of the meeting, and

        (ii) at the meeting itself.

(4) The matters to be disclosed are —

    (a) the amount of the funds provided by the company,

    (b) the purpose of the expenditure incurred or to be incurred, or that would otherwise be incurred, by the director, and

    (c) the extent of the company's liability under any transaction that is, or is connected with, the thing in question.

(5) This section does not authorise a company to enter into a transaction if the aggregate of —

    (a) the value of the transaction in question, and

    (b) the values of any relevant existing transactions or arrangements,

exceeds £50,000.

B39 Loans etc: exception for director's expenditure on defending proceedings etc

(1) A company does not need approval under section B33 or B35 (requirement of shareholder approval for loans etc) for any thing done —

    (a) to provide a director with funds to meet expenditure incurred or to be incurred by him —

        (i) in defending any criminal or civil proceedings, or

        (ii) in connection with an application for relief to which this section applies (see subsection (5)), or

    (b) to enable a director to avoid incurring such expenditure,

if it is done on the following terms.

(2) The terms are —

    (a) that the loan is to be repaid or, as the case may be, any liability of the company under any transaction connected with the thing in question is to be discharged in the event of —

        (i) the director being convicted in the proceedings,

(ii) judgment being given against him in the proceedings, or

(iii) the court refusing to grant him relief on the application; and

(b) that it is to be so repaid or discharged not later than—

(i) the date when the conviction becomes final,

(ii) the date when the judgment becomes final, or

(iii) the date when the refusal of relief becomes final.

(3) For this purpose a conviction, judgment or refusal of relief becomes final—

(a) if not appealed against, at the end of the period for bringing an appeal;

(b) if appealed against, when the appeal (or any further appeal) is disposed of.

(4) An appeal is disposed of—

(a) if it is determined and the period for bringing any further appeal has ended, or

(b) if it is abandoned or otherwise ceases to have effect.

(5) This section applies to applications for relief under—

section 144(3) or (4) of the Companies Act 1985 (c. 6) (power of court to grant relief in case of acquisition of shares by innocent nominee), or

section 727 of that Act (general power of court to grant relief in case of honest and reasonable conduct)

B40 Loans etc: exceptions for minor transactions

(1) A company does not need approval under section B33 to make a loan to a director of the company, or of its holding company, if the aggregate of—

(a) the amount of the principal of the loan, and

(b) the value of any relevant existing transactions or arrangements,

does not exceed £10,000.

(2) In section B43 (relevant existing transactions or arrangements) as it applies for the purposes of subsection (1) above the references to a person connected with a director shall be disregarded.

(3) A company does not need approval under section B33 to make a quasi-loan to a director of the company, or of its holding company, if—

(a) the quasi-loan contains a term requiring the director, or a person acting on his behalf, to reimburse the creditor his expenditure within two months of its being incurred, and

(b) the aggregate of—

(i) the amount of the quasi-loan, and

(ii) the amount outstanding under any other relevant quasi-loans,

does not exceed £10,000.

(4) For the purposes of subsection (3)(b) above—

(a) the other relevant quasi-loans are those made to the director by virtue of this section—

(i) by the creditor or its subsidiary, or

(ii) where the director is a director of the creditor's holding company, by any other subsidiary of that company; and

  (b) the amount outstanding, in relation to such a quasi-loan, is the amount of the outstanding liabilities of the person to whom the quasi-loan was made.

(5) A company does not need approval under section B35 to enter into a credit transaction, or to give a guarantee or other security in connection with a credit transaction, if the aggregate of —

  (a) the value of the transaction, and

  (b) the values of any relevant existing transactions or arrangements,

does not exceed £15,000.

(6) A company does not need approval under section B35 to enter into a credit transaction, or to give a guarantee or other security in connection with a credit transaction, if —

  (a) the transaction is entered into by the company in the ordinary course of the company's business, and

  (b) the value of the transaction is not greater, and the terms on which it is entered into are not more favourable, than it is reasonable to expect the company would have offered to, or in respect of, a person of the same financial standing but unconnected with the company.

B41 Loans etc: exceptions for intra-group transactions

(1) A company does not need approval under section B33 for —

  (a) the making of a loan or quasi-loan to an associated company, or

  (b) the giving of a guarantee or other security in connection with a loan or quasi-loan made to an associated company.

(2) A company does not need approval under section B35 —

  (a) to enter into a credit transaction as creditor for the benefit of an associated company, or

  (b) to give a guarantee or other security in connection with a credit transaction entered into by any person for the benefit of an associated company.

B42 Loans etc: exceptions for money-lending companies

(1) A money-lending company does not need approval under section B33 for the making of a loan or quasi-loan if —

  (a) the loan or quasi-loan is made by the company in the ordinary course of the company's business, and

  (b) the amount of the loan or quasi-loan is not greater, and its terms are not more favourable, than it is reasonable to expect the company would have offered to a person of the same financial standing but unconnected with the company.

(2) A money-lending company does not need approval under section B33 for the giving of a guarantee in connection with a loan or quasi-loan made by another person if —

  (a) the guarantee is given by the company in the ordinary course of the company's business, and

  (b) the amount guaranteed is not greater, and its terms are not more favourable, than it is reasonable to expect the company would have offered in respect of a person of the same financial standing but unconnected with the company.

(3) A "money-lending company" means a company whose ordinary business includes the making of loans or quasi-loans, or the giving of guarantees [or other security] in connection with loans or quasi-loans.

(4) The condition specified in subsection (1)(b) does not of itself prevent a company from making a loan to a director of the company, or of its holding company —

    (a) for the purpose of facilitating the purchase, for use as the director's only or main residence, of the whole or part of any dwelling-house together with any land to be occupied and enjoyed with it,

    (b) for the purpose of improving a dwelling-house or part of a dwelling-house so used or any land occupied and enjoyed with it, or

    (c) in substitution for any loan made by any person and falling within paragraph (a) or (b) above,

if loans of that description are ordinarily made by the company to its employees and the terms of the loan in question are no more favourable than those on which such loans are ordinarily made.

B43 Loans etc: relevant existing transactions or arrangements

(1) This section has effect for determining the "relevant existing transactions or arrangements" for the purposes of any exception to section B33 or B35.

In relation to a proposed transaction or arrangement "the relevant exception" means the exception for the purposes of which the determination falls to be made.

(2) The relevant existing transactions or arrangements, in relation to a proposed transaction or arrangement, are existing transactions or arrangements in relation to which the conditions in subsections (3) and (4) are met, but subject to subsection (5).

(3) The first condition is that the transaction or arrangement was entered into by virtue of the relevant exception —

    (a) by the company, or

    (b) where the proposed transaction or arrangement is to be made for a director of its holding company or a person connected with such a director, by the holding company or any of its subsidiaries.

(4) The second condition is that the transaction or arrangement was made —

    (a) for the director for whom the proposed transaction or arrangement is to be made, or for any person connected with that director, or

    (b) where the proposed transaction or arrangement is to be made for a person connected with a director of a company, for that director or any person connected with him.

If this condition is met in relation to a transaction it is treated as also met in relation to any arrangement relating to that transaction.

(5) Where a transaction or arrangement is entered into by a company that (at the time it is entered into) —

    (a) is a subsidiary of the company that is to make the proposed transaction or arrangement, or

    (b) is a subsidiary of that company's holding company,

it is not a relevant existing transaction or arrangement if, at the time the question arises whether the proposed transaction or arrangement falls within a relevant exception, it is no longer such a subsidiary.

B44   Loans etc: determining the value of transactions and arrangements

(1)   For the purposes of sections B33 to B48 (loans etc) —

    (a)   the value of a transaction or arrangement is determined as follows, and

    (b)   the value of a relevant existing transaction or arrangement is taken to be the value so determined reduced by any amount by which the liabilities of the person for whom the transaction or arrangement was made have been reduced.

(2)   The value of a loan is the amount of its principal.

(3)   The value of a quasi-loan is the amount, or maximum amount, that the person to whom the quasi-loan is made is liable to reimburse the creditor.

(4)   The value of a credit transaction is the price that it is reasonable to expect could be obtained for the goods, services or land to which the transaction relates if they had been supplied (at the time the transaction is entered into) in the ordinary course of business and on the same terms (apart from price) as they have been supplied, or are to be supplied, under the transaction in question.

(5)   The value of a guarantee or other security is the amount guaranteed or secured.

(6)   The value of an arrangement to which section B37 (related arrangements) applies is the value of the transaction to which the arrangement relates.

(7)   If the value of a transaction or arrangement is not capable of being expressed as a specific sum of money —

    (a)   whether because the amount of any liability arising under the transaction or arrangement is unascertainable, or for any other reason, and

    (b)   whether or not any liability under the transaction or arrangement has been reduced,

its value is deemed to exceed £100,000.

B45   Loans etc: person for whom transaction is made

For the purposes of sections B33 to B48 (loans etc) the person for whom a transaction is made is —

    (a)   in the case of a loan or quasi-loan, the person to whom it is made;

    (b)   in the case of a credit transaction, the person to whom goods or services are supplied, or land is sold or otherwise disposed of, under the transaction;

    (c)   in the case of a guarantee or security, the person for whom the transaction is made in connection with which the guarantee or security is entered into;

    (d)   in the case of an arrangement within section B37 (related arrangements), the person for whom the transaction is made to which the arrangement relates.

B46 Loans etc: civil consequences of contravention

(1) This section applies where a company enters into a transaction in contravention of section B33, B35 or B37 (requirement of shareholder approval for loans etc).

(2) The transaction is voidable at the instance of the company, unless —
  (a) restitution of any money or other asset that was the subject-matter of the transaction is no longer possible,
  (b) the company has been indemnified for any loss or damage resulting from the transaction, or
  (c) rights acquired in good faith, for value and without actual notice of the contravention by a person who is not a party to the transaction would be affected by the avoidance.

(3) Whether or not the transaction has been avoided, the persons specified in subsection (4) are liable —
  (a) to account to the company for any gain that he has made directly or indirectly by the transaction, and
  (b) (jointly and severally with any other person so liable under this section) to indemnify the company for any loss or damage resulting from the transaction.

(4) The persons so liable are —
  (a) the director of the company or its holding company, or the person connected with such a director, with whom the company entered into the transaction, and
  (b) any director of the company who authorised the transaction.
This is subject to subsections (5) and (6).

(5) In the case of a transaction entered into by a company with a person connected with a director of the company or its holding company, that director is not liable if he shows that he took all reasonable steps to secure the company's compliance with section B33, B35 or B37.

(6) In any case a person so connected, or a director who authorised the transaction, is not liable if he shows that, at the time the transaction was entered into, he did not know the relevant circumstances constituting the contravention.

(7) Nothing in this section shall be read as excluding the operation of any other enactment or rule of law by virtue of which the transaction may be called in question or any liability to the company may arise.

B47 Loans etc: effect of subsequent affirmation

Where a transaction is entered into by a company in contravention of section B33 or B35 (requirement of shareholder approval) but, within a reasonable period, it is affirmed —
  (a) in the case of a contravention of subsection (1) of that section, by resolution of the members of the company, and
  (b) in the case of a contravention of subsection (2) of that section, by resolution of the members of the holding company,
the transaction may no longer be avoided under section B46.

B48   Loans etc: shadow directors

For the purposes of sections B33 to B47 (loans etc) a shadow director is treated as a director.

B49   Loans etc: "guarantee" includes indemnity

For the purposes of sections B33 to B47 (loans etc) "guarantee" includes indemnity, and cognate expressions shall be construed accordingly.

Ex gratia payments for loss of office

B50   Payment for loss of office

(1)   The payments to which sections B51 to B53 apply (requirement of shareholder approval etc for certain payments) are payments made to a director of a company —

    (a)   by way of compensation for loss of office as director,

    (b)   by way of compensation for loss of any other office or employment with the company, or

    (c)   as consideration for or in connection with his retirement from his office as director of the company, or from any other office or employment with the company.

In those sections a payment "for loss of office" means a payment of any of the above descriptions.

(2)   Those sections do not apply to —

    (a)   payments made in good faith in fulfilment of an existing legal obligation, or

    (b)   payments under a compromise or arrangement in pursuance of section 425 of the Companies Act 1985 (c. 6) (power of company to compromise with creditors and members).

(3)   For the purposes of sections B51 to B53 —

    (a)   payment to a person connected with a director, or

    (b)   payment to any person at the direction of, or for the benefit of, a director or a person connected with him,

is treated as payment to the director.

(4)   References in those sections to payment by a person include payment by another person at the direction of, or on behalf of, the person referred to.

(5)   If in connection with any such transfer as is mentioned in section B52 or B53 —

    (a)   the price to be paid to a director of the company whose office is to be abolished or who is to retire from office for any shares in the company held by him is in excess of the price which could at the time have been obtained by other holders of like shares, or

    (b)   any valuable consideration is given to any such director,

the excess or the money value of the consideration (as the case may be) is taken for the purposes of that section to have been a payment made to him by way of compensation for loss of office or as consideration for or in connection with his retirement from office.

(6) References in this section to employment with a company include any employment under a director's service contract with the company.

B51 Payment by company to director

(1) A company may not make a payment for loss of office to a director of the company unless—

    (a) particulars of the proposed payment (including its amount) have been disclosed to the members of the company, and

    (b) the proposal has been approved by resolution of the members of the company

(2) A company ("company A") may not make a payment for loss of office to a director of an associated company ("company B") unless—

    (a) particulars of the proposed payment (including its amount) have been disclosed to the members of company A and company B, and

    (b) the proposal has been approved by resolution of the members of each of the companies.

(3) Compliance with subsection (2) is not required in relation to company A if it is a wholly-owned subsidiary of company B, or in relation to company B if it is a wholly-owned subsidiary of company A.

(4) If a payment is made in contravention of this section—

    (a) it is held by the recipient on trust for the company making the payment, and

    (b) any director who authorised the payment is jointly and severally liable to indemnify the company that made the payment for any loss resulting from it.

B52 Payment in connection with transfer of undertaking or property

(1) No payment for loss of office may be made by any person to a director of a company in connection with the transfer of the whole or any part of the undertaking or property of the company unless—

    (a) particulars of the proposed payment (including its amount) have been disclosed to the members of the company, and

    (b) the proposal has been approved by resolution of the members of the company

(2) No payment for loss of office may be made by any person to a director of a company ("company A") in connection with the transfer of the whole or any part of the undertaking or property of an associated company ("company B") unless—

    (a) particulars of the proposed payment (including its amount) have been disclosed to the members of company A and company B, and

    (b) the proposal has been approved by resolution of the members of each of the companies.

(3) Compliance with subsection (2) is not required in relation to company A if it is a wholly-owned subsidiary of company B, or in relation to company B if it is a wholly-owned subsidiary of company A.

(4) If a payment is made in contravention of this section—

> (a) it is held by the recipient on trust for the company whose undertaking or property is or is proposed to be transferred, and
>
> (b) any director, of that company or an associated company, who authorised the payment is jointly and severally liable to indemnify that company for any loss resulting from it.

(5) Where in proceedings brought by virtue of subsection (4) it is shown that—

> (a) the payment was made in pursuance of an arrangement entered into—
>
> > (i) as part of the agreement for the transfer in question, or
> >
> > (ii) within one year before or two years after that agreement, and
>
> (b) the company or any person to whom the transfer was made was privy to the arrangement,

the payment is presumed, until the contrary is shown, to be a payment for loss of office.

B53   Payment in connection with share transfer

(1) This section applies where a payment for loss of office is to be made by any person—

> (a) to a director of a company in connection with a transfer to any person of all or any of the shares in the company resulting from an offer made to some or all of the shareholders in the company, or
>
> (b) to a director of a company ("company A") in connection with a transfer to any person of all or any of the shares in an associated company ("company B") resulting from an offer made to some or all of the shareholders in company B.

(2) It is the duty—

> (a) of the director, to take all reasonable steps to secure that particulars of the proposed payment (including its amount) are included in or sent with any notice of the offer made for their shares which is given to any shareholders, and
>
> (b) of any person who is properly required to do so by the director, to include those particulars in, or send them with, any such notice.

(3) The payment may not be made unless it has been approved by a meeting of shareholders summoned for that purpose.

As to the holding of such a meeting, the persons entitled to vote and other matters, see section B54.

(4) If a payment is made in contravention of subsection (3)—

> (a) it is held by the recipient on trust for persons who have sold their shares as a result of the offer made, and
>
> (b) the expenses incurred by him in distributing that sum amongst those persons shall be borne by him and not retained out of that sum.

(5) Where in proceedings brought by virtue of subsection (4) it is shown that—

> (a) the payment was made in pursuance of an arrangement entered into—
>
> > (i) as part of the agreement for the transfer in question, or
> >
> > (ii) within one year before or two years after that agreement, and
>
> (b) the company or any person to whom the transfer was made was privy to the arrangement,

the payment is presumed, until the contrary is shown, to be a payment for loss of office.

(6)   If the payment is also in contravention of section B51 (payment by company to director), subsection (4)(a) of this section applies in priority to subsection (4)(a) of that section (payment to be held on trust for the company), unless the court directs otherwise.

(7)   A director who fails to take the steps required by subsection (2)(a) above commits an offence.

(8)   A person who fails to comply with the duty imposed on him by subsection (2)(b) above commits an offence.

(9)   A person guilty of an offence under this section is liable on summary conviction to a fine not exceeding level 3 on the standard scale.

B54   Payment in connection with share transfer: shareholders' meeting

(1)   The following provisions apply as regards the meeting required by section B53(3) (meeting to approve payment to which that section applies).

(2)   The meeting required is a meeting of the holders of the shares to which the offer relates and of other holders of shares of the same class as any of those shares.

(3)   Neither the person making the offer nor any person connected with him is entitled to vote at the meeting, but they are entitled to attend and speak (and to be given notice of the meeting) and if present (in person or by proxy) they count towards the quorum.

(4)   If no provision is made by the company's articles for summoning or regulating such a meeting —
    (a)   the provisions of this Act and of the company's articles relating to general meetings of the company apply, and
    (b)   the Secretary of State may, on the application of any person concerned, direct that they apply with such modifications as may be appropriate for the purpose of adapting them to the circumstances of the case.

(5)   If at the meeting a quorum is not present, and after the meeting has been adjourned to a later date a quorum is again not present, the payment is deemed to have been approved.

Supplementary

B55   Nature of resolution required

(1)   The resolution of the members of a company required by any provision of this Chapter is an ordinary resolution.

(2)   This is subject to anything in the company's articles requiring a higher majority (or unanimity).

CHAPTER 4

APPOINTMENT AND REMOVAL OF DIRECTORS

General

B56 Companies required to have directors

(1) A private company must have at least one director.

(2) A public company must have at least two directors.

B57 Companies required to have at least one director who is a natural person

(1) A company must have at least one director who is a natural person.

(2) This requirement is met if the office of director is held by a natural person as a corporation sole or otherwise by virtue of an office.

Appointment

B58 Minimum age for appointment as director

(1) A person may not be appointed a director of a company unless he has attained the age of 16 years.

(2) This does not affect the validity of an appointment that is not to take effect until the person appointed attains that age.

(3) Where the office of director of a company is held by a corporation sole or otherwise by virtue of another office, the appointment to that other office of a person who has not attained the age of 16 years is not effective also to make him a director of the company until he attains the age of 16 years.

(4) An appointment made in contravention of this section is void.

(5) Nothing in this section affects any liability of a person under any provision of the Companies Acts if he —
   (a) purports to act as director or
   (b) acts as a shadow director,
although he could not, by virtue of this section, be validly appointed as a director.

B59 Existing under-age directors

(1) This section applies —
   (a) where a person appointed a director of a company before the commencement of section B58 (minimum age for appointment as director) has not attained the age of 16 when this section comes into force, and
   (b) where the office of director of a company is held by a corporation sole, or otherwise by virtue of another office, and the person appointed to that other office has not attained the age of 16 years when this section comes into force.

(2) Any such person ceases to be a director on this section coming into force.

(3) The company must make the necessary consequential alteration in its register of directors in accordance with section [yet to be drafted] but need not give notice to the registrar of the change.

(4) If it appears to the registrar (from other information) that a person has ceased by virtue of this section to be a director of a company, the registrar shall note that fact on the register.

(5) A person who ceases to be a director of a company by virtue of this section is not entitled to any compensation or damages payable to him in respect of the termination of his appointment as director, or of any appointment terminating with that as director, except in pursuance of an agreement entered into before [date of publication of White Paper in March 2005].

B60 Appointment of directors of public company to be voted on individually

(1) At a general meeting of a public company a motion for the appointment of two or more persons as directors of the company by a single resolution must not be made unless a resolution that it should be so made has first been agreed to by the meeting without any vote being given against it.

(2) A resolution moved in contravention of this section is void, whether or not its being so moved was objected to at the time.

But where a resolution so moved is passed, no provision for the automatic reappointment of retiring directors in default of another appointment applies.

(3) For purposes of this section a motion for approving a person's appointment, or for nominating a person for appointment, is treated as a motion for his appointment.

(4) Nothing in this section applies to a resolution altering the company's articles.

B61 Validity of acts of directors

(1) The acts of a director are valid notwithstanding any defect that may afterwards be discovered in his appointment.

(2) This applies even if the resolution for his appointment is void under section B60 (appointment of directors of public company to be voted on individually).

Register of directors, etc

B62 Register of directors

(1) Every company must keep a register of its directors.

(2) The register —
    (a) must be kept at the company's registered office,
    (b) must contain the names and other details (see [provision yet to be drafted]) of each person who is a director of the company, and
    (c) may be kept together with any register of secretaries kept by the company in a combined register of directors and secretaries.

(3)   The register must be open to the inspection of any member of the company without charge and of any other person on payment of such fee as may be prescribed.

(4)   If default is made in complying with subsection (1) or (2), or if an inspection required under this section is refused, an offence is committed by —
    (a)   every officer of the company who is in default, and
    (b)   every responsible delegate.
For this purpose a shadow director is treated as an officer of the company.

(5)   A person guilty of an offence under this section is liable on summary conviction to a fine not exceeding level 5 on the standard scale and, for continued contravention, a daily default fine not exceeding one-tenth of level 5 on the standard scale.

(6)   In the case of a refusal of inspection of the register, the court may by order compel an immediate inspection of it.

B63   Duty to notify registrar of changes

(1)   A company must, within the period of 14 days from the occurrence of —
    (a)   any change in its directors, or
    (b)   any change in the particulars contained in its register of directors,
give notice to the registrar in the prescribed form of the change and of the date on which it occurred.

(2)   Notice of a person having become a director of the company must be accompanied by a statement by that person, appropriately authenticated, consenting to act in that capacity.

(3)   If default is made in complying with this section, an offence is committed by —
    (a)   every officer of the company who is in default, and
    (b)   every responsible delegate.
For this purpose a shadow director is treated as an officer of the company.

(4)   A person guilty of an offence under this section is liable on summary conviction to a fine not exceeding level 5 on the standard scale and, for continued contravention, a daily default fine not exceeding one-tenth of level 5 on the standard scale.

B64   Direction requiring company to make appointment

(1)   If it appears to the Secretary of State that a company is in breach of —
      section B56 (requirements as to number of directors), or
      section B57 (requirement to have at least one director who is a natural person)
the Secretary of State may give the company a direction under this section.

(2)   The direction must specify —
    (a)   the statutory requirement the company appears to be in breach of,
    (b)   what the company must do in order to comply with the direction, and
    (c)   the period within which it must do so.
That period must be not less than one month or more than three months after the date on which the direction is given.

(3) The direction must also inform the company of the consequences of failing to comply.

(4) Where the company is in breach of section B56 or B57 it must comply with the direction by —

    (a) making the necessary appointment or appointments, and

    (b) giving notice of them under section B63,

before the end of the period specified in the direction.

(5) If the company has already made the necessary appointment or appointments (or so far as it has done so), it must comply with the direction by giving notice of them under section B63 before the end of the period specified in the direction.

(6) If a company fails to comply with a direction under this section, an offence is committed by —

    (a) the company, and

    (b) every officer of the company who is in default.

For this purpose a shadow director is treated as an officer of the company.

(7) A person guilty of an offence under this section is liable on summary conviction to a fine not exceeding level 5 on the standard scale and, for continued contravention, a daily default fine not exceeding one-tenth of level 5 on the standard scale.

Removal

B65 Resolution to remove director

(1) A company may by ordinary resolution at a meeting remove a director before the expiration of his period of office, notwithstanding anything in its articles or in any agreement between it and him.

(2) Special notice is required of a resolution to remove a director under this section or to appoint somebody instead of a director so removed at the meeting at which he is removed.

(3) A vacancy created by the removal of a director under this section, if not filled at the meeting at which he is removed, may be filled as a casual vacancy.

(4) A person appointed director in place of a person removed under this section is treated, for the purpose of determining the time at which he or any other director is to retire, as if he had become director on the day on which the person in whose place he is appointed was last appointed a director.

(5) This section is not to be taken —

    (a) as depriving a person removed under it of compensation or damages payable to him in respect of the termination of his appointment as director or of any appointment terminating with that as director, or

    (b) as derogating from any power to remove a director that may exist apart from this section.

B66 Director's right to protest removal

(1) On receipt of notice of an intended resolution to remove a director under section B65, the company must forthwith send a copy of the notice to the director concerned.

(2) The director (whether or not a member of the company) is entitled to be heard on the resolution at the meeting.

(3) Where notice is given of an intended resolution to remove a director under that section, and the director concerned makes with respect to it representations in writing to the company (not exceeding a reasonable length) and requests their notification to members of the company, the company shall, unless the representations are received by it too late for it to do so—

    (a) in any notice of the resolution given to members of the company state the fact of the representations having been made; and

    (b) send a copy of the representations to every member of the company to whom notice of the meeting is sent (whether before or after receipt of the representations by the company).

(4) If a copy of the representations is not sent as required by subsection (3) because received too late or because of the company's default, the director may (without prejudice to his right to be heard orally) require that the representations shall be read out at the meeting.

(5) Copies of the representations need not be sent out and the representations need not be read out at the meeting if, on the application either of the company or of any other person who claims to be aggrieved, the court is satisfied that the rights conferred by this section are being abused to secure publicity for defamatory matter.

(6) The court may order the company's costs on an application under this section to be paid in whole or in part by the director, notwithstanding that he is not a party to the application.

CHAPTER 5

SERVICE CONTRACTS

B67 Directors' service contracts

(1) A director's "service contract" with a company means a contract with the company under which—

    (a) a director of the company undertakes personally to perform services (as director or otherwise) for the company, or

    (b) services (as director or otherwise) that a director of the company undertakes personally to perform are made available by a third party to the company.

(2) The provisions of this Part relating to directors' service contracts apply to the terms of a person's appointment as a director of a company.

They are not restricted to contracts for the performance of services outside the scope of the ordinary duties of a director.

B68   Company to keep copy of contract or memorandum of terms

(1)   A company must keep copies of —
    (a)   every director's service contract with the company, or with a subsidiary of the company, that is in writing, and
    (b)   a written memorandum setting out the terms of any such contract that is not in writing.

(2)   The copies and memoranda must be kept by the company at one of the following places —
    (a)   the company's registered office;
    (b)   the place where its register of members is kept (if it is not kept at its registered office);
    (c)   its principal place of business (if that is situated in the part of Great Britain in which the company is registered).

(3)   The company must give notice in the prescribed form to the registrar of companies —
    (a)   of the place where the copies and memoranda are kept in compliance with this section, and
    (b)   of any change in that place,
unless they have at all times been kept at the company's registered office.

(4)   If default is made in complying with subsection (1), or default is made for 14 days in complying with subsection (3), an offence is committed by —
    (a)   every officer of the company who is in default, and
    (b)   every responsible delegate.

(5)   A person guilty of an offence under this section is liable on summary conviction to a fine not exceeding level 3 on the standard scale and, for continued contravention, a daily default fine not exceeding one-tenth of level 3 on the standard scale.

(6)   The provisions of this section apply to a variation of a director's service contract as they apply to the original contract.

B69   Right of member to inspect and request copy

(1)   Every copy or memorandum required to be kept under section B68 must be open to inspection by any member of the company without charge.

(2)   Any member of the company is entitled, on request and on payment of such fee as may be prescribed, to be provided with a copy of any such copy or memorandum.
The copy must be provided within seven days after the request is received by the company.

(3)   If an inspection required under subsection (1) is refused, or default is made in complying with subsection (2), an offence is committed by —
    (a)   every officer of the company who is in default, and
    (b)   every responsible delegate.

(4)   A person guilty of an offence under this section is liable on summary conviction to a fine not exceeding level 3 on the standard scale and, for continued contravention, a daily default fine not exceeding one-tenth of level 3 on the standard scale.

(5)   In the case of any such refusal or default the court may by order compel an immediate inspection or, as the case may be, direct that the copy required be sent to the person requiring it.

B70   Directors' service contracts: application of provisions to shadow directors

A shadow director is treated as a director for the purposes of the provisions of this Part relating to directors' service contracts.

CHAPTER 6

SUPPLEMENTARY PROVISIONS

Interpretation

B71   References to company's constitution

References in this Part to a company's constitution include —
   (a)   any resolution, agreement or other decision come to in accordance with the constitution, and
   (b)   any decision by the members of the company, or a class of members, that is treated by virtue of any enactment or rule of law as equivalent to a decision by the company.

B72   References to an interest in shares or debentures

The rules set out in [Schedule 13 to the Companies Act 1985] apply to determine for the purposes of this Part whether a person is interested in shares or debentures.

B73   Persons connected with a director

(1)   This section defines what is meant by references in this Part to a person being "connected" with a director of a company (or a director being "connected" with a person).

(2)   The following persons (and only those persons) are connected with a director of a company —
   (a)   members of the director's family (see section B74);
   (b)   a body corporate with which the director is associated (see section B75);
   (c)   a person acting in his capacity as trustee of a trust —
      (i)   the beneficiaries of which include the director or a person who by virtue of paragraph (a) or (b) is connected with him, or
      (ii)   the terms of which confer a power on the trustees that may be exercised for the benefit of the director or any such person,
      other than a trust for the purposes of an employees' share scheme or a pension scheme;
   (d)   a person acting in his capacity as partner —
      (i)   of the director, or
      (ii)   of a person who, by virtue of paragraph (a), (b) or (c), is connected with that director;
   (e)   a [Scottish firm] in which —

       (i)   the director is a partner,

      (ii)   a partner is a person who, by virtue of paragraph (a), (b) or (c) is connected with the director, or

    (iii)   a partner is a [Scottish firm] in which the director is a partner or in which there is a partner who, by virtue of paragraph (a), (b) or (c), is connected with the director.

(3)   References in this Part to a person connected with a director of a company do not include a person who is himself a director of the company.

B74   Members of a director's family

(1)   This section defines what is meant by references in this Part to members of a director's family.

(2)   For the purposes of this Part the members of a director's family are —

    (a)   the director's spouse or civil partner;

    (b)   any other person with whom the director lives as partner in an enduring family relationship;

    (c)   the director's children or step-children;

    (d)   any children or step-children of a person within paragraph (b) who live with the director and have not attained the age of 18;

    (e)   the director's parents;

    (f)   the director's sister or brother.

(3)   Subsection (2)(b) does not apply if the other person is the director's parent or child, grandparent or grandchild, sister, brother, aunt or uncle, or nephew or niece.

(4)   References to relationships in subsection (3) —

    (a)   are to relationships of the full blood or half-blood or, in the case of an adopted person, such of those relationships as would exist but for adoption, and

    (b)   include the relationship of a child with his adoptive, or former adoptive, parents,

but do not include any other adoptive relationships.

B75   Director "associated with" a body corporate

(1)   This section defines what is meant by references in this Part to a director being "associated with" a body corporate.

(2)   A director of a company is associated with a body corporate if, but only if, he and the persons connected with him together —

    (a)   are interested in shares comprised in the equity share capital of that body corporate of a nominal value equal to at least 20% of that share capital, or

    (b)   are entitled to exercise or control the exercise of more than 20% of the voting power at any general meeting of that body.

(3)   The rules set out in [Schedule 13 to the Companies Act 1985] (references to interest in shares or debentures) apply for the purposes of this section.

(4) References in this section to voting power the exercise of which is controlled by a director include voting power whose exercise is controlled by a body corporate controlled by him.

(5) Shares in a company held as treasury shares, and any voting rights attached to such shares, are disregarded for the purposes of this section.

(6) For the purposes of this section—

    (a) a body corporate with which a director is associated is not treated as connected with him unless it is also connected with him by virtue of section B73(2)(c) or (d) (connection as trustee or partner); and

    (b) a trustee of a trust the beneficiaries of which include (or may include) a body corporate with which a director is associated is not treated as connected with a director by reason only of that fact.

B76 Director "controlling" a body corporate

(1) This section defines what is meant by references in this Part to a director "controlling" a body corporate.

(2) A director of a company is taken to control a body corporate if, but only if—

    (a) he or any person connected with him—

        (i) is interested in any part of the equity share capital of that body, or

        (ii) is entitled to exercise or control the exercise of any part of the voting power at any general meeting of that body, and

    (b) he, the persons connected with him and the other directors of that company, together—

        (i) are interested in more than 50% of that share capital, or

        (ii) are entitled to exercise or control the exercise of more than 50% of that voting power.

(3) The rules set out in [Schedule 13 to the Companies Act 1985] (references to interest in shares or debentures) apply for the purposes of this section.

(4) References in this section to voting power the exercise of which is controlled by a director include voting power whose exercise is controlled by a body corporate controlled by him.

(5) Shares in a company held as treasury shares, and any voting rights attached to such shares, are disregarded for the purposes of this section.

(6) For the purposes of this section—

    (a) a body corporate with which a director is associated is not treated as connected with him unless it is also connected with him by virtue of section B73(2)(c) or (d) (connection as trustee or partner); and

    (b) a trustee of a trust the beneficiaries of which include (or may include) a body corporate with which a director is associated is not treated as connected with a director by reason only of that fact.

B77 Associated bodies corporate

For the purposes of this Part bodies corporate are associated if one is a subsidiary of the other or both are subsidiaries of the same body corporate.

General

B78 **Power to increase financial limits**

(1) The Secretary of State may by order substitute for any sum of money specified in this Part a larger sum specified in the order.

(2) An order under this section shall be made by statutory instrument which shall be subject to annulment in pursuance of a resolution of either House of Parliament.

(3) An order does not have effect in relation to anything done or not done before it comes into force.

Accordingly, proceedings in respect of any liability (whether civil or criminal) incurred before that time may be continued or instituted as if the order had not been made.

B79 **Transactions under foreign law**

For the purposes of this Part it is immaterial whether the law that (apart from this Act) governs an arrangement or transaction is the law of the United Kingdom, or a part of it, or not.

Company Law Reform Bill

CONTENTS

PART C

COMPANY SECRETARIES

Private companies

Public companies

Supplementary

7 Draft Clauses

PART C

COMPANY SECRETARIES

Private companies

C1   Company's articles determine whether private company has secretary

(1)   The articles of a private company may—

     (a)   require the company to have a secretary,

     (b)   permit the company to have a secretary, or

     (c)   provide that the company is not to have a secretary.

(2)   If the company's articles make no such provision, they are treated as providing that the company is permitted (but not required) to have a secretary.

(3)   An existing private company may by ordinary resolution passed within three years after the commencement of this Chapter amend its articles—

     (a)   to make any such provision as is mentioned in subsection (1)(a), (b) or (c), or

     (b)   to remove any reference to the appointment of a secretary.

   This power may only be exercised once.

(4)   Any such resolution is subject to [section 380 of the Companies Act 1985 (c. 6)] (resolutions to be recorded by registrar).

(5)   Until such a resolution is passed, or if no such resolution is passed within three years after the commencement of this Chapter, the articles of an existing private company are treated as if they provided that the company is permitted (but not required) to have a secretary.

(6)   Subsections (3) to (5) do not apply if before the commencement of this Chapter the articles of an existing private company have been amended—

     (a)   to make any such provision as is mentioned in subsection (1)(a), (b) or (c), or

     (b)   to remove any reference to the appointment of a secretary,

   with effect from the commencement of this Chapter.

C2   Discharge of functions where company has no office of secretary

(1)   This section applies in relation to a private company where—

     (a)   the company's articles provide that the company is not to have a secretary, or

     (b)   the company's articles provide that the company may have a secretary but the company has no secretary for the time being.

(2) Anything that may be given or sent to, or served on, the company by being sent to its secretary may be so given or sent to, or served on, the company notwithstanding that it has no secretary.

(3) Anything else required or authorised to be done by or to the secretary of the company may be done by or to—
    (a) a director, or
    (b) a person authorised generally or specifically in that behalf by the directors.

C3   Discharge of functions where office vacant or secretary unable to act

(1) This section applies in relation to a private company where—
    (a) the company's articles require the company to have a secretary but—
        (i) the office of secretary is vacant, or
        (ii) there is for any other reason no secretary capable of acting;
    (b) the company's articles permit the company to have a secretary and one has been duly appointed and holds office, but he is for any reason incapable of acting.

(2) Anything required or authorised to be done by or to the secretary may be done—
    (a) by or to an assistant or deputy secretary (if any), or
    (b) if there is no assistant or deputy secretary or none capable of acting, by or to—
        (i) a director, or
        (ii) a person authorised generally or specifically in that behalf by the directors.

C4   Power to keep register of secretaries

(1) A private company—
    (a) whose articles require it to have a secretary, or
    (b) whose articles permit it to have a secretary and which appoints a secretary,
may keep a register of its secretaries.

(2) If a private company keeps a register of its secretaries, the register—
    (a) must be kept at the company's registered office,
    (b) must contain the names and other details (see [provision yet to be drafted]) of the person who is, or persons who are, the secretary or joint secretaries of the company, and
    (c) may be kept together with the company's register of directors in a combined register of directors and secretaries.

(3) must contain [the names and other details (see provision yet to be drafted)] of the person who is, or persons who are, the secretary or joint secretaries of the company.

(4) The register must be open to the inspection of any member of the company without charge and of any other person on payment of such fee as may be prescribed.

(5)   If an inspection required under this section is refused, an offence is committed by —

    (a)   every officer of the company who is in default, and

    (b)   every responsible delegate.

For this purpose a shadow director is treated as an officer of the company.

(6)   A person guilty of an offence under this section is liable on summary conviction to a fine not exceeding level 5 on the standard scale and, for continued contravention, a daily default fine not exceeding one-tenth of level 5 on the standard scale.

(7)   In the case of a refusal of inspection of the register, the court may by order compel an immediate inspection of it.

C5   Duty to notify registrar of changes

(1)   A private company whose articles require or permit it to have a secretary must, within the period of 14 days from the occurrence of any change in its secretary, give notice to the registrar in the prescribed form of the change and of the date on which it occurred.

(2)   Notice of a person having become secretary, or one of joint secretaries, of the company must be accompanied by a statement by that person, appropriately authenticated, consenting to act in the relevant capacity.

(3)   A private company that keeps a register of its secretaries must, within the period of 14 days from the occurrence of any change in the particulars contained in the register, give notice to the registrar in the prescribed form of the change and of the date on which it occurred.

(4)   If default is made in complying with this section, an offence is committed by —

    (a)   every officer of the company who is in default, and

    (b)   every responsible delegate.

For this purpose a shadow director is treated as an officer of the company.

(5)   A person guilty of an offence under this section is liable on summary conviction to a fine not exceeding level 5 on the standard scale and, for continued contravention, a daily default fine not exceeding one-tenth of level 5 on the standard scale.

C6   Execution of documents

(1)   Section 36A of the Companies Act 1985 (c. 6) (execution of documents: England and Wales) is amended as follows.

(2)   After subsection (4) insert —

    "(4AA)   In the case of a private company that —

        (a)   has only one director and no secretary (or none capable of acting), or

        (b)   has only one director who is also the secretary,

    a document signed by that director in the presence of a witness who attests the signature and that is expressed (in whatever form of words) to be executed by the company has the same effect as if executed under the common seal of the company.".

(3)   In subsection (4A) (requirement of separate signatures where person signs as director or secretary of more than one company), after "subsection (4)" insert "or (4AA)".

(4)   In subsection (6) (presumption of due execution) for "signed by a director and the secretary of the company, or by two directors of the company," substitute —

> "(a)   signed in accordance with subsection (4), or
>
> (b)   signed and witnessed in accordance with subsection (4AA)".

Public companies

C7   Public companies required to have secretary

Every public company must have a secretary.

C8   Qualifications of secretaries of public companies

(1)   It is the duty of the directors of a public company to take all reasonable steps to secure that the secretary (or each joint secretary) of the company —

> (a)   is a person who appears to them to have the requisite knowledge and experience to discharge the functions of secretary of the company, and
>
> (b)   has one or more of the following qualifications.

(2)   The qualifications are —

> (a)   that he has held the office of secretary of a public company for at least three of the five years immediately preceding his appointment as secretary;
>
> (b)   that he is a member of any of the bodies specified in subsection (3);
>
> (c)   that he is a barrister, advocate or solicitor called or admitted in any part of the United Kingdom;
>
> (d)   that he is a person who, by virtue of his holding or having held any other position or his being a member of any other body, appears to the directors to be capable of discharging the functions of secretary of the company.

(3)   The bodies referred to in subsection (2)(b) are —

> (a)   the Institute of Chartered Accountants in England and Wales;
>
> (b)   the Institute of Chartered Accountants of Scotland;
>
> (c)   the Chartered Association of Certified Accountants;
>
> (d)   the Institute of Chartered Accountants in Ireland;
>
> (e)   the Institute of Chartered Secretaries and Administrators;
>
> (f)   the Chartered Institute of Management Accountants;
>
> (g)   the Chartered Institute of Public Finance and Accountancy.

C9   Discharge of functions where office vacant or secretary unable to act

Where in the case of a public company the office of secretary is vacant, or there is for any other reason no secretary capable of acting, anything required or authorised to be done by or to the secretary may be done —

> (a)   by or to an assistant or deputy secretary (if any), or

(b)   if there is no assistant or deputy secretary or none capable of acting, by or to any person authorised generally or specially in that behalf by the directors.

C10   Duty to keep register of secretaries

(1)   A public company must keep a register of its secretaries.

(2)   The register—
   (a)   must be kept at the company's registered office,
   (b)   must contain the names and other details (see [provision yet to be drafted]) of the person who is, or persons who are, the secretary or joint secretaries of the company, and
   (c)   may be kept together with the company's register of directors as part of a combined register of directors and secretaries.

(3)   The register must be open to the inspection of any member of the company without charge and of any other person on payment of such fee as may be prescribed.

(4)   If default is made in complying with subsection (1) or (2), or if an inspection required under this section is refused, an offence is committed by—
   (a)   every officer of the company who is in default, and
   (b)   every responsible delegate.
   For this purpose a shadow director is treated as an officer of the company.

(5)   A person guilty of an offence under this section is liable on summary conviction to a fine not exceeding level 5 on the standard scale and, for continued contravention, a daily default fine not exceeding one-tenth of level 5 on the standard scale.

(6)   In the case of a refusal of inspection of the register, the court may by order compel an immediate inspection of it.

C11   Duty to notify registrar of changes

(1)   A public company must, within the period of 14 days from the occurrence of—
   (a)   any change in its secretary, or
   (b)   any change in the particulars contained in its register of secretaries,
   give notice to the registrar in the prescribed form of the change and of the date on which it occurred.

(2)   Notice of a person having become secretary, or one of joint secretaries, of the company must be accompanied by a statement by that person, appropriately authenticated, to act in the relevant capacity.

(3)   If default is made in complying with this section, an offence is committed by—
   (a)   every officer of the company who is in default, and
   (b)   every responsible delegate.
   For this purpose a shadow director is treated as an officer of the company.

(4)   A person guilty of an offence under this section is liable on summary conviction to a fine not exceeding level 5 on the standard scale and, for continued contravention, a daily default fine not exceeding one-tenth of level 5 on the standard scale.

C12 Direction requiring public company to appoint secretary

(1)   If it appears to the Secretary of State that a public company is in breach of section C7 (requirement to have secretary), the Secretary of State may give the company a direction under this section.

(2)   The direction must state that the company appears to be in breach of that section and specify —
   (a)   what the company must do in order to comply with the direction, and
   (b)   the period within which it must do so.
That period must be not less than one month or more than three months after the date on which the direction is given.

(3)   The direction must also inform the company of the consequences of failing to comply.

(4)   Where the company is in breach of section C7 it must comply with the direction by —
   (a)   making the necessary appointment, and
   (b)   giving notice of it under section C11,
before the end of the period specified in the direction.

(5)   If the company has already made the necessary appointment, it must comply with the direction by giving notice of it under section C11 before the end of the period specified in the direction.

(6)   If a company fails to comply with a direction under this section, an offence is committed by —
   (a)   the company, and
   (b)   every officer of the company who is in default.
For this purpose a shadow director is treated as an officer of the company.

(7)   A person guilty of an offence under this paragraph is liable on summary conviction to a fine not exceeding level 5 on the standard scale and, for continued contravention, a daily default fine not exceeding one-tenth of level 5 on the standard scale.

Supplementary

C13 Acts done by person in dual capacity

In the case of —
   (a)   a private company where —
      (i)   the company's articles require it to have a secretary, or
      (ii)   the company's articles permit it to have a secretary and one has been duly appointed and holds office, or
   (b)   a public company,
a provision requiring or authorising a thing to be done by or to a director and the secretary of a company is not satisfied by its being done by or to the same person acting both as director and as, or in place of, the secretary.

Company Law Reform Bill

CONTENTS

CHAPTER 4

ADDITIONAL REQUIREMENTS FOR PUBLIC COMPANIES

CHAPTER 5

ADDITIONAL REQUIREMENTS FOR QUOTED COMPANIES

CHAPTER 6

RECORDS OF RESOLUTIONS AND MEETINGS

CHAPTER 7

INTERPRETATION OF PART

7 Draft Clauses

Company Law Reform Bill
Part D — Resolutions and meetings
Chapter 1 — General provisions about resolutions

1

PART D

RESOLUTIONS AND MEETINGS

CHAPTER 1

GENERAL PROVISIONS ABOUT RESOLUTIONS

D1   Resolutions

(1)   Provisions in enactments requiring or otherwise providing for a resolution of a company are provisions for a resolution of the members of the company.

(2)   A resolution of the members (or of a class of members) of a private company is validly passed if it is passed —
    (a)   in accordance with Chapter 2 of this Part, as a written resolution, or
    (b)   in accordance with Chapter 3 of this Part, at a meeting of the members or on a poll demanded at such a meeting.

(3)   A resolution of the members (or of a class of members) of a public company is validly passed if it is passed, in accordance with Chapters 3 to 5 of this Part, at a meeting of the members or on a poll demanded at such a meeting.

D2   Ordinary resolutions

(1)   A resolution of the members of a company or of a class of members of a company is an ordinary resolution if it has been passed by a simple majority.

(2)   A written resolution is passed by a simple majority if it is passed by members representing a simple majority of the total voting rights of eligible members (see Chapter 2).

(3)   A resolution passed at a meeting on a show of hands is passed by a simple majority if it is passed by a simple majority of —
    (a)   the members who, being entitled to do so, vote in person on the resolution, and
    (b)   the persons who vote on the resolution as duly appointed proxies of members entitled to vote on it.

(4)   A resolution passed on a poll taken or demanded at a meeting is passed by a simple majority if it is passed by members representing a simple majority of the total voting rights of members who (being entitled to do so) vote in person or by proxy on the resolution.

(5)   Anything that may be done by a company by ordinary resolution may also be done by the company by special resolution.

(6)   This section has effect notwithstanding anything in the company's articles.

2

Company Law Reform Bill
Part D — Resolutions and meetings
Chapter 1 — General provisions about resolutions

D3   Special resolutions

(1)   A resolution of the members of a company or of a class of members of a company is a special resolution if it has been passed by a majority of not less than 75%.

(2)   A written resolution is passed by a majority of not less than 75% if it is passed by members representing not less than 75% of the total voting rights of eligible members (see Chapter 2).

(3)   Where a resolution of a private company is passed as a written resolution —
    (a)   the resolution is not a special resolution unless it stated that it was proposed as a special resolution, and
    (b)   if the resolution so stated, it may only be passed as a special resolution.

(4)   A resolution passed at a meeting on a show of hands is passed by a majority of not less than 75% if it is passed by not less than 75% of —
    (a)   the members who, being entitled to do so, vote in person on the resolution, and
    (b)   the persons who vote on the resolution as duly appointed proxies of members entitled to vote on it.

(5)   A resolution passed on a poll taken or demanded at a meeting is passed by a majority of not less than 75% if it is passed by members representing not less than 75% of the total voting rights of the members who (being entitled to do so) vote in person or by proxy on the resolution.

(6)   Where a resolution is passed at a meeting of the members in accordance with Chapters 3 to 5 of this Part (or on a poll demanded at such a meeting) —
    (a)   the resolution is not a special resolution unless the notice of the meeting included the text of the resolution and specified the intention to propose the resolution as a special resolution, and
    (b)   if the notice of the meeting so specified, the resolution may only be passed as a special resolution.

(7)   This section has effect notwithstanding anything in the company's articles.

D4   Votes

(1)   On a vote on a written resolution —
    (a)   in the case of a company having a share capital, every member has one vote in respect of each share or each £10 of stock held by him, and
    (b)   in any other case, every member has one vote.

(2)   On a vote on a resolution on a show of hands at a meeting —
    (a)   every member present in person has one vote, and
    (b)   (notwithstanding anything in the company's articles) every proxy present who has been duly appointed by a member entitled to vote on the resolution has one vote.

(3)   On a vote on a resolution on a poll taken or demanded at a meeting —
    (a)   in the case of a company having a share capital, every member has one vote in respect of each share or each £10 of stock held by him, and
    (b)   in any other case, every member has one vote.

Company Law Reform Bill
Part D — Resolutions and meetings
Chapter 1 — General provisions about resolutions

3

(4) Subsections (1), (2)(a) and (3) have effect subject to any provision of the company's articles, except as provided in subsection (5).

(5) In relation to a resolution that is required or otherwise provided for in an enactment, if a private company's articles provide that a member has a different number of votes in relation to a resolution when it is passed as a written resolution and when it is passed on a poll taken or demanded at a meeting—

    (a) the provision about how many votes a member has in relation to the resolution passed on a poll is void, and

    (b) a member has the same number of votes in relation to the resolution when it is passed on a poll as he has when it is passed as a written resolution.

D5 Votes of joint holders of shares

(1) In the case of joint holders of shares of a company, only the vote of the senior holder who votes (and any proxies duly authorised by him) may be counted by the company.

(2) For the purposes of this section, the senior holder of a share is determined by the order in which the names of the joint holders appear in the register of members.

(3) Subsections (1) and (2) have effect subject to any provision of the company's articles.

D6 Relationship between this Part and rules of law etc.

(1) Nothing in this Part affects any enactment or rule of law as to—

    (a) things done other than by passing a resolution,

    (b) cases in which a resolution is or is not treated as having been passed, or

    (c) cases in which a person is precluded from alleging that a resolution has not been duly passed,

except as provided in this section.

(2) References in enactments passed or made before this section comes into force to—

    (a) a resolution of a company in general meeting, or

    (b) a resolution of a meeting of a class of members of the company,

have effect as if they included references to a written resolution of the members, or of a class of members, of a private company (as appropriate).

(3) A written resolution of a private company has effect as if passed (as the case may be)—

    (a) by the company in general meeting, or

    (b) by a meeting of a class of members of the company,

and references in enactments passed or made before this section comes into force to a meeting at which a resolution is passed or to members voting in favour of a resolution shall be construed accordingly.

CHAPTER 2

WRITTEN RESOLUTIONS

General provisions about written resolutions

D7   Written resolutions of private companies

(1)   In this Act, a written resolution is a resolution of a private company proposed and passed in accordance with this Chapter.

(2)   The following resolutions may not be passed as written resolutions —
   (a)   a resolution under section 303 of the Companies Act 1985 (c. 6) removing a director before the expiration of his period of office, or
   (b)   a resolution under section 391 of that Act removing an auditor before the expiration of his term of office.

(3)   A resolution may be proposed as a written resolution —
   (a)   by the directors of a private company (see section D10), or
   (b)   by the members of a private company (see sections D11 to D13).

D8   Eligible members

(1)   In relation to a resolution proposed as a written resolution of a private company, the eligible members are the members who would have been entitled to vote on the resolution on the circulation date of the resolution (see section D9).

(2)   If the persons entitled to vote on a written resolution change during the course of the day that is the circulation date of the resolution, the eligible members are the persons entitled to vote on the resolution at the time that the first copy of the resolution is sent or submitted to a member for his agreement.

Circulation of written resolutions

D9   Circulation date

References in this Part to the circulation date of a written resolution are to the date on which copies of it are sent or submitted to members in accordance with this Chapter (or if copies are sent or submitted to members on different days, to the first of those days).

D10   Circulation of written resolutions proposed by directors

(1)   This section applies to a resolution proposed as a written resolution by the directors of the company.

(2)   The company must serve a copy of the resolution on every eligible member.

(3)   The company must do so —
   (a)   by sending copies at the same time (so far as practicable) to all eligible members in hard copy form, in electronic form or by means of a website, or

      (b)   if it is possible to do so without undue delay, by submitting the same copy to each eligible member in turn (or different copies to each of a number of eligible members in turn),

or by sending copies to some members in accordance with paragraph (a) and submitting a copy or copies to other members in accordance with paragraph (b).

(4)   The copy of the resolution must be accompanied by a statement informing the member—

      (a)   how to signify agreement to the resolution (see section D14), and

      (b)   as to the date by which the resolution must be passed if it is not to lapse (see section D15).

(5)   In the event of default in complying with this section, an offence is committed by every officer of the company who is in default.

(6)   A person guilty of an offence under this section is liable—

      (a)   on conviction on indictment, to a fine;

      (b)   on summary conviction, to a fine not exceeding the statutory maximum.

(7)   The validity of the resolution, if passed, is not affected by a failure to comply with this section.

D11 Members' requisition

(1)   Members of a private company may by requisition require the company to circulate—

      (a)   a resolution that they wish to propose as a written resolution, and

      (b)   a statement of not more than 1,000 words with respect to the subject matter of the resolution.

(2)   The requisition must be made by members representing not less than the requisite percentage of the total voting rights of all members who would be entitled to vote on the proposed resolution at the time at which the requisition is made.

(3)   In subsection (2), the "requisite percentage" is 5% or such lower percentage as is specified for this purpose in the company's articles.

(4)   The requisition must be—

      (a)   sent to the company in hard copy form or in electronic form, and

      (b)   authenticated by the requisitionists.

(5)   Where the requisition consists of more than one copy of the requisition —

      (a)   the requisition is authenticated if each copy is authenticated by the requisitionists sending the copy,

      (b)   the requisition is validly made if each copy is to the same effect and subsection (2) is satisfied by the copies of the requisition taken together, and

      (c)   the requisition is made at the time at which the company receives the last copy.

(6)   The requisition must be accompanied by, or by the tender of, a sum reasonably sufficient to meet the company's expenses in complying with section D12 (circulation of written resolution proposed by members).

(7)   A requisition is made at the time at which the requisitionists have complied with all of the requirements of this section.

D12   Circulation of written resolutions etc. proposed by members

(1)   If a requisition is made in accordance with section D11, the company must serve —
    (a)   a copy of the resolution, and
    (b)   (subject to section D13) a copy of any accompanying statement,
on every eligible member.

(2)   The company must do so —
    (a)   by sending copies at the same time (so far as practicable) to all eligible members in hard copy form, in electronic form or by means of a website, or
    (b)   if it is possible to do so without undue delay, by submitting the same copy to each eligible member in turn (or different copies to each of a number of eligible members in turn),
or by sending copies to some members in accordance with paragraph (a) and submitting a copy or copies to other members in accordance with paragraph (b).

(3)   The company must serve the copies (or, if copies are served on members on different days, the first of those copies) not more than 21 days after the date on which the requisition is made.

(4)   The copy of the resolution must be accompanied by a statement informing the member —
    (a)   how to signify agreement to the resolution (see section D14), and
    (b)   as to the date by which the resolution must be passed if it is not to lapse (see section D15).

(5)   The expenses of the company in complying with this section must be paid by the requisitionists unless the company resolves otherwise.

(6)   In the event of default in complying with this section, an offence is committed by every officer of the company who is in default.

(7)   A person guilty of an offence under this section is liable —
    (a)   on conviction on indictment, to a fine;
    (b)   on summary conviction, to a fine not exceeding the statutory maximum.

(8)   The validity of the resolution, if passed, is not affected by a failure to comply with this section.

D13   Application not to circulate members' statement

(1)   A company is not required to circulate a members' statement under section D12 if, on an application by the company or another person who claims to be aggrieved, the court is satisfied that the rights conferred by section D11 and that section are being abused to secure publicity for defamatory matter.

(2)   The court may order the requisitionists to pay the whole or part of the company's costs on such an application, even if they are not parties to the application.

Agreeing to written resolutions

D14 Procedure for signifying agreement to written resolution

(1) A member signifies his agreement to a proposed written resolution when the company receives from him (or from someone acting on his behalf) an authenticated document —

    (a) identifying the resolution to which it relates, and

    (b) indicating his agreement to the resolution.

(2) The document must be sent to the company in hard copy form or in electronic form.

(3) A member's agreement is ineffective if signified before he has seen a copy of the proposed resolution.

(4) A member's agreement to a written resolution, once signified, may not be revoked.

(5) A written resolution is passed when the required majority of eligible members have signified their agreement to it.

D15 Period for agreeing to written resolution

(1) A proposed written resolution lapses if it is not passed before the end of —

    (a) the period specified for this purpose in the company's articles, or

    (b) if none is specified, the period of 28 days beginning with the circulation date.

(2) The agreement of a member to a written resolution is ineffective if signified after the expiry of that period.

Supplementary

D16 Sending documents relating to written resolutions by electronic means

(1) Where a company has given an electronic address in any document containing or accompanying a proposed written resolution, it is deemed to have agreed that any document or information relating to that resolution may be sent by electronic means to that address (subject to any conditions or limitations specified in the document).

(2) In this section "electronic address" means any address or number used for the purposes of sending or receiving documents or information by electronic means.

D17 Publication of written resolution on website

(1) This section applies where a company sends —

    (a) a written resolution, or

    (b) a statement relating to a written resolution,

to a person by means of a website.

(2) The resolution or statement is not validly sent for the purposes of this Chapter unless the resolution is available on the website throughout the period

beginning with the circulation date and ending on the date on which the resolution lapses under section D15.

(3) For the purposes of this section, a failure to make a resolution or statement available on a website throughout the period mentioned in subsection (2) must be disregarded if—

    (a) it is made available on the website for part of that period, and

    (b) the failure to make it available throughout that period is wholly attributable to circumstances that it would not be reasonable to have expected the company to prevent or avoid.

D18 Relationship between this Chapter and provisions of company's articles

(1) In relation to a resolution of a private company that is required by or otherwise provided for in an enactment, this Chapter has effect notwithstanding anything in the company's articles.

(2) This section does not affect any power of a company to make provision in its articles for its members to pass resolutions without a meeting other than in accordance with this Chapter.

CHAPTER 3

RESOLUTIONS AT MEETINGS

General provisions about resolutions at meetings

D19 Resolutions at general meetings

(1) A resolution of the members of a company is validly passed at a general meeting (or on a poll demanded at a general meeting) if—

    (a) notice of the meeting and of the resolution is given, and

    (b) the meeting is held and conducted,

in accordance with the relevant provisions of this Part and the company's articles.

(2) The relevant provisions of this Part are this Chapter and—

    (a) in the case of a public company, Chapter 4, and

    (b) in the case of a quoted company, Chapter 5.

Calling meetings

D20 Directors' power to call general meetings

(1) The directors of a company may call a general meeting of the company.

(2) This section applies notwithstanding any contrary provision in the company's articles.

D21 Members' power to requisition general meetings

(1) The members of a company may by requisition require the directors of the company to call a general meeting of the company.

Company Law Reform Bill
Part D — Resolutions and meetings
Chapter 3 — Resolutions at meetings

9

(2)   The requisition must be made by members who, at the time at which the requisition is made—

   (a)   hold not less than 10% of such of the paid-up capital of the company as at that time carried the right of voting at general meetings of the company (excluding any paid-up capital held as treasury shares); or

   (b)   in the case of a company not having a share capital, represent not less than 10% of the total voting rights of all the members having a right to vote at general meetings at that time.

(3)   The requisition—

   (a)   must state the general nature of the business to be dealt with at the meeting, and

   (b)   may include the text of any resolution which may properly be moved and is intended to be moved at that meeting.

(4)   The requisition must be—

   (a)   sent to the directors in hard copy form or in electronic form, and

   (b)   authenticated by the requisitionists.

(5)   Where the requisition consists of more than one copy of the requisition —

   (a)   the requisition is authenticated if each copy is authenticated by the requisitionists sending the copy,

   (b)   the requisition is validly made if each copy is to the same effect and subsection (2) is satisfied by the copies of the requisition taken together, and

   (c)   the requisition is made at the time at which the company receives the last copy.

(6)   This section applies notwithstanding anything in the company's articles.

D22   Directors' duty to call meetings requisitioned by members

(1)   If a requisition is made in accordance with section D21, the directors must duly call a general meeting of the company—

   (a)   within 21 days from the date on which the requisition is made, and

   (b)   to be held on a date not less than 28 days after the date of the notice convening the meeting.

(2)   The notice of the meeting must include notice of any resolution contained in the requisition that may be properly moved at the meeting.

(3)   The business that may be dealt with at the meeting includes a resolution of which notice—

   (a)   is given in accordance with this section, or

   (b)   would have been given in accordance with this section but for the accidental omission, in giving it, of one or more members.

This subsection has effect notwithstanding anything in the company's articles.

(4)   In the case of a meeting at which a resolution is to be proposed as a special resolution, the directors are deemed not to have duly called the meeting if they do not give notice of the resolution in accordance with section D3.

7 Draft Clauses

10

Company Law Reform Bill
Part D — Resolutions and meetings
Chapter 3 — Resolutions at meetings

D23 Power of members to call requisitioned meeting at company's expense

(1) If the directors do not call a general meeting in accordance with section D22, the requisitionists, or any of them representing more than one half of the total voting rights of all of them, may themselves call a general meeting.

(2) The requisitionists may not call the meeting for a date more than 3 months after the date on which the requisition was made.

(3) The requisitionists must call the meeting in the same manner, as nearly as possible, as that in which meetings are required to be called by directors of the company.

(4) Any reasonable expenses incurred by the requisitionists by reason of the failure of the directors duly to call a meeting must be repaid to the requisitionists by the company.

(5) Any sum so repaid shall be retained by the company out of any sums due or to become due from the company by way of fees or other remuneration in respect of their services to such of the directors as were in default.

D24 Power of court to order meeting

(1) This section applies if for any reason it is impracticable—
   (a) to call a meeting of a company in any manner in which meetings of that company may be called, or
   (b) to conduct the meeting in the manner prescribed by the company's articles or this Act.

(2) The court may, either of its own motion or on the application—
   (a) of a director of the company, or
   (b) of a member of the company who would be entitled to vote at the meeting,
   order a meeting to be called, held and conducted in any manner the court thinks fit.

(3) Where such an order is made, the court may give such ancillary or consequential directions as it thinks expedient.

(4) Such directions may include a direction that one member of the company present at the meeting be deemed to constitute a quorum.

(5) A meeting called, held and conducted in accordance with an order under this section is deemed for all purposes to be a meeting of the company duly called, held and conducted.

Notice of meetings

D25 Notice of meetings

(1) A general meeting of a company (other than an adjourned meeting) may be called by 14 days' notice, unless the company's articles specify a longer period of notice.

(2) A provision of a company's articles is void in so far as it provides for the calling of a general meeting of the company (other than an adjourned meeting) by less than 14 days' notice.

Company Law Reform Bill
Part D — Resolutions and meetings
Chapter 3 — Resolutions at meetings

11

(3) A general meeting may be called by less than the period of notice required by this section or by the company's articles (as the case may be) if —

    (a) the period of notice is agreed in accordance with subsection (4), and

    (b) the meeting is not an annual general meeting of a public company.

(4) The shorter period of notice must be agreed to by a majority in number of the members having a right to attend and vote at the meeting, being a majority who —

    (a) together hold not less than the requisite percentage in nominal value of the shares giving a right to attend and vote at the meeting (excluding any shares in the company held as treasury shares), or

    (b) in the case of a company not having a share capital, together represent not less than the requisite percentage of the total voting rights at that meeting of all the members.

(5) The requisite percentage for this purpose is —

    (a) in the case of a private company, 90% or such higher percentage (not exceeding 95%) as may be specified in the company's articles;

    (b) in the case of a public company, 95%.

(6) Notice of a meeting must be given —

    (a) in hard copy form,

    (b) in electronic form, or

    (c) by means of a website (see section D26).

D26 Publication of notice of meeting on website

(1) Notice of a meeting is not validly given by a company by means of a website unless it is given in accordance with this section.

(2) When the company notifies a member of the presence of the notice on the website the notification must —

    (a) state that it concerns a notice of a company meeting,

    (b) specify the place, date and time of the meeting, and

    (c) in the case of a public company, state whether the meeting will be an annual general meeting.

(3) The notice must be available on the website throughout the period beginning with the date of that notification and ending with the conclusion of the meeting.

(4) For the purposes of this section, a failure to make a resolution or statement available on a website throughout the period mentioned in subsection (3) must be disregarded if —

    (a) it is made available on the website for part of that period, and

    (b) the failure to make it available throughout that period is wholly attributable to circumstances that it would not be reasonable to have expected the company to prevent or avoid.

D27 Persons entitled to receive notice of meetings

(1) Notice of a general meeting of a company must be sent to —

    (a) every member of the company, and

    (b) every director.

7 Draft Clauses

12

Company Law Reform Bill
Part D — Resolutions and meetings
Chapter 3 — Resolutions at meetings

(2) In subsection (1), the reference to members includes any person who is entitled to a share in consequence of the death or bankruptcy of a member, if the company has been notified of their entitlement.

(3) This section has effect subject to —
    (a) any enactment, and
    (b) any provision of the company's articles.

D28 Contents of notices of meetings

(1) Notice of a general meeting of a company must state —
    (a) the time and date of the meeting, and
    (b) the place of the meeting.
This subsection has effect notwithstanding any provision of the company's articles.

(2) Notice of a general meeting of a company must state the general nature of the business to be dealt with at the meeting.
This subsection has effect subject to any provision of the company's articles.

D29 Resolution requiring special notice

(1) Where by any provision of the Companies Acts special notice is required of a resolution, the resolution is not effective unless notice of the intention to move it has been given to the company at least 28 days before the meeting at which it is moved.

(2) The company must, where practicable, give its members notice of any such resolution in the same manner and at the same time as it gives notice of the meeting.

(3) Where that is not practicable, the company must give its members notice at least 14 days before the meeting —
    (a) by advertisement in a newspaper having an appropriate circulation, or
    (b) in any other manner allowed by the company's articles.

(4) If, after notice of the intention to move such a resolution has been given to the company, a meeting is called for a date 28 days or less after the notice has been given, the notice is deemed to have been properly given, though not given within the time required.

Members' statements

D30 Members' power to requisition circulation of statements

(1) The members of a company may by requisition require the company to circulate to members of the company entitled to receive notice of a general meeting any statement of not more than 1,000 words with respect to a matter referred to in a proposed resolution or other business to be dealt with at that meeting.

(2) The requisition must be made by —
    (a) members representing not less than 5% of the total voting rights of all the members who, at the time the requisition is made, have a relevant

Company Law Reform Bill
Part D — Resolutions and meetings
Chapter 3 — Resolutions at meetings

13

right to vote (excluding any voting rights attached to any shares in the company held as treasury shares), or

    (b)   not less than 100 members who, at the time the requisition is made, have a relevant right to vote and hold shares in the company on which there has been paid up an average sum, per member, of not less than £100.

(3)   In subsection (2), a "relevant right to vote" means —

    (a)   in relation to a statement with respect to a matter referred to in a proposed resolution, a right to vote on that resolution at the meeting to which the requisition relates, and

    (b)   in relation to any other statement, a right to vote at the meeting to which the requisition relates.

(4)   The requisition must be —

    (a)   sent to the directors in hard copy form or in electronic form not less than one week before the meeting, and

    (b)   authenticated by the requisitionists.

(5)   Where the requisition consists of more than one copy of the requisition —

    (a)   the requisition is authenticated if each copy is authenticated by the requisitionists sending the copy,

    (b)   the requisition is validly made if each copy is to the same effect and subsection (2) is satisfied by the copies of the requisition taken together, and

    (c)   the requisition is made at the time at which the company receives the last copy.

(6)   The requisition must be accompanied by, or by the tender of, a sum reasonably sufficient to meet the company's expenses in complying with section D31 (circulation of members' statement).

(7)   A requisition is made at the time at which the requisitionists have complied with all of the requirements of this section.

D31   Company's duty to circulate members' statement

(1)   If a requisition is made in accordance with section D30, the company must circulate the statement to members of the company entitled to receive notice of the meeting by sending a copy of the statement to each of them —

    (a)   in the same manner as the notice of the meeting, and

    (b)   at the same time as, or (if the requisition is received after notice of the meeting has been given) as soon as practicable after, it gives notice of the meeting.

(2)   Subsection (1) has effect subject to section D32 (application not to circulate members' statement).

(3)   The expenses of the company in complying with this section must be paid by the requisitionists, unless the company otherwise resolves.

(4)   In the event of default in complying with this section, an offence is committed by every officer of the company who is in default.

(5)   A person guilty of an offence under this section is liable —

    (a)   on conviction on indictment, to a fine;

7 Draft Clauses

14

Company Law Reform Bill
Part D — Resolutions and meetings
Chapter 3 — Resolutions at meetings

  (b) on summary conviction, to a fine not exceeding the statutory maximum.

D32 Application not to circulate members' statement

(1) A company is not required to circulate a members' statement under section D31 if, on an application by the company or another person who claims to be aggrieved, the court is satisfied that the rights conferred by section D30 and that section are being abused to secure publicity for defamatory matter.

(2) The court may order the requisitionists to pay the whole or part of the company's costs on such an application, even if they are not parties to the application.

Procedure at meetings

D33 Quorum at meetings

(1) In the case of a company limited by shares or guarantee and having only one member, one member present at a meeting is a quorum.

This subsection has effect notwithstanding any provision to the contrary in the company's articles.

(2) In any other case, subject to the provisions of the company's articles, two members present at a meeting are a quorum.

D34 Chairman of meeting

(1) A member may be elected to be the chairman of a general meeting by a resolution of the company passed at the meeting.

(2) Subsection (1) is subject to any provision of the company's articles that states who may or may not be chairman.

D35 Declaration by chairman on a show of hands

(1) On a vote on a resolution at a meeting on a show of hands, a declaration by the chairman that the resolution has or has not been passed, or passed with a particular majority, is conclusive evidence of that fact without proof of the number or proportion of the votes recorded in favour of or against the resolution.

(2) An entry in respect of such a declaration in minutes of the meeting recorded in accordance with section D60 is also conclusive evidence of that fact without such proof.

(3) This section does not have effect if a poll is demanded in respect of the resolution.

D36 Right to demand a poll

(1) A provision of a company's articles is void in so far as it would have the effect of excluding the right to demand a poll at a general meeting on any question other than—

  (a) the election of the chairman of the meeting, or

Company Law Reform

Company Law Reform Bill
Part D — Resolutions and meetings
Chapter 3 — Resolutions at meetings

15

(b)   the adjournment of the meeting.

(2)   A provision of a company's articles is void in so far as it would have the effect of making ineffective a demand for a poll on a question which is made—

    (a)   by not less than 5 members having the right to vote on the resolution; or

    (b)   by a member or members representing not less than 10% of the total voting rights of all the members having the right to vote on the resolution (excluding any voting rights attached to any shares in the company held as treasury shares); or

    (c)   by a member or members holding shares in the company conferring a right to vote on the resolution, being shares on which an aggregate sum has been paid up equal to not less than 10% of the total sum paid up on all the shares conferring that right (excluding shares in the company conferring a right to vote on the resolution which are held as treasury shares).

D37   Voting on a poll

On a poll taken or demanded at a general meeting of a company, a member entitled to more than one vote need not, if he votes, use all his votes or cast all the votes he uses in the same way.

D38   Representation of corporations at meetings

(1)   This section applies to any corporation, whether or not it is a company within the meaning of this Act.

(2)   If the corporation is a member of another corporation that is such a company, it may by resolution of its directors or other governing body authorise such person as it thinks fit to act as its representative at any meeting of the company.

(3)   A person so authorised—

    (a)   is entitled to exercise the same powers on behalf of the corporation that he represents as that corporation could exercise if it were an individual shareholder of the other corporation, and

    (b)   counts in determining whether there is a quorum at a meeting.

Proxies

D39   Statutory right to appoint proxies

(1)   Sections D40 to D48 make provision about proxies.

(2)   Those sections (other than section D45) have effect notwithstanding anything in the company's articles.

(3)   But nothing in those sections prevents a company's articles from conferring more extensive rights on members or proxies than are conferred by those sections.

D40   Rights to appoint proxies

(1)   A member of a company is entitled to appoint another person as his proxy to exercise all or any of his rights to attend and to speak and vote at a meeting of the company.

7 Draft Clauses

16

Company Law Reform Bill
Part D — Resolutions and meetings
Chapter 3 — Resolutions at meetings

(2)   The taking of a poll demanded at a meeting is for this purpose a proceeding at the meeting, even if taken later.

(3)   In the case of a company having a share capital, a member may appoint more than one proxy in relation to a meeting, provided that each proxy is appointed to exercise the rights attached to a different share or shares held by him, or (as the case may be) to a different £10, or multiple of £10, of stock held by him.

D41   Notice of meeting to contain statement of rights

(1)   In every notice calling a meeting of a company there must appear, with reasonable prominence, a statement informing the member of —
   (a)   his rights under section D40, and
   (b)   any more extensive rights conferred by the company's articles to appoint more than one proxy.

(2)   Failure to comply with this section does not affect the validity of the meeting or of anything done at the meeting.

(3)   If this section is not complied with as respects any meeting, an offence is committed by every officer of the company who is in default.

(4)   A person guilty of an offence under this section is liable on summary conviction to a fine not exceeding level 3 on the standard scale.

D42   Company-sponsored invitations to appoint proxies

(1)   If for the purposes of a meeting there are issued at the company's expense invitations to members to appoint as proxy a specified person or a number of specified persons, the invitations must be issued to all members entitled to vote at the meeting.

(2)   Subsection (1) is not contravened if —
   (a)   there is issued to a member at his request a form of appointment naming the proxy or a list of persons willing to act as proxy, and
   (b)   the form or list is available on request to all members entitled to vote at the meeting.

(3)   If subsection (1) is contravened as respects a meeting, an offence is committed by every officer of the company who is in default.

(4)   A person guilty of an offence under this section is liable on summary conviction to a fine not exceeding level 3 on the standard scale.

D43   Notice required of appointment of proxy etc.

(1)   This section applies to —
   (a)   the appointment of a proxy, and
   (b)   any document necessary to show the validity of, or otherwise relating to, the appointment of a proxy.

(2)   Any provision of the company's articles is void in so far as it would have the effect of requiring any such appointment or document to be received by the company or another person earlier than the following time —
   (a)   in the case of a meeting or adjourned meeting, 48 hours before the time for holding the meeting or adjourned meeting;

Company Law Reform Bill
Part D — Resolutions and meetings
Chapter 3 — Resolutions at meetings

17

> (b) in the case of a poll held more than 48 hours after the meeting at which it was demanded, 24 hours before the time appointed for the taking of the poll;
>
> (c) in the case of a poll held not more than 48 hours after the meeting at which it was demanded, the end of that meeting.

(3) In calculating the periods mentioned in subsection (2) no account shall be taken of any part of a Saturday or Sunday, Christmas Day, Good Friday or any day that is a bank holiday in the part of Great Britain in which the company is registered.

D44 Member present by proxy to count towards quorum

A member of a company present by proxy at a meeting of the company counts in determining whether there is a quorum.

D45 Chairing meetings

(1) A proxy may be elected to be the chairman of a general meeting by a resolution of the company passed at the meeting.

(2) Subsection (1) is subject to any provision of the company's articles that states who may or who may not be chairman.

D46 Right of proxy to demand a poll

(1) The appointment of a proxy to vote on a matter at a meeting of a company authorises the proxy to demand, or join in demanding, a poll on that matter.

(2) In applying the provisions of section D36(2) (requirements for effective demand), a demand by a proxy counts—
> (a) for the purposes of paragraph (a), as a demand by the member;
> (b) for the purposes of paragraph (b), as a demand by a member representing the voting rights that the proxy is authorised to exercise;
> (c) for the purposes of paragraph (c), as a demand by a member holding the shares to which those rights are attached.

D47 Voting on a poll

On a vote on a poll taken or demanded at a general meeting of a company, a vote by a proxy counts as a vote by a member representing the voting rights that the proxy is authorised to exercise.

D48 Notice required of determination of proxy's authority

(1) This section applies to notice of the determination of the authority of a person to act as proxy.

(2) The determination of the authority of a person to act as proxy does not affect—
> (a) the determination of whether there was a quorum at a meeting,
> (b) the validity of anything done by that person as chairman of a meeting, or
> (c) the validity of a poll demanded by that person at a meeting,

7 Draft Clauses

18

Company Law Reform Bill
Part D — Resolutions and meetings
Chapter 3 — Resolutions at meetings

unless the company received notice of the determination before the commencement of the meeting.

(3)   The determination of the authority of a person to act as proxy does not affect the validity of a vote given by that person unless the company received notice of the determination—

    (a)   before the commencement of the meeting or adjourned meeting at which the vote is given, or

    (b)   in the case of a vote on a poll taken after the day of the meeting at which the poll was demanded, before the time appointed for taking the poll.

(4)   If the company's articles require or permit members to give notice of determination to a person other than the company, the references above to the company receiving notice have effect as if they were or (as the case may be) included a reference to that person.

(5)   Any provision of the company's articles is void in so far as it would have the effect of requiring notice of determination to be received by the company or another person earlier than the following time—

    (a)   in the case of a meeting or adjourned meeting, 48 hours before the time for holding the meeting or adjourned meeting;

    (b)   in the case of a poll held more than 48 hours after the meeting at which it was demanded, 24 hours before the time appointed for the taking of the poll;

    (c)   in the case of a poll held not more than 48 hours after the meeting at which it was demanded, the end of that meeting.

(6)   In calculating the periods mentioned in subsection (5) no account shall be taken of any part of a Saturday or Sunday, Christmas Day, Good Friday or any day that is a bank holiday in the part of Great Britain in which the company is registered.

Adjourned meetings

D49   Resolution passed at adjourned meeting

Where a resolution is passed at an adjourned meeting of a company, the resolution is for all purposes to be treated as having been passed on the date on which it was in fact passed, and is not to be deemed passed on any earlier date.

Electronic communications

D50   Sending documents relating to meetings etc. in electronic form

(1)   Where a company has given an electronic address in a notice calling a meeting, it is deemed to have agreed that any document or information relating to—

    (a)   proceedings at the meeting, or

    (b)   a poll demanded at the meeting,

may be sent by electronic means to that address (subject to any conditions or limitations specified in the notice).

(2)   Where a company has given an electronic address—

    (a)   in an instrument of proxy sent out by the company in relation to the meeting, or

Company Law Reform Bill
Part D — Resolutions and meetings
Chapter 3 — Resolutions at meetings

19

(b)   in an invitation to appoint a proxy issued by the company in relation to the meeting,

it is deemed to have agreed that any document or information relating to proxies for that meeting, or for a poll demanded at that meeting, may be sent by electronic means to that address (subject to any conditions or limitations specified in the notice).

(3)   In subsection (2), documents relating to proxies include —

(a)   the appointment of a proxy in relation to a meeting or any poll demanded at the meeting,

(b)   any document necessary to show the validity of, or otherwise relating to, the appointment of a proxy, and

(c)   notice of the determination of the authority of a proxy.

(4)   In this section "electronic address" means any address or number used for the purposes of sending or receiving documents or information by electronic means.

(5)   This section has effect notwithstanding any provision to the contrary in the company's articles.

Application to class meetings

D51   Application to class meetings

(1)   The provisions of this Chapter apply (with necessary modifications) in relation to a meeting of holders of a class of shares in connection with the variation of the rights attached to such shares (a "class meeting") as they apply in relation to a general meeting, with the exception of —

(a)   sections D21 to D23 (members' power to requisition general meeting);

(b)   section D24 (power of court to order meeting);

(c)   section D33 (quorum);

(d)   section D36 (right to demand a poll).

(2)   The quorum for a class meeting is —

(a)   for a meeting other than an adjourned meeting, two persons present holding at least one-third in nominal value of the issued shares of the class in question (excluding any shares of that class held as treasury shares);

(b)   for an adjourned meeting, one person present holding shares of the class in question.

(3)   For the purposes of subsection (2), where a person is present by proxy or proxies, he is treated as holding only the shares in respect of which those proxies are authorised to exercise voting rights.

(4)   At a class meeting, any holder of shares of the class in question present may demand a poll.

(5)   For the purposes of this section —

(a)   any alteration of a provision contained in a company's articles for the variation of the rights attached to a class of shares, or the insertion of any such provision into the articles, is itself to be treated as a variation of those rights, and

7 Draft Clauses

20

Company Law Reform Bill
Part D — Resolutions and meetings
Chapter 3 — Resolutions at meetings

(b)   references to the variation of rights attached to a class of shares include references to their abrogation.

CHAPTER 4

ADDITIONAL REQUIREMENTS FOR PUBLIC COMPANIES

D52   Public companies: annual general meeting

(1)   Every public company must hold a general meeting as its annual general meeting in each period of 6 months beginning with the day following its accounting reference date (in addition to any other meetings held during that period).

(2)   A company that fails to comply with subsection (1) as result of giving of notice under section 225 of the Companies Act 1985 (c. 6) (alteration of accounting reference date) —

    (a)   specifying a new accounting reference date, and

    (b)   stating that the current accounting reference period or the previous accounting reference period is to be shortened,

shall be treated as if it had complied with subsection (1) if it holds a general meeting as its annual general meeting within 3 months of giving that notice.

(3)   If a company fails to comply with subsection (1), an offence is committed by every officer of the company who is in default.

(4)   A person guilty of an offence under this section is liable —

    (a)   on conviction on indictment, to a fine;

    (b)   on summary conviction, to a fine not exceeding the statutory maximum.

D53   Public companies: notice of AGM

(1)   A notice calling an annual general meeting of a public company must state that the meeting is an annual general meeting.

(2)   Notwithstanding that an annual general meeting is called by shorter notice than that specified in section D25 or in the company's articles (as the case may be), it is deemed to have been duly called if it is so agreed by all the members entitled to attend and vote at the meeting.

D54   Public companies: members' power to requisition circulation of resolutions for AGMs

(1)   The members of a public company may by requisition require the company to give to members of the company entitled to receive notice of the next annual general meeting notice of any resolution which may properly be moved and is intended to be moved at that meeting.

(2)   The requisition must be made by —

    (a)   members representing not less than 5% of the total voting rights of all the members who, at the time the requisition is made, have a right to vote on the resolution at the annual general meeting to which the requisition relates (excluding any voting rights attached to any shares in the company held as treasury shares), or

Company Law Reform Bill
Part D — Resolutions and meetings
Chapter 4 — Additional requirements for public companies

21

(b)   not less than 100 members who, at the time the requisition is made, have a right to vote on the resolution at the annual general meeting to which the requisition relates and hold shares in the company on which there has been paid up an average sum, per member, of not less than £100.

(3)   The requisition must be sent to the company in hard copy form or in electronic form —

      (a)   before notice of the annual general meeting to which the requisition relates is given, or

      (b)   not less than 6 weeks before that meeting.

(4)   The requisition must be authenticated by the requisitionists.

(5)   Where the requisition consists of more than one copy of the requisition —

      (a)   the requisition is authenticated if each copy is authenticated by the requisitionists sending the copy,

      (b)   the requisition is validly made if each copy is to the same effect and subsection (2) is satisfied by the copies of the requisition taken together, and

      (c)   the requisition is made at the time at which the company receives the last copy.

(6)   The requisition must be accompanied by, or by the tender of, a sum reasonably sufficient to meet the company's expenses in complying with section D55 (circulation of members' resolutions for AGMs).

(7)   A requisition is made at the time at which the requisitionists have complied with all of the requirements of this section.

D55   Public companies: company's duty to circulate members' resolutions for AGMs

(1)   If a requisition is made in accordance with section D54, the company must give notice of the resolution to members who are entitled to receive notice of the annual general meeting by sending a copy of the resolution to each of them —

      (a)   in the same manner as notice of the meeting, and

      (b)   at the same time as, or as soon as practicable after, it gives notice of the meeting.

(2)   The expenses of the company in complying with this section must be paid by the requisitionists, unless the company otherwise resolves.

(3)   Notwithstanding anything in the company's articles, the business which may be dealt with at an annual general meeting includes a resolution of which notice —

      (a)   is given in accordance with this section, or

      (b)   would have been given in accordance with this section but for the accidental omission, in giving it, of one or more members.

(4)   In the event of default in complying with this section, an offence is committed by every officer of the company who is in default.

(5)   A person guilty of an offence under this section is liable —

      (a)   on conviction on indictment, to a fine;

7 Draft Clauses

22

Company Law Reform Bill
Part D — Resolutions and meetings
Chapter 4 — Additional requirements for public companies

    (b)   on summary conviction, to a fine not exceeding the statutory maximum.

CHAPTER 5

ADDITIONAL REQUIREMENTS FOR QUOTED COMPANIES

D56   Quoted companies: notice of meeting at which annual accounts laid

(1)   A general meeting of a quoted company at which the company's annual accounts are laid must not be held less than 14 days after the expiry of the holding period.

(2)   In this section, "holding period", in relation to a company's annual accounts, means the period of 15 days beginning with the day after the day on which those accounts are published on its website.

(3)   In the event of default in complying with this section, an offence is committed by every officer of the company who is in default.

(4)   A person guilty of an offence under this section is liable —
    (a)   on conviction on indictment, to a fine;
    (b)   on summary conviction, to a fine not exceeding the statutory maximum.

(5)   This section has effect notwithstanding anything in the company's articles.

D57   Quoted companies: members' power to requisition circulation of resolutions etc. for accounts meeting

(1)   The members of a quoted company may by requisition require the company to —
    (a)   give to members of the company entitled to receive notice of the general meeting at which the company's annual accounts are to be laid (the "accounts meeting") notice of any resolution which may be properly moved and is intended to be moved by the members at that meeting;
    (b)   circulate to such members any statement of not more than 1,000 words with respect to a matter referred to in a resolution proposed to be moved at that meeting or arising from those annual accounts.

(2)   The requisition must be made by —
    (a)   members representing not less than 5% of the total voting rights of all the members who, at the time the requisition is made, have a relevant right to vote (excluding any voting rights attached to any shares in the company held as treasury shares), or
    (b)   not less than 100 members who, at the time the requisition is made, have a relevant right to vote and hold shares in the company on which there has been paid up an average sum, per member, of not less than £100.

(3)   In subsection (2), a "relevant right to vote" means —
    (a)   in relation to a resolution or to a statement with respect to a matter referred to in a proposed resolution, a right to vote on that resolution at the accounts meeting, and

Company Law Reform Bill
Part D — Resolutions and meetings
Chapter 5 — Additional requirements for quoted companies

23

    (b) in relation to any other statement, a right to vote at the accounts meeting.

 (4) The requisition must be—

    (a) sent to the company in hard copy form or in electronic form before the expiry of the period of 15 days beginning with the day after the day on which the company's annual accounts are published on its website, and

    (b) authenticated by the requisitionists.

 (5) Where the requisition consists of more than one copy of the requisition —

    (a) the requisition is authenticated if each copy is authenticated by the requisitionists sending the copy,

    (b) the requisition is validly made if each copy is to the same effect and subsection (2) is satisfied by the copies of the requisition taken together, and

    (c) the requisition is made at the time at which the company receives the last copy.

D58 **Quoted companies: company's duty to circulate members' resolutions etc. for accounts meeting**

 (1) If a requisition is made in accordance with section D57, the company must give notice of the resolution, or circulate the statement, to members who are entitled to receive notice of the accounts meeting by sending a copy of the resolution or statement to each of them—

    (a) in the same manner as notice of the meeting, and

    (b) at the same time as it gives notice of the meeting or (if the requisition is received after notice of the meeting has been given) as soon as practicable after it receives the requisition.

 (2) Subsection (1) has effect subject to section D59 (application not to circulate members' statement).

 (3) A company may not require the requisitionists to pay its expenses in complying with this section.

 (4) Notwithstanding anything in the company's articles, the business which may be dealt with at the accounts meeting includes a resolution of which notice—

    (a) is given in accordance with this section, or

    (b) would have been given in accordance with this section but for the accidental omission, in giving it, of one or more members.

 (5) In the event of default in complying with this section, an offence is committed by every officer of the company who is in default.

 (6) A person guilty of an offence under this section is liable—

    (a) on conviction on indictment, to a fine;

    (b) on summary conviction, to a fine not exceeding the statutory maximum.

D59 **Quoted companies: application not to circulate members' statement**

 (1) A quoted company is not required to circulate a statement under section D58 if, on an application by the company or another person who claims to be

7 Draft Clauses

24

Company Law Reform Bill
Part D — Resolutions and meetings
Chapter 5 — Additional requirements for quoted companies

aggrieved, the court is satisfied that the rights conferred by section D57 and that section are being abused to secure publicity for defamatory matter.

(2) The court may order the requisitionists to pay the whole or part of the company's costs on such an application, even if they are not parties to the application.

CHAPTER 6

RECORDS OF RESOLUTIONS AND MEETINGS

D60 Obligation to keep records of resolutions and meetings

(1) Every company must at all times keep records comprising—
    (a) copies of all resolutions of members passed other than at general meetings,
    (b) minutes of all proceedings of general meetings, and
    (c) details provided to the company in accordance with section D62 (decisions of sole member).

(2) The records must be kept for at least ten years from the date of the resolution, meeting or decision (as appropriate).

(3) The records—
    (a) may be kept in hard copy form or in electronic form, and
    (b) may be arranged in such manner as the directors of the company think fit,
provided they are adequately recorded for future reference.

(4) Where the records are kept in electronic form, they must be capable of being reproduced in hard copy form.

(5) Where the records are kept other than in bound books, adequate precautions must be taken—
    (a) to guard against falsification, and
    (b) to facilitate the discovery of falsification.

(6) If a company fails to comply with this section, an offence is committed by every officer of the company who is in default.

(7) A person guilty of an offence under this section is liable on summary conviction to a fine not exceeding level 3 on the standard scale and, for continued contravention, a daily default fine not exceeding one-tenth of level 3 on the standard scale.

D61 Effect of recording resolutions etc.

(1) A record of a resolution passed other than at a general meeting that is kept by the company in accordance with section D60 is evidence of the passing of the resolution if it purports to be signed by a director of the company or by the company secretary.

(2) Where a record of a written resolution of a private company is kept in accordance with section D60, the requirements of this Act with respect to the passing of the resolution are deemed to be complied with unless the contrary is proved.

Company Law Reform Bill
Part D — Resolutions and meetings
Chapter 6 — Records of resolutions and meetings

25

(3)   A minute of proceedings of a general meeting that is kept by the company in accordance with section D60 is evidence of the proceedings if it purports to be signed by the chairman of that meeting or by the chairman of the following general meeting.

(4)   Where minutes of proceedings of a general meeting have been kept in accordance with section D60, then until the contrary is proved—

   (a)   the meeting is deemed duly held and convened,

   (b)   all proceedings at the meeting are deemed to have duly taken place, and

   (c)   all appointments of directors, managers or liquidators at the meeting are deemed valid.

D62   Records of decisions by sole member

(1)   This section applies to a company limited by shares or by guarantee that has only one member.

(2)   Where the member takes any decision that—

   (a)   may be taken by the company in general meeting, and

   (b)   has effect as if agreed by the company in general meeting,

he must (unless that decision is taken by way of a written resolution) provide the company with details of that decision.

(3)   If a person fails to comply with this section he commits an offence.

(4)   A person guilty of an offence under this section is liable on summary conviction to a fine not exceeding level 2 on the standard scale.

(5)   Failure to comply with this section does not affect the validity of any decision referred to in subsection (2).

D63   Inspection of records of resolutions and meetings

(1)   The company must at all times—

   (a)   keep at its registered office those records referred to in section D60(1) that relate to the previous ten years, and

   (b)   open those records to inspection by any member without charge.

(2)   Any member is entitled on payment of such fee as may be prescribed to be furnished with a copy of any of those records.

(3)   Copies of the records must be provided—

   (a)   in hard copy form or in electronic form, and

   (b)   within seven days after the member has made a request for a copy to the company.

(4)   If an inspection required under this section is refused or if a copy requested under this section is not sent within the proper time, an offence is committed by every officer of the company who is in default.

(5)   A person guilty of an offence under this section is liable on summary conviction to a fine not exceeding level 3 on the standard scale and, for continued contravention, to a daily default fine not exceeding one-tenth of level 3 on the standard scale.

7 Draft Clauses

26

Company Law Reform Bill
Part D — Resolutions and meetings
Chapter 6 — Records of resolutions and meetings

(6)   In the case of any such refusal or default, the court may by order compel an immediate inspection of the records or direct that the copies required be sent to the persons who requested them.

D64 Records of resolutions and meetings of class of members

The provisions of this Chapter apply (with necessary modifications) in relation to resolutions and meetings of holders of a class of shares in connection with the variation of the rights attached to such shares as they apply in relation to resolutions of members generally and to general meetings.

CHAPTER 7

INTERPRETATION OF PART

D65 Interpretation

(1)   In this Part—

"circulation date", in relation to a written resolution, has the meaning given by section D9;

"eligible members", in relation to a written resolution, has the meaning given in section D8;

"enactment" includes a provision comprised in an Act of the Scottish Parliament or subordinate legislation made under such an Act;

"quoted company" has the same meaning as in Part 7 of the Companies Act 1985 (c. 6);

"written resolution" has the meaning given in section D7.

(2)   In this Part, as it applies in Scotland—

(a)   references to costs are references to expenses, and

(b)   references to evidence are references to sufficient evidence.

Company Law Reform Bill

CONTENTS

7 Draft Clauses

PART E

EXERCISE OF RIGHTS OF MEMBERS

E1 Enjoyment or exercise of members' rights

(1) This section applies where provision is made by a company's articles enabling a member to identify another person or persons as entitled to enjoy or exercise all or any specified rights of the member in relation to the company.

(2) So far as is necessary to give effect to that provision, anything required or authorised by any provision of the Companies Acts to be done by or in relation to the member shall instead be done, or (as the case may be) may instead be done, by or in relation to the person so identified (or each of them) as if he were a member of the company.

(3) This applies, in particular, to the rights conferred by —
    (a) section 238(1)(a) of the Companies Act 1985 (c. 6) (right to be sent a copy of the annual accounts and certain other documents);
    (b) sections D10 and D12 (right to be sent proposed written resolution);
    (c) section D11 (right to requisition written resolution);
    (d) section D21 (right to requisition general meeting);
    (e) section D27 (right to notice of general meetings);
    (f) section D30 (right to requisition circulation of a statement);
    (g) section D40 (right to appoint proxy to act at meeting);
    (h) section D54 (right to requisition circulation of resolution for AGM of public company);
    (i) section D57 (right to requisition circulation of resolution or statement for accounts meeting of quoted company).

(4) This section and any such provision as is mentioned in subsection (1) do not confer rights enforceable against the company by anyone other than the member.

(5) The requirements for an effective transfer or other disposition of the whole or part of a member's interest in the company are not affected by this section.

E2 Power of Secretary of State to make regulations about exercise of certain rights of members

(1) The Secretary of State may by regulations made by statutory instrument require companies to enable a member to identify another person or persons as entitled to receive documents and information that the member is entitled to receive from the company.

(2)   Where such regulations are made, a company may provide in its articles that such persons are only entitled to receive the documents in electronic form or by means of the company's website.

(3)   So far as is necessary to give effect to regulations made under this section, any documents or information required or authorised by any provision of the Companies Acts to be sent or supplied to a member shall, or (as the case may be) may, instead be sent or supplied to the person so identified (or each of them) as if he were a member of the company.

(4)   Regulations under this section may —
    (a)   create summary criminal offences punishable with a fine not exceeding level 5 on the standard scale or such lower amount as may be specified;
    (b)   make provision only in respect of a particular class or description of company;
    (c)   make provision only in respect of a particular document or a particular class of documents.

(5)   Rights under regulations made under this section have effect as if they were rights under the company's articles and may be enforced by members accordingly.

(6)   This section and regulations made under this section do not confer rights enforceable against the company by anyone other than a member (except to the extent that such regulations create offences).

(7)   Regulations may not be made under this section unless a draft of the statutory instrument containing the regulations has been laid before and approved by a resolution of each House of Parliament.

(8)   The requirements for an effective transfer or other disposition of the whole or part of a member's interest in the company are not affected by regulations made under this section.

Company Law Reform Bill

CONTENTS

7 Draft Clauses

PART F

SENDING AND SUPPLYING DOCUMENTS AND INFORMATION

F1   Application of this Part

(1)   The provisions of this Part have effect for the purposes of any provision of the Companies Acts that authorises or requires documents or information to be sent or supplied by or to a company.

(2)   As regards documents or information to be sent or supplied to the registrar of companies this Part has effect subject to [provisions on registrar of companies].

F2   Sending or supplying documents or information

(1)   Documents or information to be sent or supplied to a company must be sent or supplied in accordance with the provisions of Schedule F1.

(2)   Documents or information to be sent or supplied by a company must be sent or supplied —
    (a)   in the case of a company other than a traded company, in accordance with the provisions of Schedule F2;
    (b)   in the case of a traded company, in accordance with the provisions of Schedule F3.

(3)   Those Schedules apply notwithstanding anything in the company's articles.

(4)   The provisions referred to in subsection (2) apply (and those referred to in subsection (1) do not apply) in relation to documents or information that are to be sent or supplied by one company to another.

F3   Meaning of "in hard copy form", "in electronic form" and "by means of a website"

(1)   A document or information is sent or supplied "in hard copy form" if it is sent or supplied in a paper copy or similar form capable of being read with the naked eye.

(2)   A document or information is sent or supplied "in electronic form" if it is sent or supplied —
    (a)   by electronic means (for example, by e-mail or fax), or
    (b)   by any other means while in an electronic form (for example, sending a disk by post).

(3)   A document or information authorised or required to be sent or supplied in hard copy or electronic form must be sent or supplied in a form, and by a means, that the sender or supplier reasonably considers will enable the recipient —

     (a)   to read it, and

     (b)   to retain a copy of it.

(4)   A provision that requires a document or information to be sent or supplied in hard copy form, and does not authorise its being sent or supplied in electronic form, is not complied with by sending or supplying it by electronic means.

(5)   A provision that authorises documents or information to be sent or supplied in hard copy form, in electronic form or by means of a website only authorises them to be sent or supplied in accordance with this Part (unless it expressly states otherwise).

(6)   A requirement to send or supply documents or information in hard copy form, in electronic form or by means of a website is a requirement to send or supply them in accordance with this Part (unless it expressly states otherwise).

F4   Right to hard copy version

(1)   Where a member of a company or a holder of a company's debentures has received a document or information from the company otherwise than in hard copy form, he is entitled to require the company to send him a version of the document or information in hard copy form.

(2)   The company must send the document or information in hard copy form within 21 days of receipt of the request from the member or debenture holder.

(3)   The company may not make a charge for providing the document or information in that form.

(4)   If a company fails to comply with this section, an offence is committed by the company and every officer of it who is in default.

(5)   A person guilty of an offence under this section is liable on summary conviction to a fine not exceeding level 3 on the standard scale and, for continued contravention, a daily default fine not exceeding one-tenth of level 3 on the standard scale.

(6)   This section has effect subject to any contrary provision in an enactment.

F5   Meaning of "authenticated"

A document or information sent or supplied by a person to a company is authenticated if—

     (a)   in the case of a document or information in hard copy form, it is signed by the person sending or supplying it;

     (b)   in the case of a document or information in electronic form, the identity of the sender or supplier of the document is confirmed—

          (i)   in a manner specified by the company, or

          (ii)   if no such manner has been specified by the company, [in accordance with normal commercial practice].

F6   Deemed delivery of documents and information sent by post or electronic means

(1)   This section applies in relation to documents and information sent or supplied by a company.

(2) Where—
  (a) the document or information was sent by post (whether in hard copy or electronic form) to an address in the United Kingdom, and
  (b) the company is able to show that it was properly addressed, prepaid and posted,

it is deemed to have been received by the intended recipient 48 hours after it was sent.

(3) Where—
  (a) the document or information is sent or supplied by electronic means, and
  (b) the company is able to show that it was properly addressed,

it is deemed to have been received by the intended recipient 48 hours after it was sent.

(4) In calculating a period of hours for the purposes of this section, no account shall be taken of any part of a Saturday or Sunday, Christmas Day, Good Friday or any day that is a bank holiday in the part of Great Britain in which the company is registered.

(5) This section has effect—
  (a) subject to any contrary provision in the Companies Acts, and
  (b) in its application to documents or information sent by a company to its members, subject to any contrary provision in the company's articles.

F7   Interpretation

(1) In this Part—
    "address" includes a number or address used for the purposes of sending or receiving documents or information by electronic means;
    "document" includes summons, notice, order or other legal process and registers;
    "traded company" means a company whose securities are admitted to trading on a regulated market within the meaning of Directive 2004/39 of the European Parliament and the Council of 21 April 2004 on markets in financial instruments.

(2) References in this Part to provisions of the Companies Acts authorising or requiring a document or information to be sent or supplied include all such provisions, whatever expression is used, and references to documents or information being sent or supplied shall be construed accordingly.

(3) References in this Part to documents or information being sent or supplied by or to a company include references to documents or information being sent or supplied by or to the directors of a company acting on behalf of the company.

SCHEDULES

SCHEDULE F1

Section F2(1)

DOCUMENTS AND INFORMATION SENT OR SUPPLIED TO A COMPANY

PART 1

INTRODUCTION

Application of Schedule

1   This Schedule does not apply to documents or information sent or supplied by one company to another (see section F2(4) and Schedules F2 and F3).

PART 2

COMMUNICATIONS IN HARD COPY FORM

Introduction

2   A document or information is validly sent or supplied to a company if it is sent or supplied in hard copy form in accordance with this Part of this Schedule.

Method of communication in hard copy form

3   (1) A document or information in hard copy form may be sent or supplied by hand or by post to an address (in accordance with paragraph 4).

     (2) For the purposes of this Schedule, a person sends a document or information by post if he prepays and posts an envelope containing the document or information.

Address for communications in hard copy form

4   A document or information in hard copy form may be sent or supplied —
      (a)   to an address specified by the company for the purpose;
      (b)   to the company's registered office;
      (c)   to an address to which any provision of the Companies Acts authorises the document or information to be sent or supplied.

Company Law Reform Bill
Schedule F1 — Documents and information sent or supplied to a company
Part 3 — Communications in electronic form

5

PART 3

COMMUNICATIONS IN ELECTRONIC FORM

Introduction

5 (1) A document or information is validly sent or supplied to a company if it is sent or supplied in electronic form in accordance with this Part of this Schedule.

(2) This paragraph has effect subject to any requirements or contrary provision in the Companies Acts.

Conditions for use of communications in electronic form

6 (1) A document or information may only be sent or supplied to a company in an electronic form if —
   (a) the company has agreed (generally or specifically) that the document or information may be sent or supplied in that form (and has not revoked that agreement), or
   (b) the company is deemed to have so agreed by a provision in the Companies Acts.

(2) Where the company has specified (generally or specifically) that the identity of the sender or supplier of the document or information must be confirmed in a particular manner, it must be confirmed in that manner.

Address for communications in electronic form

7 (1) Where the document or information is sent or supplied by electronic means, it may only be sent or supplied in electronic form to an address —
   (a) specified for the purpose by the company (generally or specifically), or
   (b) deemed by a provision in the Companies Acts to have been so specified.

(2) Where the document or information is sent or supplied in electronic form by hand or by post, it must be sent or supplied to an address to which it could be validly sent if it were in hard copy form.

PART 4

OTHER AGREED FORMS OF COMMUNICATION

8 (1) A document or information that is sent or supplied to a company otherwise than in hard copy form or electronic form is validly sent or supplied if it is sent or supplied in a form or manner that has been agreed by the company.

(2) This paragraph has effect subject to any requirements or contrary provision in the Companies Acts.

6

Company Law Reform Bill
Schedule F2 — Communications by a company other than a traded company
Part 1 — Introduction

SCHEDULE F2   Section F2(2)

COMMUNICATIONS BY A COMPANY OTHER THAN A TRADED COMPANY

PART 1

INTRODUCTION

Application of this Schedule

1   This Schedule applies to documents or information sent or supplied by companies that are not traded companies.

PART 2

COMMUNICATIONS IN HARD COPY FORM

Introduction

2   A document or information is validly sent or supplied by a company in hard copy form if it is sent or supplied in accordance with this Part of this Schedule.

Method of communication in hard copy form

3   (1) A document or information in hard copy form must be—
        (a)   handed to the intended recipient, or
        (b)   sent or supplied by hand or by post to an address (in accordance with paragraph 4).

     (2) For the purposes of this Schedule, a person sends a document or information by post if he prepays and posts an envelope containing the document or information.

Address for communications in hard copy form

4   (1) A document or information in hard copy form may be sent or supplied by the company—
        (a)   to an address specified for the purpose by the intended recipient;
        (b)   to a company at its registered office;
        (c)   to a person in his capacity as a member of the company at his address as shown in the company's register of members;
        (d)   to a person in his capacity as a director of the company at his address as shown in the company's register of directors;
        (e)   to an address to which any provision of the Companies Acts authorises the document or information to be sent or supplied.

     (2) Where the company is unable to obtain an address falling within sub-paragraph (1), the document or information may be sent or supplied to the intended recipient's last address known to the company.

Company Law Reform Bill
Schedule F2 — Communications by a company other than a traded company
Part 3 — Communications in electronic form

7

PART 3

COMMUNICATIONS IN ELECTRONIC FORM

Introduction

5   (1)   A document or information is validly sent or supplied by a company if it is sent in electronic form in accordance with this Part of this Schedule.

     (2)   This paragraph has effect subject to any requirements or contrary provision in the Companies Acts.

Agreement to communications in electronic form

6   (1)   A document or information may only be sent or supplied by a company in electronic form —
        (a)   to a person who has agreed (generally or specifically) that the document or information may be sent or supplied in that form (and has not revoked that agreement), or
        (b)   to a company that is deemed to have so agreed by a provision in the Companies Acts.

     (2)   Where the intended recipient has specified (generally or specifically) that the identity of the sender or supplier of the document or information must be confirmed in a particular manner, it must be confirmed in that manner.

Address for communications in electronic form

7   (1)   Where the document or information is sent or supplied by electronic means, it may only be sent or supplied to an address —
        (a)   specified for the purpose by the intended recipient (generally or specifically), or
        (b)   where the intended recipient is a company, deemed by a provision of the Companies Acts to have been so specified.

     (2)   Where the document or information is sent or supplied in electronic form by hand or by post, it must be —
        (a)   handed to the intended recipient, or
        (b)   sent or supplied to an address to which it could be validly sent if it were in hard copy form.

PART 4

COMMUNICATIONS BY MEANS OF A WEBSITE

Use of website

8   (1)   A document or information is validly sent or supplied by a company if it is made available on a website in accordance with this Part of this Schedule.

     (2)   This paragraph has effect subject to any requirements or contrary provision in the Companies Acts.

7 Draft Clauses

8

Company Law Reform Bill
Schedule F2 — Communications by a company other than a traded company
Part 4 — Communications by means of a website

Agreement to use of website

9   A document or information may only be sent or supplied by the company to a person by being made available on a website if the person—

    (a)   has agreed (generally or specifically) that the document or information may be sent or supplied to him in that manner, or

    (b)   is taken to have so agreed under—

        (i)   paragraph 10 (members of the company etc.), or

        (ii)   paragraph 11 (debenture holders),

and has not revoked that agreement.

Deemed agreement of members of company etc. to use of website

10   (1)   This paragraph applies to a document or information to be sent or supplied to a person—

    (a)   as a member of the company, or

    (b)   as a person identified by a member (in accordance with the company's articles or regulations made under section E2) as entitled to enjoy or exercise all or any specified rights of the member in relation to the company (an "entitled person").

    (2)   To the extent that—

    (a)   the members of the company have resolved that the company may send or supply documents or information to members by making them available on a website, or

    (b)   the company's articles contain provision to that effect,

a member of the company or entitled person in relation to whom the following conditions are met is taken to have agreed that the company may send or supply documents or information to him in that manner.

    (3)   The conditions are that the member or entitled person—

    (a)   has been asked individually by the company to agree that the company may send or supply documents or information generally, or the documents or information in question, to him by means of a website, and

    (b)   failed to respond within the period of 28 days beginning with the date on which the company's request was sent.

    (4)   A member or entitled person is not taken to have so agreed if the company's request—

    (a)   did not state clearly what the effect of a failure to respond would be, or

    (b)   was sent less than twelve months after a previous request made to him for the purposes of this paragraph in respect of the same or a similar class of documents or information.

    (5)   A resolution under this paragraph is subject to [section 380 of the Companies Act 1985 (c. 6)] (copy to be forwarded to registrar within 15 days).

Deemed agreement of debenture holders to use of website

11   (1)   This paragraph applies to a document or information to be sent or supplied to a person as holder of a company's debentures.

(2) To the extent that the relevant debenture holders have duly resolved that the company may send or supply documents or information to them by making them available on a website, a debenture holder in relation to whom the following conditions are met is taken to have agreed that the company may send or supply documents or information to him in that manner.

(3) The conditions are that the debenture holder —

    (a) has been asked individually by the company to agree that the company may send or supply documents or information generally, or the documents or information in question, to him by means of a website, and

    (b) failed to respond within the period of 28 days beginning with the date on which the company's request was sent.

(4) A person is not taken to have so agreed if the company's request —

    (a) did not state clearly what the effect of a failure to respond would be, or

    (b) was sent less than twelve months after a previous request made to him for the purposes of this paragraph in respect of the same or a similar class of documents or information.

(5) For the purposes of this paragraph —

    (a) the relevant debenture holders are the holders of debentures of the company ranking pari passu for all purposes with the intended recipient, and

    (b) a resolution of the relevant debenture holders is duly passed if they agree in accordance with the provisions of the instruments creating the debentures.

Notification of availability

12 (1) The company must notify the intended recipient of —

    (a) the presence of the document or information on the website,

    (b) the address of the website,

    (c) the place on the website where it may be accessed, and

    (d) how to access the document or information.

(2) The document or information is taken to be sent —

    (a) on the date on which the notification required by this paragraph is sent, or

    (b) if later, the date on which the document or information first appears on the website after that notification is sent.

Period of availability on website

13 (1) The company must make the document or information available on the website throughout —

    (a) the period specified by any applicable provision of the Companies Acts, or

    (b) if no such period is specified, the period of 28 days beginning with the date on which the notification required under paragraph 12 is sent to the person in question.

10

Company Law Reform Bill
Schedule F2 — Communications by a company other than a traded company
Part 4 — Communications by means of a website

(2) For the purposes of this paragraph, a failure to make a document or information available on a website throughout the period mentioned in sub-paragraph (1) shall be disregarded if—

    (a) it is made available on the website for part of that period, and

    (b) the failure to make it available throughout that period is wholly attributable to circumstances that it would not be reasonable to have expected the company to prevent or avoid.

PART 5

OTHER AGREED FORMS OF COMMUNICATION

14 (1) A document or information that is sent or supplied otherwise than in hard copy or electronic form or by means of a website is validly sent or supplied if it is sent or supplied in a form or manner that has been agreed by the intended recipient.

    (2) This paragraph has effect subject to any requirements or contrary provision in the Companies Acts.

PART 6

SUPPLEMENTARY PROVISIONS

Joint holders of shares

15 (1) This paragraph applies in relation to documents or information to be sent or supplied to joint holders of shares of a company.

    (2) Anything to be agreed or specified by the member must be agreed or specified by all of the joint holders.

    (3) Anything authorised or required to be sent or supplied to the member may be sent or supplied either—

        (a) to each of the joint holders, or

        (b) to the holder whose name appears first in the register of members.

    (4) This paragraph has effect subject to anything in the company's articles.

Death or bankruptcy of holder of shares

16 (1) This paragraph has effect in the case of the death or bankruptcy of a holder of a company's shares.

    (2) Documents or information required or authorised to be sent or supplied to the member may be sent or supplied to the persons claiming to be entitled to the shares in consequence of the death or bankruptcy—

        (a) by name, or

        (b) by the title of representatives of the deceased, or trustee of the bankrupt, or by any like description,

at the address in the United Kingdom supplied for the purpose by those so claiming.

    (3) Until such an address has been so supplied, a document or information may be sent or supplied in any manner in which it might have been sent or supplied if the death or bankruptcy had not occurred.

Company Law Reform Bill
Schedule F2 — Communications by a company other than a traded company
Part 6 — Supplementary provisions

11

(4) This paragraph has effect subject to anything in the company's articles.

SCHEDULE F3

Section F2(2)

COMMUNICATIONS BY A TRADED COMPANY

PART 1

INTRODUCTION

Application of this Schedule

1   This Schedule applies to documents or information sent or supplied by traded companies.

PART 2

COMMUNICATIONS IN HARD COPY FORM

Introduction

2   A document or information is validly sent or supplied by a traded company in hard copy form if it is sent or supplied in accordance with this Part of this Schedule.

Method of communication in hard copy form

3   (1) A document or information in hard copy form must be—
   (a) handed to the intended recipient, or
   (b) sent or supplied by hand or by post to an address (in accordance with paragraph 4).

   (2) For the purposes of this Schedule, a person sends a document or information by post if he prepays and posts an envelope containing the document or information.

Address for communications in hard copy form

4   (1) Documents or information in hard copy form may be sent or supplied by the traded company—
   (a) to an address specified for the purpose by the intended recipient;
   (b) to a company at its registered office;
   (c) to a person in his capacity as a member of the company at his address as shown in the company's register of members;
   (d) to a person in his capacity as a director of the company at his address as shown in the company's register of directors;
   (e) to an address to which any provision of the Companies Acts authorises the document or information to be sent or supplied.

   (2) Where the traded company is unable to obtain an address falling within sub-paragraph (1), the documents or information may be sent or supplied to the intended recipient's last address known to the company.

12

Company Law Reform Bill
Schedule F3 — Communications by a traded company
Part 3 — Communications in electronic form

PART 3

COMMUNICATIONS IN ELECTRONIC FORM

Introduction

5   (1) A document or information is validly sent or supplied by a traded company if it is sent in electronic form in accordance with this Part of this Schedule.

     (2) This paragraph has effect subject to any requirements or contrary provision in the Companies Acts.

Agreement to communications in electronic form

6   (1) A document or information may only be sent or supplied by a traded company in electronic form —

         (a) to a person who has agreed (generally or specifically) that the document or information may be sent or supplied in that form (and has not revoked that agreement), or

         (b) to a company that is deemed to have so agreed by a provision in the Companies Acts.

     (2) A document or information may not be sent or supplied by a traded company in electronic form to —

         (a)   a member of the company,

         (b) a person identified by a member (in accordance with the company's articles or regulations made under section E2) as entitled to enjoy or exercise all or any specified rights of the member in relation to the company, or

         (c) a holder of debt securities of the company,

         except in accordance with paragraph 7 or 8 (resolution required before documents and information sent or supplied in electronic form).

     (3) Where the intended recipient has specified (generally or specifically) that the identity of the sender or supplier of the document or information must be confirmed in a particular manner, it must be confirmed in that manner.

Resolution required for communications in electronic form with members of traded company etc.

7   (1) This paragraph applies to documents or information to be sent or supplied to a person —

         (a) as a member of a traded company, or

         (b) as a person identified by a member (in accordance with the company's articles or regulations made under section E2) as entitled to enjoy or exercise all or any specified rights of the member in relation to the company.

     (2) The traded company may not send or supply such documents or information in electronic form except to the extent that the members of the company have resolved that the company may do so.

     (3) A resolution under this paragraph is subject to [section 380 of the Companies Act 1985 (c. 6)] (copy to be forwarded to registrar within 15 days).

Company Law Reform Bill
Schedule F3 — Communications by a traded company
Part 3 — Communications in electronic form

13

Resolution required for communications in electronic form with holders of debt securities

8   (1)   This paragraph applies to documents or information to be sent or supplied to a person as holder of debt securities of traded company.

      (2)   The company may not send or supply such documents or information in electronic form except to the extent that the relevant holders of debt securities have duly resolved that the company may do so.

      (3)   For the purposes of this paragraph—

          (a)   the relevant holders of debt securities are the holders of debt securities of the company ranking pari passu for all purposes with the intended recipient, and

          (b)   a resolution of the relevant holders of debt securities is duly passed if they agree in accordance with the provisions of the instruments creating the debt securities.

      (4)   In this Part, "debt securities" means bonds or other forms of transferable securitised debts, with the exception of securities—

          (a)   that are equivalent to shares in companies, or

          (b)   that if converted, or if the rights conferred by them are exercised, give rise to a right to acquire shares or securities equivalent to shares.

Address for communications in electronic form

9   (1)   Where the document or information is sent or supplied by electronic means, it may only be sent or supplied to an address—

          (a)   specified for the purpose by the intended recipient (generally or specifically), or

          (b)   where the intended recipient is a company, deemed by a provision of the Companies Acts to have been so specified.

      (2)   Where the document or information is sent or supplied in electronic form by hand or by post, it must be—

          (a)   handed to the intended recipient, or

          (b)   sent or supplied to an address to which it could be validly sent if it were in hard copy form.

PART 4

COMMUNICATIONS BY MEANS OF A WEBSITE

Use of website

10   (1)   A document or information is validly sent or supplied by a traded company if it is made available on a website in accordance with this Part of this Schedule.

      (2)   This paragraph has effect subject to any requirements or contrary provision in the Companies Acts.

Use of website to communicate with members of traded company etc.

11   (1)   This paragraph applies to a document or information to be sent or supplied by a traded company to a person—

7 Draft Clauses

14

Company Law Reform Bill
Schedule F3 — Communications by a traded company
Part 4 — Communications by means of a website

(a)   as a member of the company, or

(b)   as a person identified by a member (in accordance with the company's articles or regulations made under section E2) as entitled to enjoy or exercise all or any specified rights of the member in relation to the company (an "entitled person").

(2)   The traded company may not send or supply such documents or information by making them available on a website except to the extent that the members of the company have resolved that the company may do so.

(3)   The traded company may only send or supply such documents or information in that manner to members or entitled persons who —

(a)   have agreed that the company may send or supply documents or information generally, or the documents or information in question, to them in that manner, or

(b)   are taken to have so agreed under the following provisions,

and have not revoked that agreement.

(4)   A person is taken to have so agreed if —

(a)   he has been asked individually by the company to agree that the company may send or supply documents or information generally, or the documents or information in question, to him in that manner, and

(b)   he has failed to respond within the period of 28 days beginning with the date on which the company's request was sent.

(5)   A person is not taken to have so agreed if the company's request —

(a)   did not state clearly what the effect of a failure to respond would be, or

(b)   was sent less than twelve months after a previous request made to him in respect of the same or a similar class of documents or information.

(6)   A resolution under this paragraph is subject to [section 380 of the Companies Act 1985 (c. 6)] (copy to be forwarded to registrar within 15 days).

Use of website to communicate with holders of debt securities

12   (1)   This paragraph applies to a document or information to be sent or supplied by a traded company to a person as a holder of debt securities of the company.

(2)   The company may not send or supply such documents or information by making them available on a website except to the extent that the relevant holders of debt securities have duly resolved that the company may do so.

(3)   The traded company may only send or supply such documents in that manner to holders of debt securities who —

(a)   have agreed that the company may send or supply documents or information generally, or the documents or information in question, to them in that manner, or

(b)   are taken to have so agreed under the following provisions,

and have not revoked that agreement.

(4)   A person is taken to have so agreed if —

Company Law Reform Bill
Schedule F3 — Communications by a traded company
Part 4 — Communications by means of a website

15

      (a)   he has been asked individually by the company to agree that the company may send or supply documents or information generally, or the documents or information in question, to him in that manner, and

      (b)   he has failed to respond within the period of 28 days beginning with the date on which the company's request was sent.

  (5) A person is not taken to have so agreed if the company's request—

      (a)   did not state clearly what the effect of a failure to respond would be, or

      (b)   was sent less than twelve months after any previous request made to him in respect of the same or a similar class of documents or information.

  (6) For the purposes of this paragraph—

      (a)   the relevant holders of debt securities are the holders of debt securities of the company ranking pari passu for all purposes with the intended recipient, and

      (b)   a resolution of the relevant holders of debt securities is duly passed if they agree in accordance with the provisions of the instruments creating the debt securities.

  (7) In this Part, "debt securities" means bonds or other forms of transferable securitised debts, with the exception of securities—

      (a)   that are equivalent to shares in companies, or

      (b)   that if converted, or if the rights conferred by them are exercised, give rise to a right to acquire shares or securities equivalent to shares.

Use of website to communicate with other debenture holders

13 (1) A document or information may only be sent or supplied by the company to a person as a holder of debentures of the company (other than debt securities) by being made available on a website if the person—

      (a)   has agreed (generally or specifically) that the document or information may be sent or supplied to him in that manner, or

      (b)   is taken to have so agreed under this paragraph,

and has not revoked that agreement.

  (2) To the extent that the relevant debenture holders have duly resolved that the company may send or supply documents or information to them by making them available on a website, a debenture holder in relation to whom the following conditions are met is taken to have agreed that documents or information may be sent or supplied to him by the company in that manner.

  (3) The conditions are that the debenture holder—

      (a)   has been asked individually by the company to agree that the company may send or supply documents or information generally, or the documents or information in question, to him by means of a website, and

      (b)   failed to respond within the period of 28 days beginning with the date on which the company's request was sent.

  (4) A person is not taken to have so agreed if the company's request—

      (a)   did not state clearly what the effect of a failure to respond would be, or

16

Company Law Reform Bill
Schedule F3 — Communications by a traded company
Part 4 — Communications by means of a website

    (b)   was sent less than twelve months after a previous request made to him for the purposes of this paragraph in respect of the same or a similar class of documents or information.

(5)   For the purposes of this paragraph —

    (a)   the relevant debenture holders are the holders of debentures of the company (other than debt securities) ranking pari passu for all purposes with the intended recipient, and

    (b)   a resolution of the relevant debenture holders is duly passed if they agree in accordance with the provisions of the instruments creating the debentures.

Use of website to communicate with other persons

14   A document or information may only be sent or supplied by a traded company to a person who is not —

    (a)   a member of the company or an entitled person, or

    (b)   a holder of debentures of the company,

by being made available on a website if the person has agreed (generally or specifically) that the document or information may be sent or supplied to him in that manner (and has not revoked that agreement).

Notification of availability

15   (1)   The traded company must notify the intended recipient of —

    (a)   the presence of the document or information on the website,

    (b)   the address of the website,

    (c)   the place on the website where it may be accessed, and

    (d)   how to access the document or information.

(2)   The document or information is taken to be sent —

    (a)   on the date on which the notification required by this paragraph is sent, or

    (b)   if later, the date on which the document or information first appears on the website after that notification is sent.

Period of availability on website

16   (1)   The traded company must make the document or information available on the website throughout —

    (a)   the period specified by any applicable provision of the Companies Acts, or

    (b)   if no such period is specified, the period of 28 days beginning with the date on which the notification required under paragraph 15 is sent to the person in question.

(2)   For the purposes of this paragraph, a failure to make a document or information available on a website throughout the period mentioned in sub-paragraph (1) shall be disregarded if —

    (a)   it is made available on the website for part of that period, and

    (b)   the failure to make it available throughout that period is wholly attributable to circumstances that it would not be reasonable to have expected the company to prevent or avoid.

Company Law Reform Bill
Schedule F3 — Communications by a traded company
Part 5 — Other agreed forms of communication

17

PART 5

OTHER AGREED FORMS OF COMMUNICATION

17 (1) A document or information that is sent or supplied otherwise than in hard copy or electronic form or by means of a website is validly sent or supplied if it is sent or supplied in a form or manner that has been agreed by the intended recipient.

(2) This paragraph has effect subject to any requirements or contrary provision in the Companies Acts.

PART 6

SUPPLEMENTARY PROVISIONS

Joint holders of shares

18 (1) This paragraph applies in relation to documents or information to be sent or supplied to joint holders of shares of a traded company.

(2) Anything to be agreed or specified by the member must be agreed or specified by all of the joint holders.

(3) Anything authorised or required to be sent or supplied to the member may be sent or supplied either —
   (a) to each of the joint holders, or
   (b) to the holder whose name appears first in the register of members.

(4) This paragraph has effect subject to anything in the company's articles.

Death or bankruptcy of holder of shares

19 (1) This paragraph has effect in the case of the death or bankruptcy of a holder of a traded company's shares.

(2) Documents or information required or authorised to be sent or supplied to the member may be sent or supplied to the persons claiming to be entitled to the shares in consequence of the death or bankruptcy —
   (a) by name, or
   (b) by the title of representatives of the deceased, or trustee of the bankrupt, or by any like description,
   at the address in the United Kingdom supplied for the purpose by those so claiming.

(3) Until such an address has been so supplied, a document or information may be sent or supplied in any manner in which it might have been sent or supplied if the death or bankruptcy had not occurred.

(4) This paragraph has effect subject to anything in the company's articles.

7 Draft Clauses

Company Law Reform Bill

CONTENTS

PART G

ACCOUNTS AND REPORTS (SMALL COMPANIES)

CHAPTER 1

INTRODUCTION

G1 Companies subject to the small companies regime

The small companies regime for accounts and reports applies to a company for a financial year in relation to which the company —
(a) qualifies as small (see sections G2 and G3), and
(b) is not excluded from the regime (see section G4).

G2 Companies qualifying as small: general

(1) A company qualifies as small in relation to a financial year if the qualifying conditions are met —
(a) in the case of the company's first financial year, in that year, and
(b) in the case of any subsequent financial year, in that year and the preceding year.

(2) A company is treated as qualifying as small in relation to a financial year (other than its first financial year) —
(a) if the qualifying conditions are not met in relation to the financial year in question but it qualified under subsection (1) in relation to the previous financial year; or
(b) if the qualifying conditions are met in relation to the financial year in question and it was treated as qualifying in relation to the previous year by virtue of paragraph (a); or
(c) if the qualifying conditions are not met in relation to the financial year in question but it qualified under paragraph (b) in relation to the previous financial year.

(3) The qualifying conditions are met by a company in a year in which it satisfies two or more of the following requirements —

1. Turnover	Not more than £5.6 million
2. Balance sheet total	Not more than £2.8 million
3. Number of employees	Not more than 50

(4) For a period that is a company's financial year but not in fact a year the maximum figures for turnover must be proportionately adjusted.

(5) The balance sheet total means—

    (a) where the company prepares Companies Act individual accounts—

        (i) the aggregate of the amounts shown in the balance sheet under the headings corresponding to items A to D of Format 1 in Schedule G1, or

        (ii) if Format 2 is adopted, the aggregate of the amounts shown under the general heading "ASSETS";

    (b) where the company prepares IAS individual accounts, the aggregate of the amounts shown as assets in the balance sheet.

(6) The number of employees means the average number of persons employed by the company in the year, determined as follows—

    (a) find for each month in the financial year the number of persons employed under contracts of service by the company in that month (whether throughout the month or not),

    (b) add together the monthly totals, and

    (c) divide by the number of months in the financial year.

(7) This section is subject to section G3 (companies qualifying as small: parent companies).

G3 Companies qualifying as small: parent companies

(1) A parent company qualifies as a small company in relation to a financial year only if the group headed by it qualifies as a small group.

(2) A group qualifies as small in relation to a financial year if the qualifying conditions are met—

    (a) in the case of the parent company's first financial year, in that year, and

    (b) in the case of any subsequent financial year, in that year and the preceding year.

(3) A group is treated as qualifying as small in relation to a financial year (other than the parent company's first financial year)—

    (a) if the qualifying conditions are not met in relation to the financial year in question but it qualified under subsection (2) in relation to the previous financial year; or

    (b) if the qualifying conditions are met in relation to the financial year in question and it was treated as qualifying in relation to the previous year by virtue of paragraph (a); or

    (c) if the qualifying conditions are not met in relation to the financial year in question but it qualified under paragraph (b) in relation to the previous financial year.

(4) The qualifying conditions are met by a group in a year in which it satisfies two or more of the following requirements—

1. Aggregate turnover	Not more than £5.6 million net (or £6.72 million gross)

2. Aggregate balance sheet total	Not more than £2.8 million net (or £3.36 million gross)
3. Aggregate number of employees	Not more than 50

(5) The aggregate figures are ascertained by aggregating the relevant figures determined in accordance with section G2 for each member of the group.

(6) In relation to the aggregate figures for turnover and balance sheet total —

"net" means with the set-offs and other adjustments required by Schedule G2

"gross" means without those set-offs and other adjustments.

A company may satisfy the relevant requirements on the basis of either the net or the gross figure.

(7) The figures for each subsidiary undertaking shall be those included in its individual accounts for the relevant financial year, that is —

(a) if its financial year ends with that of the parent company, that financial year, and

(b) if not, its financial year ending last before the end of the financial year of the parent company.

If those figures cannot be obtained without disproportionate expense or undue delay, the latest available figures shall be taken.

G4 Companies excluded from the small companies regime

(1) The small companies regime does not apply to a company that is, or was at any time within the financial year to which the accounts relate —

(a) a public company,

(b) a company that —

    (i) has permission under Part 4 of the Financial Services and Markets Act 2000 (c. 8) to carry on one or more regulated activities, or

    (ii) carries on insurance market activity, or

(c) a member of an ineligible group.

(2) A group is ineligible if any of its members is —

(a) a public company,

(b) a body corporate (other than a company) that has power under its constitution to offer its shares or debentures to the public and may lawfully exercise that power, or

(c) a person who —

    (i) has permission under Part 4 of the Financial Services and Markets Act 2000 to carry on one or more regulated activities, or

    (ii) carries on insurance market activity.

(3) In this section —

"regulated activity" has the meaning given in section 22 of the Financial Services and Markets Act 2000; and

"insurance market activity" has the meaning given in section 316(3) of that Act.

CHAPTER 2

ACCOUNTING RECORDS

G5 Duty to keep accounting records

(1) Every small company must keep adequate accounting records.

(2) Adequate accounting records means records that are sufficient—
    (a) to show and explain the company's transactions,
    (b) to disclose with reasonable accuracy, at any time, the financial position of the company at that time, and
    (c) to enable the directors to ensure that any accounts required to be prepared comply with the requirements of this Act.

(3) Accounting records must, in particular, contain—
    (a) entries from day to day of all sums of money received and expended by the company and the matters in respect of which the receipt and expenditure takes place, and
    (b) a record of the assets and liabilities of the company.

(4) If the company's business involves dealing in goods, the accounting records must contain—
    (a) statements of stock held by the company at the end of each financial year of the company,
    (b) all statements of stocktakings from which any statement of stock as is mentioned in paragraph (a) has been or is to be prepared, and
    (c) except in the case of goods sold by way of ordinary retail trade, statements of all goods sold and purchased, showing the goods and the buyers and sellers in sufficient detail to enable all these to be identified.

(5) A parent company that has a subsidiary undertaking in relation to which the above requirements do not apply must take reasonable steps to secure that the undertaking keeps such accounting records as to enable the directors of the parent company to ensure that any accounts required to be prepared under this Part comply with the requirements of this Act.

(6) If a company fails to comply with any provision of this section, every officer of the company who is in default is guilty of an offence unless he shows that he acted honestly and that in the circumstances in which the company's business was carried on the default was excusable.

(7) A person guilty of an offence under this section is liable to imprisonment or a fine, or both.

G6 Where and for how long records to be kept

(1) A small company's accounting records must be kept at its registered office or such other place as the directors think fit, and must at all times be open to inspection by the company's officers.

(2) If accounting records are kept at a place outside Great Britain, accounts and returns with respect to the business dealt with in the accounting records so kept must be sent to, and kept at, a place in Great Britain, and must at all times be to such inspection.

(3) The accounts and returns to be sent to Great Britain must be such as to —

    (a) disclose with reasonable accuracy the financial position of the business in question at intervals of not more than six months, and

    (b) enable the directors to ensure that the accounts required to be prepared under this Part comply with the requirements of this Act.

(4) If a company fails to comply with any provision of subsections (1) to (3), every officer of the company who is in default is guilty of an offence, and liable to imprisonment or a fine or both, unless he shows that he acted honestly and that in the circumstances in which the company's business was carried on the default was excusable.

(5) Accounting records that a company is required by section G5 to keep must be preserved by it for three years from the date on which they are made.

This is subject to any provision contained in rules made under section 411 of the Insolvency Act 1986 (company insolvency rules).

(6) An officer of a company is guilty of an offence, and liable to imprisonment or a fine or both, if he fails to take all reasonable steps for securing compliance by the company with subsection (5) or intentionally causes any default by the company under that subsection.

CHAPTER 3

A COMPANY'S FINANCIAL YEAR

G7 A company's financial year

(1) A small company's financial year is determined as follows.

(2) Its first financial year begins with the first day of its first accounting reference period and ends with the last day of that period or such other date, not more than seven days before or after the end of that period, as the directors may determine.

(3) Subsequent financial years begin with the day immediately following the end of the company's previous financial year and end with the last day of its next accounting reference period or such other date, not more than seven days before or after the end of that period, as the directors may determine.

(4) In relation to an undertaking that is not a company, references in this Act to its financial year are to any period in respect of which a profit and loss account of the undertaking is required to be made up (by its constitution or by the law under which it is established), whether that period is a year or not.

(5) The directors of a parent company must secure that, except where in their opinion there are good reasons against it, the financial year of each of its subsidiary undertakings coincides with the company's own financial year.

G8 Accounting reference periods and accounting reference date

(1) A small company's accounting reference periods are determined according to its accounting reference date.

(2) The accounting reference date of a company incorporated before 1st April 1996 is —

6

Company Law Reform Bill
Part G — Accounts and reports (small companies)
Chapter 3 — A company's financial year

   (a)   the date specified by notice to the registrar in accordance with section 224(2) of the Companies Act 1985 (notice specifying accounting reference date given within nine months of incorporation), or

   (b)   failing such notice —

       (i)   in the case of a company incorporated before 1st April 1990, 31st March, and

      (ii)   in the case of a company incorporated on or after 1st April 1990, the last day of the month in which the anniversary of its incorporation falls.

(3)   The accounting reference date of a company incorporated on or after 1st April 1996 is the last day of the month in which the anniversary of its incorporation falls.

(4)   A company's first accounting reference period is the period of more than six months, but not more than 18 months, beginning with the date of its incorporation and ending with its accounting reference date.

(5)   Its subsequent accounting reference periods are successive periods of twelve months beginning immediately after the end of the previous accounting reference period and ending with its accounting reference date.

(6)   This section has effect subject to the provisions of section G9 (alteration of accounting reference date).

G9   Alteration of accounting reference date

(1)   A small company may by notice in the prescribed form given to the registrar specify a new accounting reference date having effect in relation to —

   (a)   the company's current accounting reference period and subsequent periods, or

   (b)   the company's previous accounting reference period and subsequent periods.

A company's "previous accounting reference period" means the one immediately preceding its current accounting reference period.

(2)   The notice must state whether the current or previous accounting reference period —

   (a)   is to be shortened, so as to come to an end on the first occasion on which the new accounting reference date falls or fell after the beginning of the period, or

   (b)   is to be extended, so as to come to an end on the second occasion on which that date falls or fell after the beginning of the period.

(3)   A notice extending a company's current or previous accounting reference is not effective if given less than five years after the end of an earlier accounting reference period of the company that was extended under this section.

This does not apply —

   (a)   to a notice given by a company that is a subsidiary undertaking or parent undertaking of another EEA undertaking if the new accounting reference date coincides with that of the other EEA undertaking or, where that undertaking is not a company, with the last day of its financial year, or

   (b)   where an administration order is in force under Part 2 of the Insolvency Act 1986, or

Company Law Reform Bill
Part G — Accounts and reports (small companies)
Chapter 3 — A company's financial year

7

(c) where the Secretary of State directs that it should not apply, which he may do with respect to a notice that has been given or that may be given.

(4) A notice under this section may not be given in respect of a previous accounting reference period if the period allowed for circulating accounts and reports for that period has already expired.

(5) An accounting reference period may not be extended so as to exceed 18 months and a notice under this section is ineffective if the current or previous accounting reference period as extended in accordance with the notice would exceed that limit.

This does not apply where an administration order is in force under Part 2 of the Insolvency Act 1986.

CHAPTER 4

ANNUAL ACCOUNTS

Individual accounts

G10 Duty to prepare individual accounts

(1) The directors of every small company must prepare accounts for the company for each of its financial years.

Those accounts are referred to as the company's "individual accounts".

(2) A company's individual accounts may be prepared —
  (a) in accordance with section G11 ("Companies Act individual accounts"), or
  (b) in accordance with international accounting standards ("IAS individual accounts").

This is subject to the following provisions of this section and to section G16 (consistency of accounts).

(3) The individual accounts of a company that is a charity must be Companies Act individual accounts.

(4) After the first financial year in which the directors of a company prepare IAS individual accounts ("the first IAS year"), all subsequent individual accounts of the company must be prepared in accordance with international accounting standards unless there is a relevant change of circumstance.

(5) There is relevant change of circumstance if, at any time during or after the first IAS year —
  (a) the company becomes a subsidiary undertaking of another undertaking that does not prepare IAS individual accounts,
  (b) the company ceases to be a company with securities admitted to trading on a regulated market, or
  (c) a parent undertaking of the company ceases to be an undertaking with securities admitted to trading on a regulated market.

In this subsection "regulated market" has the same meaning as it has in Council Directive 93/22/EEC on investment services in the securities field.

(6)   If, having changed to preparing Companies Act individual accounts following a relevant change of circumstance, the directors again prepare IAS individual accounts for the company, subsections (4) and (5) apply again as if the first financial year for which such accounts are again prepared were the first IAS year.

G11   Companies Act individual accounts

(1)   Companies Act individual accounts of a small company must comprise—
 (a)   a balance sheet as at the last day of the financial year, and
 (b)   a profit and loss account.

(2)   The balance sheet must give a true and fair view of the state of affairs of the company as at the end of the financial year; and the profit and loss account must give a true and fair view of the profit or loss of the company for the financial year.

(3)   Companies Act individual accounts must comply with the provisions of Schedule G1 as to the form and content of the balance sheet and profit and loss account and additional information to be provided by way of notes to the accounts.

(4)   If compliance with those provisions, and the other provisions of this Act as to the matters to be included in a company's individual accounts or in notes to those accounts, would not be sufficient to give a true and fair view, the necessary additional information must be given in the accounts or in a note to them.

(5)   If in special circumstances compliance with any of those provisions is inconsistent with the requirement to give a true and fair view, the directors must depart from that provision to the extent necessary to give a true and fair view.

 Particulars of any such departure, the reasons for it and its effect must be given in a note to the accounts.

(6)   A company is treated as having complied with any provision of Schedule G1 if it complies instead with the corresponding provision of Schedule 4 to the Companies Act 1985 (c. 6) (provisions applicable to companies not subject to the small companies regime).

G12   IAS individual accounts

 Where the directors of a small company prepare IAS individual accounts, they must state in the notes to the accounts that the accounts have been prepared in accordance with international accounting standards.

Group accounts

G13   Option to prepare group accounts

(1)   If at the end of a financial year a small company is a parent company the directors, as well as preparing individual accounts for the year, may prepare consolidated accounts for the group for the year.

 Those accounts are referred to in this Act as the company's "group accounts".

(2) If group accounts are prepared, they may be prepared—
  (a) in accordance with section G14 ("Companies Act group accounts"), or
  (b) in accordance with international accounting standards ("IAS group accounts").
  This is subject to the following provisions of this section.

(3) The group accounts of a parent company that is a charity must be Companies Act group accounts.

(4) After the first financial year in which the directors of a parent company prepare IAS group accounts ("the first IAS year"), all subsequent group accounts of the company must be prepared in accordance with international accounting standards unless there is a relevant change of circumstance.

(5) There is a relevant change of circumstance if, at any time during or after the first IAS year—
  (a) the company becomes a subsidiary undertaking of another undertaking that does not prepare IAS group accounts,
  (b) the company ceases to be a company with securities admitted to trading on a regulated market, or
  (c) a parent undertaking of the company ceases to be an undertaking with securities admitted to trading on a regulated market.
  In this subsection "regulated market" has the same meaning as it has in Council Directive 93/22/EEC on investment services in the securities field.

(6) If, having changed to preparing Companies Act group accounts following a relevant change of circumstance, the directors again prepare IAS group accounts for the company, subsections (4) and (5) apply again as if the first financial year for which such accounts are again prepared were the first IAS year.

G14 Companies Act group accounts

(1) Companies Act group accounts of a small company must comprise—
  (a) a consolidated balance sheet dealing with the state of affairs of the parent company and its subsidiary undertakings, and
  (b) a consolidated profit and loss account dealing with the profit or loss of the parent company and its subsidiary undertakings.

(2) The accounts must give a true and fair view of the state of affairs as at the end of the financial year, and the profit or loss for the financial year, of the undertakings included in the consolidation as a whole, so far as concerns members of the company.

(3) All the subsidiary undertakings of the parent company must be included in the consolidation, subject to the following exceptions.

(4) A subsidiary undertaking may be excluded from consolidation if its inclusion is not material for the purpose of giving a true and fair view (but two or more undertakings may be excluded only if they are not material taken together);

(5) A subsidiary undertaking may be excluded from consolidation where—
  (a) severe long-term restrictions substantially hinder the exercise of the rights of the parent company over the assets or management of that undertaking, or

(b)   the information necessary for the preparation of group accounts cannot be obtained without disproportionate expense or undue delay, or

(c)   the interest of the parent company is held exclusively with a view to subsequent resale.

The reference in paragraph (a) to the rights of the parent company and the reference in paragraph (c) to the interest of the parent company are, respectively, to the rights and interest held by or attributed to the company for the purposes of section 258 of the Companies Act 1985 (definition of "parent undertaking") in the absence of which it would not be the parent company.

(6)   The group accounts must comply so far as practicable with the provisions of Schedule G1 (Companies Act individual accounts) as if the undertakings included in the consolidation ("the group") were a single company.
But a company is treated as having complied with any provision of that Schedule if it complies instead with the corresponding provision of Schedule 4 to the Companies Act 1985 (c. 6) (provisions applicable to companies not subject to the small companies regime).

(7)   Companies Act group accounts must comply with the provisions of Schedule G2 as to —

(a)   the form and content of the consolidated balance sheet and consolidated profit and loss account, and

(b)   additional information to be provided by way of notes to the accounts.

(8)   If compliance with those provisions, and the other provisions of this Act as to the matters to be included in a company's group accounts or in notes to those accounts, would not be sufficient to give a true and fair view, the necessary additional information must be given in the accounts or in a note to them.

(9)   If in special circumstances compliance with any of those provisions is inconsistent with the requirement to give a true and fair view, the directors must depart from that provision to the extent necessary to give a true and fair view.

Particulars of any such departure, the reasons for it and its effect must be given in a note to the accounts.

G15   IAS group accounts

Where the directors of a small company prepare IAS group accounts, they must state in the notes to those accounts that the acounts have been prepared in accordance with international accounting standards.

G16   Consistency of financial reporting within group

(1)   The directors of a small company that is a parent company must secure that the individual accounts of —

(a)   the parent company, and

(b)   each of its subsidiary undertakings,

are all prepared using the same financial reporting framework, except to the extent that in their opinion there are good reasons for not doing so.

(2)   Subsection (1) does not apply if the directors do not prepare group accounts for the parent company.

(3) Subsection (1) only applies to accounts of subsidiary undertakings that are required to be prepared under this Part.

(4) Subsection (1) does not require accounts of undertakings that are charities to be prepared using the same financial reporting framework as accounts of undertakings which are not charities.

(5) Subsection (1)(a) does not apply where the directors of a parent company prepare IAS group accounts and IAS individual accounts.

G17 Individual profit and loss account where group accounts prepared

(1) This section applies where—
   (a) a small company prepares group accounts in accordance with this Act, and
   (b) the notes to the company's individual balance sheet show the company's profit or loss for the financial year determined in accordance with this Act.

(2) Where the company prepares Companies Act individual accounts, the profit and loss account need not contain the information specified in [paragraphs 58 to 60 of Schedule G1] (information supplementing the profit and loss account).

(3) The company's individual profit and loss account must be approved in accordance with section G21(1) (approval by directors) but may be omitted from the company's annual accounts for the purposes of the other provisions below in this Act.

(4) The exemption conferred by this section is conditional upon its being disclosed in the company's annual accounts that the exemption applies.

G18 Information about related undertakings

(1) The information specified in Schedule G3 must be given in notes to a small company's annual accounts—
   (a) if the company does not prepare group accounts, the information specified in Part 1 of that Schedule must be given;
   (b) if the company prepares group accounts, the information specified in Part 2 of that Schedule must be given.

(2) The information required by that Schedule need not be disclosed with respect to an undertaking that—
   (a) is established under the law of a country outside the United Kingdom, or
   (b) carries on business outside the United Kingdom,
   if in the opinion of the directors of the company the disclosure would be seriously prejudicial to the business of that undertaking, or to the business of the company or any of its subsidiary undertakings, and the Secretary of State agrees that the information need not be disclosed.
   This subsection does not apply in relation to the information required under paragraph 4, 8, 16 or 25 of that Schedule.

(3) Where advantage is taken of subsection (2), that fact must be stated in a note to the company's annual accounts.

(4)   If the directors of the company are of the opinion that the number of undertakings in respect of which the company is required to disclose information under any provision of Schedule G3 is such that compliance with that provision would result in information of excessive length being given, the information need only be given in respect of —

    (a)   the undertakings whose results or financial position, in the opinion of the directors, principally affected the figures shown in the company's annual accounts, and

    (b)   undertakings excluded from consolidation under paragraph 1(3) of Schedule G2.

(5)   If advantage is taken of subsection (4) —

    (a)   there must be included in the notes to the company's annual accounts a statement that the information is given only with respect to such undertakings as are mentioned in that subsection, and

    (b)   the full information (both that which is disclosed in the notes to the accounts and that which is not) must be annexed to the company's next annual return.

For this purpose the "next annual return" means that next delivered to the registrar after the accounts in question have been approved under section G21.

(6)   If a company fails to comply with subsection (5)(b), the company and every officer of it who is in default is liable to a fine and, for continued contravention, to a daily default fine.

Information to be given in notes to the accounts

G19   Information about employee numbers and costs

(1)   The following information with respect to the employees of a small company must be given in notes to the company's annual accounts —

    (a)   the average number of persons employed by the company in the financial year, and

    (b)   the average number of persons so employed within each category of persons employed by the company.

(2)   The categories by reference to which the number required to be disclosed by subsection (1)(b) is to be determined must be such as the directors may select having regard to the manner in which the company's activities are organised.

(3)   The average number required by subsection (1)(a) or (b) is determined by dividing the relevant annual number by the number of months in the financial year.

(4)   The relevant annual number is determined by ascertaining for each month in the financial year —

    (a)   for the purposes of subsection (1)(a), the number of persons employed under contracts of service by the company in that month (whether throughout the month or not);

    (b)   for the purposes of subsection (1)(b), the number of persons in the category in question of persons so employed;

and adding together all the monthly numbers.

(5)   In respect of all persons employed by the company during the financial year who are taken into account in determining the relevant annual number for the

purposes of subsection (1)(a) there must also be stated the aggregate amounts respectively of —

    (a)   wages and salaries paid or payable in respect of that year to those persons;

    (b)   social security costs incurred by the company on their behalf; and

    (c)   other pension costs so incurred.

This does not apply in so far as those amounts, or any of them, are stated elsewhere in the company's accounts.

(6)   In subsection (4) —

"pension costs" includes any costs incurred by the company in respect of —

    (a)   any pension scheme established for the purpose of providing pensions for persons currently or formerly employed by the company,

    (b)   any sums set aside for the future payment of pensions directly by the company to current or former employees, and

    (c)   any pensions paid directly to such persons without having first been set aside;

"social security costs" means any contributions by the company to any state social security or pension scheme, fund or arrangements.

(7)   This section applies in relation to group accounts as if the undertakings included in the consolidation were a single company.

G20   Information about benefits of directors and others

(1)   The information specified in Schedule G4 must be given in notes to a small company's annual accounts.

(2)   In that Schedule —

Part 1 relates to the emoluments of directors (including emoluments waived), pensions of directors and past directors, compensation for loss of office to directors and past directors and sums paid to third parties in respect of directors' services,

Part 2 relates to loans, quasi-loans and other dealings in favour of directors and connected persons, and

Part 3 relates to transactions, arrangements and agreements made by the company or a subsidiary undertaking for officers of the company other than directors.

(3)   It is the duty of any director of a company, and any person who is or has at any time in the preceding five years been an officer of the company, to give notice to the company of such matters relating to himself, as may be necessary for the purposes of Part 1 of that Schedule.

(4)   A person who makes default in complying with subsection (3) commits an offence and is liable to a fine.

Approval and signing of accounts

G21 Approval and signing of accounts

(1) A small company's annual accounts must be approved by the board of directors and signed on behalf of the board by a director of the company.

(2) The signature must be on the company's balance sheet.

(3) Every copy of the balance sheet that is circulated, published or issued, or laid before the company in general meeting, must state the name of the person who signed the balance sheet on behalf of the board.

(4) The copy of the company's balance sheet that is delivered to the registrar must be signed on behalf of the board by a director of the company.

(5) The balance sheet must contain a statement in a prominent position, above the signature required by subsection (2) or (4), that the accounts are prepared in accordance with [the small companies regime].

This does not apply if the directors have taken advantage of the exemption from audit conferred by section 249AA of the Companies Act 1985 (dormant companies).

(6) If annual accounts are approved that do not comply with the requirements of this Act, every director of the company who is party to their approval and who knows that they do not comply or is reckless as to whether they comply is guilty of an offence and liable to a fine.

For this purpose every director of the company at the time the accounts are approved must be taken to be a party to their approval unless he shows that he took all reasonable steps to prevent their being approved.

(7) If a copy of the balance sheet —

    (a) is laid before the company, or otherwise circulated, published or issued, without the balance sheet having been signed as required by this section or without the required statement of the signatory's name being included, or

    (b) is delivered to the registrar without being signed as required by this section,

the company and every officer of it who is in default is guilty of an offence and liable to a fine.

CHAPTER 5

DIRECTORS' REPORT

Directors' report

G22 Duty to prepare directors' report

(1) The directors of a small company shall for each financial year prepare a report (a "directors' report") complying with the general requirements of section G23.

(2) For a financial year in which —

    (a) the company is a parent company, and

    (b) the directors of the company prepare group accounts,

the directors' report must be a consolidated report (a "group directors' report") relating, to the extent specified in the following provisions of this Part, to the company and its subsidiary undertakings included in the consolidation.

(3) A group directors' report may, where appropriate, give greater emphasis to the matters that are significant to the company and its subsidiary undertakings included in the consolidation, taken as a whole.

(4) If a directors' report does not comply with the provisions of this Part relating to the preparation and contents of the report, every director of the company who—

    (a) knew that it did not comply or was reckless as to whether it complied, and

    (b) failed to take all reasonable steps to secure compliance with the provision in question,

is guilty of an offence and liable to a fine.

G23 Directors' report: general requirements

(1) In the case of a small company the directors' report for a financial year must state—

    (a) the names of the persons who, at any time during the financial year, were directors of the company, and

    (b) the principal activities of the company in the course of the year.

(2) In relation to a group directors' report subsection (1)(b) has effect as if the reference to the company was to the company and its subsidiary undertakings included in the consolidation.

(3) The report must also comply with Schedule G5 as regards the disclosure of the matters mentioned there.

(4) The report must contain a statement in a prominent position in the report, above the signature required by section G25, that it is prepared in accordance with [the small companies regime].

This does not apply if the directors have taken advantage of the exemption from audit conferred by section 249AA of the Companies Act 1985 (dormant companies).

G24 Statement as to disclosure of information to auditors

(1) If for any financial year the directors of a small company [are not entitled to, or do not take advantage of, exemption from audit], the directors' report must contain the statement required by this section.

(2) The statement required is to the effect that, in the case of each of the persons who are directors at the time the directors' report is approved—

    (a) so far as the director is aware, there is no relevant audit information of which the company's auditors are unaware, and

    (b) he has taken all the steps that he ought to have taken as a director in order to make himself aware of any relevant audit information and to establish that the company's auditors are aware of that information.

(3) For this purpose—

    (a) "relevant audit information" means information needed by the company's auditors in connection with preparing their report, and

(b) a director is regarded as having taken all the steps that he ought to have taken as a director in order to do the things mentioned in subsection (2)(b) if he has—

  (i) made such enquiries of his fellow directors and of the company's auditors for that purpose, and

  (ii) taken such other steps (if any) for that purpose,

as were required by his duty as a director of the company to exercise due care, skill and diligence.

(4) In determining for the purposes of subsection (2) the extent of that duty in the case of a particular director, the following considerations (in particular) are relevant—

  (a) the knowledge, skill and experience that may reasonably be expected of a person carrying out the same functions as are carried out by the director in relation to the company, and

  (b) (so far as they exceed what may reasonably be so expected) the knowledge, skill and experience that the director in fact has.

(5) Where a directors' report containing the statement required by this section is approved under section G25 but the statement is false, every director of the company who—

  (a) knew that the statement was false, or was reckless as to whether it was false, and

  (b) failed to take reasonable steps to prevent the report from being approved,

is guilty of an offence and liable to imprisonment or a fine, or both.

G25 Approval and signing of directors' report

(1) The directors' report must be approved by the board of directors and signed on behalf of the board by a director or the secretary of the company.

(2) Every copy of the directors' report that is circulated, published or issued, or laid before the company in general meeting, must state the name of the person who signed it on behalf of the board.

(3) The copy of the directors' report that is delivered to the registrar must be signed on behalf of the board by a director or the secretary of the company.

(4) If a copy of the directors' report—

  (a) is laid before the company, or otherwise circulated, published or issued, without the report having been signed as required by this section or without the required statement of the signatory's name being included, or

  (b) is delivered to the registrar without being signed as required by this section,

the company and every officer of it who is in default is guilty of an offence and liable to a fine.

Company Law Reform Bill

CONTENTS

PART H

SHARE CAPITAL

Share capital and how it may be altered

H1 Shares of limited companies to have fixed nominal value

(1) Shares in a limited company having a share capital must each have a fixed nominal value.

(2) An allotment of a share that does not have a fixed nominal value is void.

(3) Shares in a limited company having a share capital may be denominated in any currency, and different classes of shares may be denominated in different currencies.

(4) If a company purports to allot shares in contravention of this section, an offence is committed by every officer of the company who is in default.

(5) A person guilty of an offence under this section is liable —
    (a) on conviction on indictment, to a fine, and
    (b) on summary conviction, to a fine not exceeding the statutory maximum

H2 Alteration of share capital of limited company

(1) A limited company having a share capital may not alter its share capital except in the following ways.

(2) The company may —
    (a) increase its share capital by allotting new shares in accordance with Part 4 of the Companies Act 1985 (c. 6), or
    (b) reduce its share capital in accordance with Chapter 4 of Part 5 of that Act.

(3) The company may —
    (a) sub-divide or consolidate all or any of its share capital in accordance with section H3 of this Act, or
    (b) reconvert stock into shares in accordance with section H4 of this Act.

(4) The company may redenominate all or any of its shares in accordance with section H27 of this Act.

(5) Nothing in this section affects the power of a company to redeem shares, or to purchase its own shares, in accordance with Chapter 7 of Part 5 of the Companies Act 1985.

H3   Sub-division or consolidation of shares

(1)   A limited company having a share capital may—

  (a)   sub-divide its shares, or any of them, into shares of a smaller nominal amount than its existing shares, or

  (b)   consolidate and divide all of any of its share capital into shares of a larger nominal amount than its existing shares.

(2)   In any sub-division, consolidation or division of shares under this section, the proportion between the amount paid and the amount (if any) unpaid on each resulting share must be the same as it was in the case of the share from which that share is derived.

(3)   The powers conferred by this section are exercisable by ordinary resolution of the company.

(4)   If a company exercises any of the powers conferred by this section it must, within one month after doing so, give notice to the registrar specifying the shares affected.

(5)   The notice must—

  (a)   be in the prescribed form, and

  (b)   include a statement of capital.

(6)   The statement of capital must be in the prescribed form and must state with respect to the company's share capital immediately following the exercise of the power—

  (a)   the total number of shares of the company,

  (b)   the aggregate nominal value of those shares,

  (c)   for each class of shares—

    (i)   prescribed particulars of the rights attached to the shares,

    (ii)   the total number of shares of that class, and

    (iii) the aggregate nominal value of shares of that class, and

  (d)   the amount paid up and the amount (if any) unpaid on each share (whether on account of the nominal value of the share or by way of premium).

(7)   For the purpose of subsection (6)—

  (a)   shares are of one class if the rights attached to them are in all respects uniform, and

  (b)   the rights attached to shares are not regarded as different from those attached to other shares by reason only that they do not carry the same rights to dividends in the twelve months immediately following their allotment.

(8)   If a company makes default in complying with subsection (4) or (5), an offence is committed by—

  (a)   the company,

  (b)   every officer of the company who is in default, and

  (c)   every responsible delegate.

(9)   A person guilty of an offence under this section is liable on summary conviction to a fine not exceeding level 3 on the standard scale and, for continued contravention, a daily default fine not exceeding one-tenth of level 3 on the standard scale.

(10)   The company's articles may exclude or restrict the exercise of all or any of the powers conferred by this section.

H4   Re-conversion of stock into shares

(1)   A company that has converted paid-up shares into stock (before the repeal by this Act of the power to do so) may re-convert that stock into paid-up shares of any nominal value.

(2)   The power conferred by this section is exercisable by ordinary resolution of the company.

(3)   If a company exercises the power conferred by this section it must, within one month after doing so, give notice to the registrar specifying the stock affected.

(4)   The notice must—
    (a)   be in the prescribed form, and
    (b)   include a statement of capital.

(5)   The statement of capital must be in the prescribed form and must state with respect to the company's share capital immediately following the reconversion—
    (a)   the total number of shares of the company,
    (b)   the aggregate nominal value of those shares,
    (c)   for each class of shares—
        (i)   prescribed particulars of the rights attached to the shares,
        (ii)   the total number of shares of that class, and
        (iii)   the aggregate nominal value of shares of that class, and
    (d)   the amount paid up and the amount (if any) unpaid on each share (whether on account of the nominal value of the share or by way of premium).

(6)   For the purpose of subsection (5)—
    (a)   shares are of one class if the rights attached to them are in all respects uniform, and
    (b)   the rights attached to shares are not regarded as different from those attached to other shares by reason only that they do not carry the same rights to dividends in the twelve months immediately following their allotment.

(7)   If a company makes default in complying with subsection (3) or (4), an offence is committed by—
    (a)   the company,
    (b)   every officer of the company who is in default, and
    (c)   every responsible delegate.

(8)   A person guilty of an offence under this section is liable on summary conviction to a fine not exceeding level 3 on the standard scale and, for continued contravention, a daily default fine not exceeding one-tenth of level 3 on the standard scale.

Allotment of shares

H5   Exercise by directors of power to allot shares etc.

(1)   For section 80 of the Companies Act 1985 (c. 6) (authority of company required for certain allotments) substitute —

> **"80   Exercise by directors of power to allot shares etc.**
>
> (1)   The directors of a company must not exercise any power of the company —
>> (a)   to allot shares in the company, or
>> (b)   to grant rights to subscribe for, or to convert any security into, shares in the company,
>
> except in accordance with section 80ZA (private company with single class of shares) or section 80ZB (authorisation by company).
>
> (2)   Subsection (1) does not apply —
>> (a)   to the allotment of shares in pursuance of an employees' share scheme, or
>> (b)   to the grant of a right to subscribe for, or to convert any security into, shares so allotted.
>
> (3)   Where this section applies in relation to the grant of a right to subscribe for, or to convert any security into, shares, it does not apply in relation to the allotment of shares pursuant to that right.
>
> (4)   This section does not apply to the deemed allotment of shares to the subscribers to the company's memorandum on the formation of the company.
>
> (5)   A director who knowingly and willingly contravenes, or permits or authorises a contravention of, this section commits an offence and is liable to a fine.
>
> (6)   Nothing in this section affects the validity of an allotment or other transaction.
>
> **80ZA Power of directors to allot shares etc.: private company with only one class of shares**
>
> (1)   Where a private company has only one class of shares, the directors may exercise any power of the company —
>> (a)   to allot shares of that class, or
>> (b)   to grant rights to subscribe for, or to convert any security into, such shares,
>
> except to the extent that they are prohibited from doing so by the company's articles.
>
> (2)   For this purpose —
>> (a)   shares are of one class if the rights attached to them are in all respects uniform, and
>> (b)   the rights attached to shares are not regarded as different from those attached to other shares by reason only that they do not carry the same rights to dividends in the twelve months immediately following their allotment.

80ZB Power of directors to allot shares etc.: authorisation by company

(1) The directors of a company may exercise a power of the company—

    (a)   to allot shares in the company, or

    (b)   to grant rights to subscribe for, or to convert any security into, shares in the company,

if they are, in accordance with this section, authorised to do so by the company's articles or by resolution of the company.

(2) Authority under this section may be given for a particular exercise of the power or for its exercise generally, and may be unconditional or subject to conditions.

(3) The authority must—

    (a)   state the maximum amount of shares that may be allotted under it, and

    (b)   specify the date on which it will expire, which must be not more than five years from—

        (i)   in the case of an authority contained in the company's articles at the time of its original incorporation, the date of that incorporation;

        (ii) in any other case, the date on which the resolution is passed by virtue of which the authority is given.

(4) Authority under this section—

    (a)   may be renewed or further renewed by resolution of the company for a further period not exceeding five years, and

    (b)   may at any time be revoked or varied by resolution of the company.

(5) A resolution renewing an authority under this section must—

    (a)   state (or restate) the maximum amount of shares that may be allotted under the authority or, as the case may be, the amount remaining to be allotted under it, and

    (b)   specify the date on which the renewed authority will expire.

(6) In relation to rights to subscribe for, or to convert any security into, shares in the company, references in this section to the maximum amount of shares that may be allotted under the authority are to the maximum amount of shares that may be allotted pursuant to the rights.

(7) The directors may allot shares, or grant rights to subscribe for or to convert any security into shares, after an authority under this section has expired if—

    (a)   the shares are allotted, or the rights are granted, in pursuance of an offer or agreement made by the company before the authority expired, and

    (b)   the authority allowed it to make an offer or agreement which would or might require shares to be allotted, or rights to be granted, after the authority expired.

(8) A resolution of a company to give, vary, revoke or renew an authority under this section—

    (a)   may be an ordinary resolution, even though it alters the company's articles, and

      (b)   is subject to [section 380 of the Companies Act 1985] (resolutions to be recorded by registrar).".

(2)   In Schedule 24 to the Companies Act 1985 (c. 6) (punishment of offences), in the entry in respect of section 80(9), in the first column, for "80(9)" substitute "80(5)".

H6   Abolition of election of private companies as to duration of authority for directors to allot shares etc.

Section 80A of the Companies Act 1985 (election by private company as to duration of authority) shall cease to have effect.

H7   Return of allotments

(1)   Section 88 of the Companies Act 1985 (return as to allotments etc) is amended as follows.

(2)   For subsection (2) substitute—

    "(2)   The company must, within one month of making an allotment of shares, deliver to the registrar for registration a return of the allotments.

    (2A)   The return of allotments must—
        (a)   be in the prescribed form,
        (b)   contain the prescribed information, and
        (c)   include a statement of capital.

    (2B)   The statement of capital must be in the prescribed form and must state with respect to the company's share capital at the date to which the return is made up—
        (a)   the total number of shares of the company,
        (b)   the aggregate nominal value of those shares,
        (c)   for each class of shares—
            (i)   prescribed particulars of the rights attached to the shares,
            (ii)   the total number of shares of that class, and
            (iii)   the aggregate nominal value of shares of that class, and
        (d)   the amount paid up and the amount (if any) unpaid on each share (whether on account of the nominal value of the share or by way of premium).".

(3)   Omit subsection (3).

(4)   After that subsection insert—

    "(3A)   For the purposes of this section—
        (a)   shares are of one class if the rights attached to them are in all respects uniform, and
        (b)   the rights attached to shares are not regarded as different from those attached to other shares by reason only that they do not carry the same rights to dividends in the twelve months immediately following their allotment.

(3B)   In relation to rights attached to a class of shares, the Secretary of State may prescribe different particulars to be included in a statement of capital in different cases.

(3C)   In this section, an allotment of shares does not include the deemed allotment of shares to the subscribers to the memorandum.".

H8   Return of allotment of new class of shares by unlimited company

(1)   After section 88 of the Companies Act 1985 (c. 6) insert—

"88A   Return of allotment of shares of new class of unlimited company

(1)   If an unlimited company allots shares with rights that are not in all respects uniform with shares previously allotted, the company must, within one month of making an allotment of shares, deliver to the registrar for registration a return of allotments—

(a)   in the prescribed form, and

(b)   containing prescribed particulars of those rights.

(2)   For the purposes of this section, shares are not to be treated as different from shares previously allotted by reason only that the former do not carry the same rights to dividends as the latter during the 12 months immediately following the former's allotment.

(3)   If a company fails to comply with this section, an offence is committed by—

(a)   every officer of the company who is in default, and

(b)   every responsible delegate.

(4)   A person guilty of an offence under this section is liable to a fine and, for continued contravention, to a daily default fine.".

(2)   In section 128 of the Companies Act 1985 (registration of particulars of special rights), omit subsections (1) and (2).

(3)   In Schedule 24 to the Companies Act 1985 (punishment of offences)—

(a)   in the entry in respect of section 88(5), in the second column, for "company" substitute "limited company";

(b)   in the appropriate place insert—

"Section of Act creating offence	*General nature of offence*	*Mode of prosecution*	*Punishment*	*Daily default fine (where applicable)*
88A(3)	Officer of unlimited company failing to deliver return of allotment of shares of new class to registrar	1. On indictment 2. Summary	1. A fine 2. The statutory maximum	One-tenth of the statutory maximum."

H9   Time for acceptance of pre-emption offers

(1)   Section 90 of the Companies Act 1985 (c. 6) (communication of pre-emption offers to shareholders) is amended as follows.

(2)   After subsection (6) insert —

"(6A)   The Secretary of State may by regulations made by statutory instrument —
  (a)   reduce the period specified in subsection (6) (but not to less than 14 days), or
  (b)   increase that period.

(6B)   A statutory instrument containing regulations made under subsection (6A) may not be made unless a draft of the instrument has been laid before Parliament and approved by a resolution of each House.".

H10   Pre-emption rights

(1)   Section 95 of the Companies Act 1985 (disapplication of pre-emption rights) is amended as follows.

(2)   Before subsection (1) insert —

"(A1)   The directors of a private company that has only one class of shares (within the meaning of section 80ZA) may be given power by the articles, or by a special resolution of the company, to allot equity securities of that class as if —
  (a)   section 89(1) did not apply to the allotment, or
  (b)   that subsection applied to the allotment with such modifications as the directors may determine;
and where the directors make an allotment under this subsection, sections 89 to 94 have effect accordingly.".

(3)   In subsection (1), for "section 80" substitute "section 80ZB".

(4)   In subsection (2), for "section 80" substitute "section 80ZB".

Reserve capital

H11   Abolition of reserve capital

(1)   Section 120 of the Companies Act 1985 (reserve liability of limited company) shall cease to have effect.

(2)   Section 124 of that Act (reserve capital of unlimited company) shall cease to have effect.

(3)   The repeals made by this section do not affect the validity of —
  (a)   a special resolution passed by a company under section 120 of the Companies Act 1985 before the date on which this section came into force, provided that the resolution is forwarded to the registrar in accordance with section 380 of that Act, or
  (b)   the exercise of either of the powers under section 124 of the Companies Act 1985 before that date.

Class rights

H12 Registration of class rights

(1) In section 128 of the Companies Act 1985 (c. 6) (registration of particulars of special rights) —

    (a) in subsection (3) (notification of variation of class rights), omit from "otherwise than" to "section 380";

    (b) in subsection (4) omit from "(otherwise than" to "above)".

(2) In section 129 of the Companies Act 1985 (registration of newly created class rights of company without share capital) —

    (a) in subsection (1) (notification of new class of members) —

        (i) for "a class of members" substitute "a new class of members", and

        (ii) omit from "with rights which" to "section 380 applies";

    (b) in subsection (2) (notification of variation of class rights), omit from "otherwise than" to "section 380".

Share premiums

H13 Application of share premiums

In section 130 of the Companies Act 1985 (application of share premiums) for subsection (2) substitute —

"(1A) Where, on issuing shares, a company has transferred a sum to the share premium account, it may use that sum to write off —

    (a) the expenses of the issue of those shares;

    (b) any commission paid on the issue of those shares.

(2) The company may use the share premium account to pay up new shares to be allotted to members as fully paid bonus shares.".

Reduction of share capital

H14 Circumstances in which companies may reduce share capital

(1) Before section 135 of the Companies Act 1985 (special resolution for reduction of share capital) insert —

"Circumstances in which limited companies may reduce share capital".

(2) Section 135 (special resolution for reduction of share capital) is amended as follows.

(3) For subsection (1) substitute —

"(1) A private company limited by shares may reduce its share capital in any way by special resolution if the resolution is supported by a solvency statement in accordance with section 135A.

(1A) Any limited company may reduce its share capital in any way by special resolution if the reduction is confirmed by the court in accordance with sections 136 to 139.".

(4) In subsection (2)—

(a) for "subsection (1)" substitute "subsections (1) and (1A)";

(b) omit the words following paragraph (c).

(5) After subsection (2) insert—

"(2A) A special resolution under this section may not provide for a reduction of share capital to take effect later than the date on which the resolution has effect in accordance with this Chapter.

(2B) This Chapter (apart from subsection (2A)) has effect subject to any provision of the company's articles restricting or prohibiting the reduction of the company's share capital.".

H15 Reduction of capital supported by solvency statement

(1) After section 135 of the Companies Act 1985 (c. 6) insert—

"Reduction of capital of private company supported by solvency statement

135A Requirement for solvency statement

(1) A resolution for reducing share capital of a private company limited by shares is supported by a solvency statement if—

(a) the directors of the company make a statement of the solvency of the company in accordance with section 135B (a "solvency statement") not more than 15 days before the date on which the resolution is passed, and

(b) the resolution and solvency statement are registered in accordance with section 135C.

(2) Where the resolution is proposed as a written resolution, the solvency statement must be sent or submitted to every eligible member at or before the time at which the proposed resolution is served on him.

(3) Where the resolution is proposed at a general meeting, the solvency statement must be made available for inspection by members of the company throughout that meeting.

(4) The validity of a resolution is not affected by a failure to comply with subsection (2) or (3).

135B Solvency statement

(1) A solvency statement is a statement that the directors—

(a) have formed the opinion, as regards the company's situation at the date of the statement, that there is no ground on which the company could then be found to be unable to pay its debts; and

(b) have also formed the opinion—

(i) if it is intended to commence the winding up of the company within 12 months of that date, that the company will be able to pay its debts in full within 12 months of the commencement of the winding up; or

      (ii)   in any other case, that the company will be able to pay its debts as they fall due during the year immediately following that date.

(2)   In forming those opinions, the directors must take into account the same liabilities (including contingent and prospective liabilities) as would be relevant under section 122 of the Insolvency Act (winding up by the court) to the question whether the company is unable to pay its debts.

(3)   The solvency statement must state—

    (a)   the date on which it is made, and

    (b)   the name of each director of the company.

(4)   A director of a company who makes a solvency statement without having reasonable grounds for the opinion expressed in it is guilty of an offence and liable to imprisonment or a fine, or both, if the statement is delivered to the registrar.

135C Registration of resolution and solvency statement

(1)   Within 15 days after the resolution for reducing share capital is passed, in addition to the copy of the resolution required to be delivered under section 380, the company must deliver to the registrar—

    (a)   a copy of the solvency statement, and

    (b)   a statement of capital.

(2)   The statement of capital must be in the prescribed form and must state with respect to the company's share capital as reduced by the resolution—

    (a)   the total number of shares of the company,

    (b)   the aggregate nominal value of those shares,

    (c)   for each class of shares—

        (i)   prescribed particulars of the rights attached to the shares,

        (ii)   the total number of shares of that class, and

        (iii)   the aggregate nominal value of shares of that class, and

    (d)   the amount paid up and the amount (if any) unpaid on each share (whether on account of the nominal value of the share or by way of premium).

(3)   For the purpose of subsection (2)—

    (a)   shares are of one class if the rights attached to them are in all respects uniform, and

    (b)   the rights attached to shares are not regarded as different from those attached to other shares by reason only that they do not carry the same rights to dividends in the twelve months immediately following their allotment.

(4)   When he has received all of the documents specified in subsection (1), the registrar must register the documents.

(5)   The resolution does not take effect until those documents are registered.

(6)   The company must also deliver to the registrar, within 15 days after the resolution is passed, a statement made by the directors confirming that the solvency statement was —

    (a)   made not more than 15 days before the date on which the resolution was passed, and

    (b)   provided to members in accordance with section 135A(2) or (3).

(7)   The validity of a resolution is not affected by —

    (a)   a failure to deliver the documents specified in subsection (1) to the registrar within the time specified in that subsection, or

    (b)   a failure to comply with subsection (6) (confirmation of date etc. of solvency statement).

(8)   If the company delivers to the registrar a solvency statement that was not provided to members in accordance with section 135A(2) or (3), every officer of the company who is in default is guilty of an offence and liable to a fine.

(9)   If the company delivers the documents specified in subsection (1) to the registrar more than 15 days after the resolution is passed, the company and every officer of the company who is in default is guilty of an offence and liable to a fine.

(10)   If the company delivers to the registrar a statement made by the directors under subsection (6) that is false, a director who —

    (a)   knew that it was false, or

    (b)   did not have reasonable grounds for believing it to be true,

is guilty of an offence and liable to imprisonment or a fine, or both.

Reduction of capital confirmed by court".

(2)   In Schedule 24 to the Companies Act 1985 (c. 6) (punishment of offences) at the appropriate place insert —

Section of Act creating offence	General nature of offence	Mode of prosecution	Punishment	Daily default fine (where applicable)
135B(4)	Director making solvency statement without having reasonable grounds for opinion expressed in it	1. On indictment 2. Summary	1. 2 years or a fine; or both 2. 6 months or the statutory maximum; or both	
135C(8)	Delivery to registrar of solvency statement that was not provided to members	1. On indictment 2. Summary	1. A fine 2. The statutory maximum	

Section of Act creating offence	General nature of offence	Mode of prosecution	Punishment	Daily default fine (where applicable)
135C(9)	Late delivery to registrar of documents evidencing solvency statement	1. On indictment 2. Summary	1. A fine 2. The statutory maximum	
135C(10)	Director making false statement about timing etc. of solvency statement that he knows is false or does not believe to be true	1. On indictment 2. Summary	1. 2 years or a fine; or both 2. 6 months or the statutory maximum; or both	

H16   Registration of court order

(1)   Section 138 of the Companies Act 1985 (c. 6) (registration of order and minute of reduction) is amended as follows.

(2)   In subsection (1), for paragraphs (a) to (c) substitute —

"(a)   the total number of shares of the company,

(b)   the aggregate nominal value of those shares,

(c)   for each class of shares —

(i)   prescribed particulars of the rights attached to the shares,

(ii)   the total number of shares of that class, and

(iii)   the aggregate nominal value of shares of that class, and

(d)   the amount paid up and the amount (if any) unpaid on each share (whether on account of the nominal value of the share or by way of premium),".

(3)   After that subsection insert —

"(1A)   For the purpose of subsection (1) —

(a)   shares are of one class if the rights attached to them are in all respects uniform, and

(b)   the rights attached to shares are not regarded as different from those attached to other shares by reason only that they do not carry the same rights to dividends in the twelve months immediately following their allotment.".

(4)   For subsection (2) substitute —

"(2)   The resolution for reducing share capital as confirmed by the order so registered takes effect —

(a)   if the reduction of share capital forms part of a compromise or arrangement sanctioned by the court under section 425 (power of company to compromise with creditors and members), on delivery of the order and minute to the registrar, and

(b) otherwise, on the registration of the order and minute.".

(5) Omit subsections (5) and (6).

H17 Liability of members on reduced shares

(1) After section 139 of the Companies Act 1985 (c. 6) insert—

"Supplementary"

(2) In section 140 of the Companies Act 1985 (liability of members on reduced shares)—

    (a) in subsection (1), for "as fixed by the minute" substitute "as notified to the registrar in accordance with section 135C(1) or 138(1)".

    (b) in subsection (2) after "if" insert "a reduction of capital is confirmed by the court and".

Financial assistance

H18 Financial assistance by company for acquisition of shares

(1) Chapter 6 of Part 5 of the Companies Act 1985 (financial assistance by a company for acquisition of its own shares) is amended as follows.

(2) For section 151 (financial assistance generally prohibited) substitute—

"151 Prohibited financial assistance: acquisition of shares in public company

(1) Where a person is acquiring or proposing to acquire shares in a public company, it is not lawful for the company or any of its subsidiaries to give financial assistance directly or indirectly for the purpose of the acquisition before or at the same time as the acquisition takes place.

(2) Where—

    (a) a person has acquired shares in a public company, and

    (b) any liability has been incurred (by that or another person) for the purpose of the acquisition,

it is not lawful for the company or any of its subsidiaries to give financial assistance directly or indirectly for the purpose of reducing or discharging the liability so incurred.

(3) Subsections (1) and (2) have effect subject to section 153 (transactions not prohibited).

(4) If a company contravenes this section—

    (a) the company is guilty of an offence and liable to a fine, and

    (b) every officer of it who is in default is guilty of an offence and liable to imprisonment or a fine, or both.

151A Prohibited financial assistance: acquisition of shares in private company

(1) Where a person is acquiring or proposing to acquire shares in a private company, it is not lawful for—

    (a) a public company that is a subsidiary of that company, or

(b)   any subsidiary of such a public company,

to give financial assistance directly or indirectly for the purpose of the acquisition before or at the same time as the acquisition takes place.

(2)   Where a person has acquired shares in a private company and any liability has been incurred (by that or another person) for the purpose of the acquisition, it is not lawful for—

(a)   a public company that is a subsidiary of that company, or

(b)   any subsidiary of such a public company,

to give financial assistance directly or indirectly for the purpose of reducing or discharging the liability so incurred.

(3)   Subsections (1) and (2) have effect subject to section 153 (transactions not prohibited).

(4)   If a company contravenes this section—

(a)   the company is guilty of an offence and liable to a fine, and

(b)   every officer of it who is in default is guilty of an offence and liable to imprisonment or a fine, or both.".

(3)   Sections 155 to 158 (relaxation of prohibitions for private companies) shall cease to have effect.

(4)   In Schedule 24 to the Companies Act 1985 (c. 6) (punishment of offences)—

(a)   for the entry for section 151(3) substitute—

"Section of Act creating offence	General nature of offence	Mode of prosecution	Punishment	Daily default fine (where applicable)
151(4)	Company giving prohibited financial assistance towards acquisition of shares of public company	1. On indictment	1. Where the company is convicted, a fine Where an officer of the company is convicted, 2 years or a fine, or both	
		2. Summary	2. Where the company is convicted, the statutory maximum Where an officer of the company is convicted, 6 months or the statutory maximum, or both"	

"Section of Act creating offence	General nature of offence	Mode of prosecution	Punishment	Daily default fine (where applicable)
151A(4)	Company giving prohibited financial assistance towards acquisition of shares of private company	1. On indictment	1. Where the company is convicted, a fine Where an officer of the company is convicted, 2 years or a fine, or both	
		2. Summary	2. Where the company is convicted, the statutory maximum Where an officer of the company is convicted, 6 months or the statutory maximum, or both	

    (b)   omit the entries relating to section 156(6) and (7).

H19 Circumstances in which financial assistance is not prohibited

(1)   Section 153 of the Companies Act 1985 (c. 6) (transactions not prohibited by section 151) is amended as follows.

(2)   In the section heading, for "s 151" substitute "this Chapter".

(3)   In subsection (1) —
        (a)   for "Section 151(1) does not" substitute "Sections 151(1) and 151A(1) do not"; and
        (b)   for "an acquisition of shares in it or its holding company" substitute "an acquisition of shares in a company in relation to which it is a restricted company".

(4)   In subsection (2) —
        (a)   for "Section 151(2) does not" substitute "Sections 151(2) and 151A(2) do not"; and
        (b)   in paragraph (a), for "the acquisition of shares in the company or its holding company" substitute "an acquisition of shares in a company in relation to which it is a restricted company".

(5)   After subsection (2) insert —

    "(2A)   In subsections (1) and (2)(a) "restricted company" means —
        (a)   in relation to an acquisition of shares in a public company, the company itself or a subsidiary of the company; and

(b) in relation to an acquisition of shares in a private company —

(i) a public company that is a subsidiary of that company, or

(ii) any subsidiary of such a public company.".

(6) In subsection (3), for "Section 151 does not" substitute "Sections 151 and 151A do not".

(7) In subsection (4), for "Section 151 does not" substitute "Sections 151 and 151A do not".

Redeemable shares

H20 Redeemable shares

(1) Section 159 of the Companies Act 1985 (c. 6) (power to issue redeemable shares) is amended as follows.

(2) In subsection (1) —

(a) omit ", if authorised to do so by its articles,", and

(b) at the end insert "("redeemable shares")".

(3) After subsection (1) insert —

"(1A) A public company may not issue redeemable shares unless it is authorised to do so by its articles.".

(4) After that section insert —

"159A Terms and manner of redemption determined by directors

(1) The directors of a company may determine the terms, conditions and manner of redemption of shares if they are authorised to do so by —

(a) a resolution of the company, or

(b) the company's articles.

(2) Where the directors are authorised to determine the terms, conditions or manner of redemption of shares, they must do so before the shares are allotted.".

(5) In section 160 of that Act (financing etc of redemption), omit subsection (3).

H21 Notifying registrar of allotment of redeemable shares

In section 88 of the Companies Act 1985 (return as to allotments etc), after subsection (2B) (inserted by this Act) insert —

"(2C) If a company allots redeemable shares (within the meaning of section 159), the return must contain prescribed particulars of the terms, conditions and manner of redemption.".

Purchase by company of its own shares

H22 Power of company to purchase own shares

In section 162 of the Companies Act 1985 (power of company to purchase own shares) for subsection (1) substitute —

> "(1) A company limited by shares or limited by guarantee and having a share capital may purchase its own shares (including any redeemable shares), subject to —
>> (a) the following provisions of this Chapter, and
>> (b) any restriction or prohibition in the company's articles.".

H23 Repeal of power of private companies to redeem or purchase own shares out of capital

(1) Sections 171 to 177 of the Companies Act 1985 (c. 6) (redemption or purchase by private company of own shares out of capital) shall cease to have effect.

(2) In section 160(1) of the Companies Act 1985 (financing etc of redemption) for "sections 171 (private companies redeeming or purchasing own shares out of capital) and 178(4)" substitute "section 178(4)".

(3) In section 263(2) of the Companies Act 1985 (meaning of "distribution"), for paragraph (b) substitute —

> "(b) the redemption or purchase of any of the company's own shares out of the proceeds of a fresh issue of shares made for the purposes of the redemption or purchase in accordance with Chapter 7 of Part 5,".

(4) In the Insolvency Act 1986 (c. 45) the following provisions shall cease to have effect —

> (a) section 76 (liability of past directors and shareholders on winding up in respect of redemption or purchase of shares out of capital);
> (b) section 79(3) (meaning of "contributory");
> (c) section 124(3) (application for winding up by contributory).

(5) The repeals and amendments made by this section in the Companies Act 1985 do not have effect in relation to a redemption or purchase of shares of a private limited company out of capital which is approved by a special resolution of the company before the date on which this section has effect.

(6) The repeals made by this section in the Insolvency Act 1986 do not have effect in relation to a person who is liable to contribute to a company's assets in the event of its being wound up under section 76 of that Act as the result of such a redemption or purchase.

Transfers of shares etc.

H24 Registration of transfers of shares and debentures

(1) In section 183 of the Companies Act 1985 (transfer and registration) —

> (a) in the title, omit "and registration";
> (b) omit subsections (4) to (6).

(2)   After that section insert—

"183A Registration of allotment and transfer of shares and debentures

(1)   A company must register an allotment of shares or debentures as soon as practicable and in any event within 2 months after the date of the allotment.

(2)   A company must—
   (a)   register a transfer of shares or debentures, or
   (b)   send to the transferee notice of refusal to register the transfer, giving reasons for the refusal,
as soon as practicable and in any event within 2 months after the date on which the transfer is lodged with it.

(3)   The directors must provide the transferee with such further information about the reasons for the refusal as the transferee may reasonably request, but such information does not include copies of minutes of meetings of directors.

(4)   On the application of the transferor of any share or interest in a company, the company must enter in its register of members the name of the transferee in the same manner and subject to the same conditions as if the application for the entry were made by the transferee.

(5)   If a company fails to comply with this section, an offence is committed by—
   (a)   every officer of the company who is in default, and
   (b)   every responsible delegate.

(6)   A person guilty of an offence under this section is liable to a fine and, for continued contravention, a daily default fine.

(7)   This section does not apply—
   (a)   in relation to an allotment or transfer of shares if the company has issued a share warrant in respect of the shares (under section 188);
   (b)   in relation to the transmission of shares by operation of law.".

(3)   After section 183A insert—

"183B Obligation to register transmission of shares by operation of law

(1)   This section applies where a person to whom the right to any shares in the company has been transmitted by operation of law gives notice requiring the company to enter his name in the register of members as the holder of the shares.

(2)   The person must provide the directors of the company with such evidence of his entitlement as they reasonably require.

(3)   The company must register the person as a member of the company as soon as practicable and in any event within 2 months of the later of—
   (a)   the date on which the notice is received, or
   (b)   if the directors request evidence of entitlement, the date on which the directors receive that evidence.

(4) If a person fails to provide the directors of the company with such evidence of his entitlement as they reasonably require, the directors must send the person notice of refusal to register his name in the register of members, setting out the reasons for the refusal.

(5) The directors must provide the person with such further information about the reasons for the refusal as the person may reasonably request, but such information does not include copies of minutes of meetings of directors.

(6) If a company fails to comply with this section, an offence is committed by —
    (a) every officer of the company who is in default, and
    (b) every responsible delegate.

(7) A person guilty of an offence under this section is liable to a fine and, for continued contravention, a daily default fine.".

(4) Subsection (2) has effect in relation to allotments and transfers of shares and debentures that take effect after this section comes into force.

(5) In Schedule 24 to the Companies Act 1985 (c. 6) (punishment of offences),
    (a) omit the entry in respect of section 183(6), and
    (b) in the appropriate place insert —

"Section of Act creating offence	*General nature of offence*	*Mode of prosecution*	*Punishment*	*Daily default fine (where applicable)*
183A(5)	Company failing to register allotment or transfer of share or debentures or to give reasons for refusal to register	Summary	Level 3 on the standard scale	One-tenth of level 3 on the standard scale.
183B(6)	Company failing to register transmission of shares by operation of law or to give reasons for refusal to register	Summary	Level 3 on the standard scale	One-tenth of level 3 on the standard scale."

H25 Share certificates and share warrants

In section 185 of the Companies Act 1985 (duty of company as to issue of certificates), after subsection (2) insert —

"(2A) Subsection (1) does not apply in relation to an allotment or transfer of shares if, following the allotment or transfer, the company has issued a share warrant in respect of the shares (under section 188).

(2B)   A company must, within 2 months of the surrender of a share warrant for cancellation, complete and have ready for delivery the certificates of the shares specified in the warrant (unless its articles provide otherwise).".

Distributions

H26   Distributions in kind

(1)   Part 8 of the Companies Act 1985 (c. 6) (distributions) is amended as follows.

(2)   After section 275 insert—

"Distributions in kind

275A   Distributions in kind: determination of amount

(1)   This section applies for the purpose of determining the amount of any distribution arising from the sale, transfer or other disposition by a company of a non-cash asset.

(2)   If the following conditions are met, the amount of the distribution is the amount by which the book value of the asset exceeds the amount or value of the consideration for the disposition.

(3)   The conditions are—
  (a)   that at the time of the disposition of the asset, the company has profits available for distribution, and
  (b)   that if the amount of the distribution were determined in accordance with subsection (2), the company could make the distribution without contravening—
      (i)   section 263 (general limit on distributions),
      (ii) section 264 (restriction on distribution of assets by public companies), or
      (iii) section 265 (distributions by investment companies).

(4)   If those conditions are not met, the amount of the distribution is the amount by which the market value of the asset as at the date of the disposition exceeds the amount or value of the consideration for the disposition.

(5)   In this section "book value", in relation to an asset, means the amount at which the asset is stated in the accounts relevant for the purposes of the distribution in accordance with sections 270 to 275.

(6)   The provisions of sections 270 to 275 (distribution to be justified by reference to company's accounts) have effect subject to this section.".

(3)   In section 276 (distributions in kind), at the end of the heading insert ": **treatment of unrealised profits**".

(4)   After section 280 insert —

"280A Application of rules of law restricting distribution

(1)   Except as provided in this section, the provisions of this Part are without prejudice to any rule of law restricting the sums out of which, or the cases in which, a distribution may be made.

(2)   For the purposes of any rule of law requiring distributions to be paid out of profits or restricting the return of capital to members —

   (a)   the amount of any distribution or return of capital arising from the sale, transfer or other disposition by a company of a non-cash asset must be determined in accordance with section 275A (distributions in kind: determination of amount); and

   (b)   section 276 (distributions in kind: treatment of unrealised profits) applies as it applies for the purposes of this Part.

(3)   In this section references to distributions are to amounts regarded as distributions for the purposes of any such rule of law as is referred to in subsection (1).".

(5)   In section 281 (saving for other restraints on distribution), omit "or rule of law".

Redenomination of share capital

H27   Redenomination of share capital

(1)   A limited company having a share capital may by ordinary resolution redenominate its share capital or any class of its share capital.

"Redenominate" means convert shares from having a fixed nominal value in one currency to having a fixed nominal value in another currency.

(2)   The conversion must be made at an appropriate spot rate of exchange specified in the resolution.

(3)   The rate must be either —

   (a)   a rate prevailing on the day the resolution is passed,

   (b)   a rate prevailing on another day specified in the resolution, or

   (c)   a rate determined by taking the average of rates prevailing on each consecutive day of a period specified in the resolution.

The day or period specified for the purposes of paragraph (b) or (c) must be within 28 days before the resolution is passed.

(4)   A resolution under this section takes effect on the day it is passed.

(5)   A company's articles may prohibit or restrict the exercise of the power conferred by this section.

H28   Calculation of new nominal values

For each class of share the new nominal value of each share is calculated as follows:

Step One

Take the aggregate of the old nominal values of all the shares of that class.

Step Two

Translate that amount into the new currency at the rate of exchange specified in the resolution.

Step Three

Round the resulting figure to the nearest unit or sub-unit of the new currency.

Step Four

Divide that amount by the number of shares in the class.

H29 Effect of redenomination

(1) The redenomination of shares does not affect any rights or obligations of members under the company's constitution, or any restrictions affecting members under the company's constitution.

In particular, it does not affect entitlement to dividends, voting rights or any liability in respect of amounts unpaid on shares.

(2) For this purpose the company's constitution means the company's articles, together with —

    (a) any resolution of the members of the company or any class of members,

    (b) any resolution or agreement within [section 380 of the Companies Act 1985] (resolutions and agreements to be recorded by registrar), and

    (c) the terms on which any shares of the company are allotted or held.

(3) Subject to subsection (1), references to the old nominal value of the shares in any agreement or statement, or in any deed, instrument or document, shall (unless the context otherwise requires) be read after the resolution takes effect as references to the new nominal value of the shares.

H30 Notice to registrar of redenomination

(1) If a company having a share capital redenominates any of its share capital, it must within one month after doing so give notice to the registrar, specifying the shares redenominated.

(2) The notice must —

    (a) be in the prescribed form,

    (b) state the date on which the resolution was passed, and

    (c) include a statement of capital.

(3) The statement of capital must be in the prescribed form and must state with respect to the company's share capital as redenominated by the resolution —

    (a) the total number of shares of the company,

    (b) the aggregate nominal value of those shares,

    (c) for each class of shares —

        (i) prescribed particulars of the rights attached to the shares,

        (ii) the total number of shares of that class, and

        (iii) the aggregate nominal value of shares of that class, and

    (d) the amount paid up and the amount (if any) unpaid on each share (whether on account of the nominal value of the share or by way of premium).

(4) For the purpose of subsection (3) —

    (a) shares are of one class if the rights attached to them are in all respects uniform, and

    (b)   the rights attached to shares are not regarded as different from those attached to other shares by reason only that they do not carry the same rights to dividends in the twelve months immediately following their allotment.

(5)   If default is made in complying with this section, an offence is committed by —

    (a)   the company,

    (b)   every officer of the company who is in default, and

    (c)   every responsible delegate.

(6)   A person guilty of an offence under this section is liable on summary conviction to a fine not exceeding level 3 on the standard scale and, for continued contravention, a daily default fine not exceeding one-tenth of level 3 on the standard scale.

H31   Reduction of capital in connection with redenomination

(1)   A company that passes a resolution redenominating some or all of its shares may, for the purpose of adjusting the nominal values of the redenominated shares to obtain values that are, in the opinion of the company, more suitable, reduce its share capital under this section.

(2)   A reduction of capital under this section requires a special resolution of the company.

(3)   Any such resolution must be passed within twelve months of the resolution effecting the redenomination.

(4)   The amount by which a company's share capital is reduced under this section must not exceed 10% of the nominal value of the company's allotted share capital immediately after the reduction.

(5)   A reduction of capital under this section does not extinguish or reduce any liability in respect of share capital not paid up.

(6)   Nothing in —

    (a)   sections 135 to 135C of the Companies Act 1985 (c. 6) (reduction of capital supported by solvency statement), or

    (b)   sections 135 and 136 to 141 of that Act (reduction of capital requiring confirmation by court),

applies to a reduction of capital under this section.

H32   Notice to registrar of reduction of capital in connection with redenomination

(1)   A company that passes a resolution under section H31 (reduction of capital in connection with redenomination) must give notice to the registrar within 15 days after the resolution is passed.

(2)   The notice must —

    (a)   be in the prescribed form,

    (b)   state —

        (i)   the date of the resolution, and

        (ii)   the date of the resolution under section H27 in connection with which it was passed, and

    (c)   include a statement of capital.

(3) The statement of capital must be in the prescribed form and must state with respect to the company's share capital as reduced by the resolution—

    (a) the total number of shares of the company,

    (b) the aggregate nominal value of those shares,

    (c) for each class of shares—

        (i) prescribed particulars of the rights attached to the shares,

        (ii) the total number of shares of that class, and

        (iii) the aggregate nominal value of shares of that class, and

    (d) the amount paid up and the amount (if any) unpaid on each share (whether on account of the nominal value of the share or by way of premium).

(4) For the purpose of subsection (3)—

    (a) shares are of one class if the rights attached to them are in all respects uniform, and

    (b) the rights attached to shares are not regarded as different from those attached to other shares by reason only that they do not carry the same rights to dividends in the twelve months immediately following their allotment.

(5) On receipt of the notice required by this section the registrar shall register it.

(6) The reduction of capital is not effective until entry of that notice on the register.

(7) If a company fails to comply with this section, an offence is committed by—

    (a) the company, and

    (b) every officer of the company who is in default.

(8) A person guilty of an offence under this section is liable—

    (a) on conviction on indictment to a fine, and

    (b) on summary conviction to a fine not exceeding the statutory maximum.

H33 Redenomination reserve

(1) The amount by which a company's share capital is reduced under section H31 (reduction of capital in connection with redenomination) must be transferred to a reserve, called "the redenomination reserve".

(2) The redenomination reserve may be applied by the company in paying up shares to be allotted to members as fully paid bonus shares.

(3) Subject to that, the provisions of the Companies Acts relating to the reduction of a company's share capital apply as if the redenomination reserve were paid-up share capital of the company.

Public company minimum share capital requirement

H34 Requirement as to minimum share capital of public company

(1) A public company must not do business or exercise any borrowing powers unless the registrar has issued it with a certificate under this section.

(2) This does not affect the validity of a transaction entered into by the company, but if a company—

    (a) enters into a transaction in contravention of this section, and

(b) fails to comply with its obligations in connection with the transaction within 21 days from being called on to do so,

the directors of the company are jointly and severally liable to indemnify the other party to the transaction in respect of any loss or damage suffered by him by reason of the company's failure to comply with its obligations.

(3) The directors who are so liable are those who were directors at the time the company entered into the transaction.

(4) The registrar shall issue a certificate under this section if, on an application made in accordance with section H35, he is satisfied that the nominal value of the company's allotted share capital is not less than the authorised minimum.

(5) For this purpose a share allotted in pursuance of an employees' share scheme shall not be taken into account unless paid up as to—

(a) at least one-quarter of the nominal value of the share, and
(b) the whole of any premium on the share.

(6) A certificate under this section has effect from the date on which it is issued and is conclusive evidence that the company is entitled to do business and exercise any borrowing powers.

H35 Procedure for obtaining certificate

(1) An application for a certificate under section H34 must be in the prescribed form and must—

(a) state that the nominal value of the company's allotted share capital is not less than the authorised minimum,
(b) specify the amount, or estimated amount, of the company's preliminary expenses,
(c) specify any amount or benefit paid or given, or intended to be paid or given, to any promoter of the company, and the consideration for the payment or benefit, and
(d) be accompanied by a statement of compliance.

(2) The statement of compliance is a statement by a director or secretary of the company that the company meets the requirements for the issue of a certificate under section H34.

(3) The statement of compliance must be in the prescribed form and must be signed by the person by whom it is made.

(4) The registrar may accept the statement of compliance as sufficient evidence of the matters stated in it.

H36 The authorised minimum

For the purposes of sections H34 and H35 (requirement as to minimum share capital of public company) the authorised minimum is £50,000.

Company Law Reform Bill

CONTENTS

7 Draft Clauses

PART I

COMPANY REGISTERS

I1   Register of members: period after which entry may be removed etc

In section 352 of the Companies Act 1985 (c. 6) (register of members) —

    (a)   in subsection (6) (period after which entry relating to former member may be removed), and

    (b)   in subsection (7) (period after which liability in connection with making or deletion of entry becomes unenforceable),

for "20 years" substitute "ten years".

I2   Register of members: share warrants

    (1)   Section 355 of the Companies Act 1985 (entries in register in relation to share warrants) is amended as follows.

    (2)   In subsection (1) omit from "shall strike out" to "had ceased to be a member, and".

    (3)   After subsection (1) insert —

    "(1A)   On the issue of a share warrant the company must, if necessary, amend the register so that no person is named on the register as the holder of the shares specified in the warrant.".

I3   Register of members: inspection or provision of copy

    (1)   Section 356 of the Companies Act 1985 (inspection of register of members and index of members' names) is amended as follows.

    (2)   After subsection (3) insert —

    "(3A)   When a person inspects the register or the company provides him with a copy of the register, or any part of it, the company must inform him of the most recent date (if any) on which alterations were made to the register and there were no further alterations to be made.

    (3B)   When a person inspects the index of members' names, the company must inform him whether there is any alteration to the register that is not reflected in the index.".

    (3)   [Subsections (5) and (6) to be replaced.]

(4)   After subsection (6) insert—

"(7)   If a company fails to provide the information required under subsection (3A) or (3B), every officer of the company who is in default is guilty of an offence and liable to a fine.".

(5)   In Schedule 24 to that Act (punishment of offences), at the appropriate place insert—

Section of Act creating offence	General nature of offence	Mode of prosecution	Punishment	Daily default fine (where applicable)
"356(7)	Company failing to provide information about state of register or index of members	Summary	Level 3 on the standard scale"	

I4   Register of members: removal of power to close register

(1)   Section 358 of the Companies Act 1985 (c. 6) (power to close register of members) shall cease to have effect.

(2)   In section 356 of that Act (inspection of register and index), in subsection (1) omit "Except when the register of members is closed under the provisions of this Act,".

(3)   In Schedule 14 to that Act (overseas branch registers), in paragraph 2(2) omit from ", except that the advertisement before closing the register" to the end.

I5   Form of company registers etc

(1)   In section 722 of the Companies Act 1985 (form of company registers, etc), for subsection (1) substitute—

"(1)   Any register, index, minute book or accounting records required by the Companies Acts to be kept by a company—
   (a)   may be kept in hard copy or electronic form, and
   (b)   may be arranged in such manner as the directors of the company think fit,

provided the information in question is adequately recorded for future reference.".

(2)   In section 723 of that Act (use of computers for company records)—
   (a)   omit subsections (1) and (3) to (5) (which are superseded by the amendment in subsection (1) above), and
   (b)   in subsection (2) (adaptation of pre-1979 instruments providing for register of debenture holders) for "in a legible form" substitute "in hard copy form" and for "in a legible or non-legible form" substitute "in hard copy or electronic form".

Company Law Reform Bill

CONTENTS

PART J

OFFENCES

7 Draft Clauses

PART J

OFFENCES

Liability of officer in default or responsible delegate

J1   Liability of officer in default

  (1)   This section has effect for the purposes of any provision of the Companies Act 1985 (c. 6) or this Act to the effect that, in the event of contravention of an enactment in relation to a company, an offence is committed by every "officer" of the company who is "in default".

  (2)   The "officers" to whom the provision applies (whether or not they would otherwise be regarded as an officer of the company) are—

      (a)   any director of the company;

      (b)   any secretary of the company—

           (i)   on whom the function of securing compliance with the enactment is conferred by the company's articles, or

          (ii)   to whom that function has been properly delegated by one or more of the directors;

      (c)   any senior executive of the company whose functions include securing compliance with the enactment;

      (d)   any other person who is to be treated as an officer of the company for the purposes of the provision in question.

  (3)   Any such person is "in default" for the purposes of the provision if he authorises or permits, participates in or fails to take all reasonable steps to prevent the contravention.

  (4)   For the purposes of this section a function is "properly delegated" to a person if its delegation to that person—

      (a)   is not prohibited by the company's articles, and

      (b)   is reasonable in all the circumstances.

  (5)   In this section "senior executive" means a person who is responsible at a senior level for decision-making, or managerial or advisory functions.

The expression does not include—

      (a)   a director or secretary of the company, or

      (b)   a person whose functions do not affect a significant part of the company's operations or the business of the company as a whole.

J2   Liability of responsible delegate

  (1)   This section has effect for the purposes of any provision of the Companies Act 1985 or this Act to the effect that, in the event of contravention of an enactment

in relation to a company, an offence is committed by every "responsible delegate".

(2) A "delegate" means a person to whom the function of securing compliance with the enactment in question has been properly delegated by the directors, or by a director or secretary, of the company.

(3) Any such person is "responsible" if he authorises or permits, participates in or fails to take all reasonable steps to prevent the contravention.

(4) For the purposes of this section a function is "properly delegated" to a person if its delegation to that person—

    (a) is not prohibited by the company's articles, and

    (b) is reasonable in all the circumstances.

J3   Liability of company as officer in default or responsible delegate

(1) A company does not commit an offence as an officer in default or responsible delegate unless—

    (a) an officer of the company is in default, or

    (b) a delegate of the company is responsible.

(2) Where any such offence is committed by a company the officer or delegate in question also commits the offence and is liable to be proceeded against and punished accordingly.

(3) In this section—

    (a) "officer" and "in default" have the meanings given by section J1, and

    (b) "delegate" and "responsible" have the meanings given by section J2.

J4   Application of provisions to bodies other than companies

(1) Sections J1 to J3 (liability of officers in default and responsible delegates) apply to a body other than a company as they apply to a company.

(2) As they apply in relation to a body corporate other than a company—

    (a) any reference to a director of the company shall be read as referring—

        (i) where the body's affairs are managed by its members, to a member of the body,

        (ii) in any other case, to any corresponding officer of the body,

    (b) any reference to a secretary of the company shall be read as referring to any secretary or similar officer of the body, and

    (c) any reference to the company's articles shall be read as referring to the body's constitution.

(3) As they apply in relation to a partnership—

    (a) any reference to a director of the company shall be read as referring to a member of the partnership,

    (b) any reference to a secretary of the company shall be read as referring to any secretary or similar officer of the partnership, and

    (c) any reference to the company's articles shall be read as referring to the partnership agreement.

(4) As they apply in relation to an unincorporated body other than a partnership—

(a) any reference to a director of the company shall be read as referring to a member of the governing body,

(b) any reference to a secretary of the company shall be read as referring to any secretary or similar officer of the governing body, and

(c) any reference to the company's articles shall be read as referring to the body's constitution.

J5 Criminal proceedings against unincorporated bodies

(1) Proceedings for an offence alleged to have been committed by virtue of any provision of sections J1 to J4 (liability of officer in default or responsible delegate) by an unincorporated body may be brought in the name of the body.

(2) For the purposes of such proceedings—

(a) any rules of court relating to the service of documents have effect as if the body were a body corporate, and

(b) the following provisions apply as they apply in relation to a body corporate—

section 33 of the Criminal Justice Act 1925 (c. 86) and Schedule 3 to the Magistrates' Courts Act 1980 (c. 43),

sections 70 and 143 of the Criminal Procedure (Scotland) Act 1995 (c. 46).

(3) A fine imposed on an unincorporated body on its conviction of an offence shall be paid out of the funds of the body.

Dishonesty offences

J6 Approval of defective accounts

(1) In section 233 of the Companies Act 1985 (c. 6) (approval and signing of accounts), for subsection (5) substitute—

"(5) If annual accounts are approved that do not comply with the requirements of this Act, every director of the company who—

(a) knew that they did not comply, or was reckless as to whether they complied, and

(b) failed to take reasonable steps to prevent them from being approved,

is guilty of an offence and liable to imprisonment or a fine, or both.".

(2) In Schedule 24 to that Act (punishment of offences), for the entry relating to section 233(5) substitute—

"233(5)	Approval of defective accounts	1. On indictment 2. Summary	7 years or a fine; or both 12 months or the statutory maximum; or both	—"

(3) The amendment in subsection (2) above has effect—

    (a)   in relation to England and Wales, in the case of an offence committed before section 154(1) of the Criminal Justice Act 2003 (c. 44) comes into force, and

    (b)   in relation to Scotland,

as if for "12 months" there were substituted "6 months".

J7   Failure to keep accounting records

(1)   In section 221 of the Companies Act 1985 (duty to keep accounting records), for subsections (5) and (6) substitute —

    "(5)   If a company fails to comply with any provision of this section, an offence is committed by —

        (a)   every officer of the company who is in default, and

        (b)   every responsible delegate.

    (6)   Subject to subsection (7), a person guilty of an offence under this section is liable to a fine.

    (7)   If in committing an offence under this section a person acts dishonestly he is liable to imprisonment or a fine, or both.".

(2)   In Schedule 24 to that Act (punishment of offences), in the entry relating to sections 221(5) and 222(4) omit "221(5) or" and after that entry insert —

| "221(6) | Failure to keep accounting records | 1. On indictment 2. Summary | A fine The statutory maximum | — |
| 221(7) | Dishonest failure to keep accounting records | 1. On indictment 2. Summary | 7 years or a fine; or both 12 months or the statutory maximum; or both | —" |

(3)   The amendment in subsection (2) above has effect —

    (a)   in relation to England and Wales, in the case of an offence committed before section 154(1) of the Criminal Justice Act 2003 comes into force, and

    (b)   in relation to Scotland,

as if for "12 months" there were substituted "6 months".

J8   Penalty for fraudulent trading

In Schedule 24 to the Companies Act 1985 (c. 6) (punishment of offences), in the entry relating to offences under section 458 of that Act (fraudulent trading), for "7 years" substitute "10 years".

Supplementary

J9   Transitional provision

The provisions of this Part do not apply to offences committed before the commencement of this section.

7 Draft Clauses

Company Law Reform

CONTENTS

PART K

REFORM POWER

7 Draft Clauses

PART K

REFORM POWER

K1   Power to reform company law

(1)   The Secretary of State may by order made in accordance with this Part make provision for the purpose of reforming the law relating to companies.
Such an order is referred to in this Part as a "company law reform order".

(2)   A company law reform order may make provision—
    (a)   amending the law relating to companies,
    (b)   restating statutory provisions relating to companies,
    (c)   codifying rules of law relating to companies,
and may make such consequential modifications, repeals and revocations in statutory provisions as the Secretary of State considers appropriate.

(3)   The provision that may be made under subsection (2) includes any such provision as might be made by Act of Parliament, subject to the following provisions of this Part.

(4)   In this Part—
    "amend" includes making new provision and repealing or abolishing existing statutory provisions or rules of law;
    "codify", in relation to a rule of law, means replace with statutory provisions;
    "statutory provision" means a provision comprised in—
        (a)   an Act of Parliament or subordinate legislation made under such an Act, whenever passed or made, or
        (b)   an Act of the Scottish Parliament or subordinate legislation made under such an Act, whenever passed or made;
    "restate", in relation to a statutory provision, means replace with alterations only of form or arrangement;
    "subordinate legislation" means orders, rules, regulations, schemes, warrants, byelaws and other subordinate instruments.

K2   Definition of "company" etc.

(1)   The following definitions apply for the purposes of this Part.

(2)   "Company" means—
    (a)   a company within the meaning of this Act,
    (b)   an unregistered company within the meaning of section 718 of the Companies Act 1985 (c. 6), or
    (c)   an oversea company within the meaning of section 744 of that Act.

(3) "Law relating to companies" means statutory provisions and rules of law relating to the creation, operation, regulation or dissolution of companies.

(4) "Statutory provisions relating to companies" means any statutory provision to the extent that it relates to the creation, operation, regulation or dissolution of companies.

(5) Statutory provisions relating to companies include such provisions as they are applied to other persons or bodies or for other purposes.

(6) Statutory provisions relating to companies —
    (a)   include company law reform orders;
    (b)   do not include the provisions of this Part of this Act.

(7) "Rule of law relating to companies" means any rule of law to the extent that it relates to the creation, operation, regulation or dissolution of companies.

K3   No power to impose taxation

(1) A company law reform order may not make provision imposing or increasing taxation.

(2) Nothing in this section affects the power to restate statutory provisions or codify rules of law.

K4   Restrictions on penalties for criminal offences

(1) A company law reform order may not create a new offence that is punishable, or increase the penalty for an existing offence so that it is punishable —
    (a)   on indictment, with imprisonment for a term exceeding two years, or
    (b)   on summary conviction, with imprisonment for a term exceeding the normal maximum term or a fine exceeding —
        (i)   where the offence is a summary offence, level 5 on the standard scale, or
        (ii)   where the offence is triable either way, the statutory maximum.

(2) In subsection (2), "the normal maximum term" means —
    (a)   in England and Wales —
        (i)   in the case of a summary offence, 51 weeks, and
        (ii)   in the case of an offence triable either way, 12 months;
    (b)   in Scotland, six months.

(3) If a company law reform order creating an offence, or altering the penalty for an offence, is made before the date on which section 281(5) of the Criminal Justice Act 2003 (c. 44) comes into force, the order must provide that, in relation to a summary offence committed before that date, any reference to a term of imprisonment of 51 weeks is to be read as a reference to six months.

(4) If a company law reform order creating an offence, or altering the penalty for an offence, is made before the date on which section 154(1) of the Criminal Justice Act 2003 comes into force, the order must provide that, in relation to an offence triable either way committed before that date, any reference to a term of imprisonment of 12 months is to be read as a reference to six months.

(5) Nothing in this section affects the power to restate statutory provisions or codify rules of law.

K5 Restrictions on provisions for forcible entry etc.

(1) A company law reform order must not contain any provision—
    (a) providing for forcible entry, seizure or search, or
    (b) compelling the giving of evidence.

(2) This does not prevent a company law reform order extending existing statutory provisions or rules of law for purposes of the like nature as those to which they applied before the order was made.

(3) Nothing in this section affects the power to restate statutory provisions or codify rules of law.

K6 Restrictions on powers to legislate

(1) A company law reform order may not confer a power or duty to legislate except in accordance with this section.

(2) A company law reform order may confer power on the Secretary of State (a "new power") to make subordinate legislation—
    (a) imposing or making provision about the amount of fees or charges (other than charges in the nature of taxation),
    (b) making procedural or other administrative provision, or
    (c) making provision about technical matters.

(3) The order must provide that the new power may only be exercised by statutory instrument.

(4) The order must provide that such a statutory instrument—
    (a) is subject to annulment in pursuance of a resolution of either House of Parliament, or
    (b) is not to be made unless a draft of the statutory instrument has been laid before and approved by a resolution of each House of Parliament.

(5) Nothing in this section affects the power to restate statutory provisions.

(6) In particular, where—
    (a) a company law reform order restates a statutory provision, and
    (b) immediately prior to the restatement, there was a power to modify, restate or apply that provision by subordinate legislation,
the order may provide for the restated provision to be modified, restated or applied by subordinate legislation in the same way.

(7) In this section "legislate" means legislate by orders, rules, regulations or other subordinate instrument.

K7 Restrictions on delegation of legislative functions

(1) A company law reform order may not make provision enabling a person or body on whom a legislative function is conferred to delegate the performance of that function, except in accordance with this section.

(2) Where an existing statutory provision enables a person or body to delegate the performance of a legislative function, a company law reform order may extend the provision so as to make it applicable in additional circumstances of the like nature as those in which it was exercisable before the order was made.

(3) Nothing in this section affects the power to restate statutory provisions.

(4) Where —
    (a) a company law reform order restates a provision for the delegation of a legislative function, and
    (b) immediately prior to the restatement, the delegation was required to be done by statutory instrument,

the order may not remove that requirement or alter the Parliamentary procedure specified.

(5) In this section, "legislative function" means a power or duty to legislate by orders, rules, regulations or other subordinate instrument.

K8 No power to make provision with retrospective effect

A company law reform order may not make provision taking effect from a date earlier than that of the making of the instrument containing the provision.

K9 Procedure for making orders

(1) A company law reform order must be made by statutory instrument.

(2) Such an order may not be made unless a draft of the statutory instrument containing the order has been laid before and approved by a resolution of each House of Parliament.

(3) The Secretary of State may not make a company law reform order unless —
    (a) he has consulted in accordance with section K10 on the proposal to make the order,
    (b) following that consultation, he has laid a document containing a proposed order before Parliament in accordance with section K11,
    (c) the period for Parliament to consider that document under section K14 has expired, and
    (d) on laying the order before Parliament, he has also laid the statement required by that section.

K10 Consultation

(1) If the Secretary of State proposes to make company law reform order, he must —
    (a) consult such organisations as appear to him to be representative of interests substantially affected by the proposals,
    (b) in such cases as he considers appropriate, consult the Law Commission or the Scottish Law Commission, and
    (c) consult such other persons as he considers appropriate,

except to the extent that subsection (2) applies.

(2) In relation to proposals, or parts of proposals, implementing a recommendation of the Law Commission or the Scottish Law Commission without material changes, the Secretary of State must carry out such consultation as he considers appropriate, having regard to the consultation carried out by the Law Commission or the Scottish Law Commission.

(3) If, as a result of the consultation, it appears to the Secretary of State that it is appropriate to vary the whole or any part of his proposals, he must undertake

such further consultation with respect to the variations as appears to him to be appropriate.

(4) The requirements of this section may be satisfied by consultation undertaken before the day on which this Act is passed.

K11 Document to be laid before Parliament

(1) If, after the conclusion of the consultation required by section K10, the Secretary of State considers it appropriate to proceed with the making of an order, he must lay before Parliament a document containing—
  (a) the proposed order,
  (b) the information required by this section, and
  (c) the explanation required under section K12 (reasons for order).

(2) The document must explain the manner in which the order is intended—
  (a) to amend the law relating to companies,
  (b) to restate statutory provisions relating to companies, and
  (c) to codify rules of law relating to companies.

(3) Where the proposed order restates statutory provisions, the document must explain which provisions it restates.

(4) The document must identify any new powers conferred by the order to make subordinate legislation.

(5) If the order makes provisions implementing or responding to recommendations of the Law Commission or the Scottish Law Commission, the document must—
  (a) identify the recommendations and the report of the Law Commission or the Scottish Law Commission in which they appeared,
  (b) identify the manner in which the order is intended to implement or respond to each of the recommendations, and
  (c) give details of, and reasons for, any differences between the recommendations and the Secretary of State's proposals.

(6) The document must give details of—
  (a) who was consulted about the proposals for the order,
  (b) any representations received as a result of that consultation (subject to section K13 (confidential representations)), and
  (c) the changes (if any) that the Secretary of State has made to the proposals in response to those representations.

K12 Reasons for proposed order

(1) In relation to provisions of the order that amend the law, the document must explain the Secretary of State's reasons for making the order, including (where appropriate) the ways in which the Secretary of State considers that the amendment would—
  (a) remove inconsistencies or anomalies in the existing law,
  (b) make companies (or particular types of company) a more effective vehicle for conducting business, or
  (c) increase the effectiveness of the system of regulating companies in Great Britain.

(2) In relation to provisions of the order that restate statutory provisions or codify rules of law, the document must explain the ways in which the Secretary of State considers that the restatement or codification would make the law more accessible to, or more easily understood by, those affected by it.

K13 Representations made in confidence etc.

(1) This section applies where a person ("the respondent") makes representations in response to consultation on proposals for an order under this Part.

(2) If the respondent asks the Secretary of State not to disclose his representations, in the document laid before Parliament in accordance with section K11 in respect of the order, the Secretary of State —

  (a) must disclose the fact that the respondent has made representations, but

  (b) must not disclose those representations unless he can do so in accordance with subsection (3).

(3) Representations are disclosed in accordance with this subsection if the disclosure is made —

  (a) with the consent both of the respondent and of any person to whom, or who is carrying on a business to which, the information in the representations relates, or

  (b) in such a manner that the representations cannot be identified with the respondent or with such a person or business.

(4) If information in the representations relates to a person other than the respondent, the Secretary of State is not obliged to disclose that information in the document laid before Parliament in accordance with section K11 in respect of the order if, or to the extent that —

  (a) it appears to the Secretary of State that the disclosure of that information could adversely affect the interests of that person, and

  (b) the Secretary of State has been unable to —

    (i) verify the information, or

    (ii) obtain the consent of that person to the disclosure.

(5) This section does not affect any disclosure that, during the period for Parliamentary consideration (as defined in section K14), is requested by, and made to, a committee of either House of Parliament charged with reporting on the draft order.

K14 Parliamentary consideration of proposals

(1) Where a document has been laid before Parliament under section K11, a draft of an order to give effect (with or without variations) to proposals in that document may not be laid before Parliament before the expiry of the period for Parliamentary consideration.

(2) In this section —

  the "period for Parliamentary consideration", in relation to a document, means the period of sixty sitting days beginning on the day on which it was laid before Parliament;

  "sitting day" means any day other than a day during a time in which Parliament is dissolved or prorogued or in which either House is adjourned for more than four days.

(3) In preparing a draft order to give effect (with or without variations) to proposals in a document laid before Parliament under section K11, the Secretary of State must have regard —

    (a) to any representations made during the period for Parliamentary consideration with regard to the document, and

    (b) in particular, to any resolution or report of, or of any committee of, either House of Parliament with regard to the document.

(4) When he lays the draft order before Parliament, the Secretary of State must also lay a statement giving details of —

    (a) any such representations, resolutions or reports (subject to subsection (5)), and

    (b) the changes (if any) that he has made to his proposals in the light of those representations, resolutions or reports.

(5) Subsections (1) to (4) of section K13 (confidential representations) apply in relation to representations made during the period for Parliamentary consideration as they apply in relation to representations made in response to consultation on a proposal for a draft order.

8 Draft Model Articles of Association for Private Companies Limited by Shares

("THE PRIVATE COMPANY ARTICLES")

GENERAL

1 DEFINITIONS

The special meanings given to certain words and phrases in the articles are set out in the index of defined terms.

DIRECTORS' FUNCTIONS

2 DIRECTORS' GENERAL AUTHORITY TO MANAGE THE COMPANY

(1) The directors' functions are:

   (a) to manage the company's business; and

   (b) to exercise all the powers of the company for any purpose connected with managing the company's business.

(2) The directors may delegate their functions in accordance with the articles.

3 LIMITS ON DIRECTORS' FUNCTIONS

(1) The shareholders may, by special resolution:

   (a) alter the scope of the directors' functions; or

   (b) require the directors to act in a specified manner.

(2) No special resolution passed under paragraph (1) shall have retrospective effect.

DECISION-MAKING BY DIRECTORS

4 SCOPE OF RULES AND POSITION OF SOLE DIRECTORS

(1) References in the articles to decisions of directors are to decisions of directors which are connected with their functions.

(2) Except where the articles expressly provide otherwise, provisions of the articles about how the directors take decisions do not apply:

    (a) when the company only has one director; or

    (b) (when the company has more than one director), to decisions delegated to a single director.

5 DIRECTORS TO TAKE DECISIONS COLLECTIVELY

(1) Any decision which the directors take:

    (a) must be either a unanimous decision or a majority decision; and

    (b) may, but need not, be taken at a meeting of directors.

(2) Except where the articles specify otherwise, the directors may take either a unanimous decision or a majority decision on any matter.

6 UNANIMOUS DECISIONS

(1) The directors take a unanimous decision when they all indicate to each other that they share a common view on a matter.

(2) A unanimous decision need not involve any discussion between directors.

7 MAJORITY DECISIONS

(1) The directors take a majority decision if:

    (a) a matter to be decided has been communicated to every director (other than those whom it is not practicable to contact);

    (b) all the directors who indicate that they wish to discuss the matter have had a reasonable opportunity to communicate their views on it to each other; and

    (c) those directors have together reached a conclusion which a majority of them support.

(2) Directors participating in the taking of a majority decision otherwise than at a meeting of directors:

    (a) may be in different places, and may participate at different times; and

    (b) may communicate with each other by any means.

8   MEETINGS OF DIRECTORS

(1) Any director may call a meeting of directors.

(2) Every director must be given reasonable notice of a meeting of directors.

(3) Paragraph (2) does not require notice to be given:

    (a) in writing; or

    (b) to directors to whom it is not practicable to give notice, or who have waived their entitlement to notice.

(4) Directors participating at a meeting of directors:

    (a) must participate at the same time, but may be in different places; and

    (b) may communicate with each other by any means.

9   MAJORITY DECISIONS – VIEWS OF INTERESTED DIRECTORS NOT TO BE COUNTED

(1) This article applies to any director who has an interest of any kind in an actual or proposed transaction or arrangement with the company.

(2) Subject to paragraphs (3) and (4), when the directors take a majority decision on a matter relating to such a transaction or arrangement, they must disregard the views of any such interested director.

(3) Paragraph (2) does not apply:

    (a) if the director's interest cannot reasonably be regarded as giving rise to any real possibility of a conflict between the interests of the director and the company; or

    (b) if the director's interest only arises because the director has given, or has been given, a guarantee, security or indemnity in respect of an obligation incurred by or on behalf of the company or any of its subsidiaries.

(4) The shareholders may by ordinary resolution decide, either in relation to majority decisions generally or in relation to a particular decision, that the directors shall not disregard the views of interested directors.

10 RECORDS TO BE KEPT

(1) The directors are responsible for ensuring that the company keeps a record of:

    (a) every unanimous or majority decision taken by the directors; and

    (b) every declaration by a director of an interest in an actual or proposed transaction with the company.

(2) Any record kept under paragraph (1) must be kept for at least ten years from the date of the decision or declaration recorded in it.

11 SPECIFIED NUMBER OF DIRECTORS FOR MAJORITY DECISIONS

(1) The directors may make a rule that no majority decision shall be taken unless a specified minimum number of directors participate in the process by which it is taken (a "quorum rule").

(2) A decision to make a quorum rule must be a unanimous decision.

(3) If a quorum rule is in force and the company has one or more directors, but the total number of directors is less than the specified number, the directors must not take any decision other than:

    (a) a decision to appoint further directors;

    (b) a decision that will enable the shareholders to appoint further directors; or

    (c) a decision to modify or abolish the quorum rule and seek the shareholders' approval for such revocation or modification.

(4) In the circumstances specified in paragraph (3), a decision to abolish or modify a quorum rule is of no effect unless it is approved by an ordinary resolution of the shareholders.

12 CHAIRING OF MAJORITY DECISION MAKING PROCESSES

(1) The directors may appoint a director to chair:

    (a) all of the processes by which a majority decision may be taken; or

    (b) a particular process, or processes of a particular type, by which a majority decision may be taken.

(2) The directors may terminate an appointment made under paragraph (1) at any time.

13 CASTING VOTE

(1) The directors may make a rule (a "casting vote rule") that if:

    (a) a majority decision is to be taken on a matter; and

    (b) equal numbers of directors hold differing views on the matter,

    then, subject to paragraph (3), the views of a specified director shall determine the majority decision which is taken on that matter.

(2) A decision to make a rule under paragraph (1) must be a unanimous decision.

(3) A casting vote rule shall not apply if the views of the specified director are to be disregarded as a result of an actual or potential conflict of interest.

14 DIRECTORS' DISCRETION TO MAKE FURTHER RULES

(1) Subject to the articles, the directors may make any rule which they think fit about how they take decisions.

(2) The directors must ensure that any such rule is communicated to all persons who are directors while it remains in force.

DELEGATION

15 DIRECTORS' GENERAL AUTHORITY TO DELEGATE FUNCTIONS

(1) Subject to the articles, the directors may delegate any of their functions to any person they think fit.

(2) The directors must not delegate to any person who is not a director any decision connected with:

   (a) the taking of decisions by directors;

   (b) the appointment of a director or the termination of a director's appointment; or

   (c) the declaration of a dividend.

(3) Any delegation under paragraph (1) may authorise further delegation of the directors' functions by any person to whom they are delegated.

16 COMMITTEES OF DIRECTORS

(1) Two or more directors are a "committee" if the directors have:

   (a) delegated a directors' function to them; and

   (b) indicated that they should act together in relation to that function.

(2) The provisions of the articles about how the directors take decisions shall apply, as far as possible, to the taking of decisions by committees.

APPOINTMENT OF DIRECTORS

17 METHODS OF APPOINTING DIRECTORS

Any person who is willing to act as a director, and is permitted by law to do so, may be appointed to be a director:

   (a) by ordinary resolution of the shareholders; or

   (b) by a decision of the directors.

18 TERMINATION OF DIRECTOR'S APPOINTMENT

A person ceases to be a director as soon as:

   (a) that person ceases to be a director by virtue of any provision of the Acts, or is prohibited by law from being a director;

   (b) any notification to the company that that person is resigning or retiring from office as director takes effect;

(c) the shareholders pass an ordinary resolution removing that person from office;

(d) the directors decide that that person, having repeatedly and without reasonable excuse failed to participate in processes by which majority decisions may be taken, should cease to be a director; or

(e) any contract under which that person was appointed as a director of, or personally performs services for, the company or any of its subsidiaries terminates, unless, immediately after its termination, the contract is renewed or replaced with another similar contract.

19 DIRECTORS' TERMS OF SERVICE

(1) Subject to the provisions of the Acts, the directors may decide the terms (including as to remuneration) on which a director is to perform directors' functions, or otherwise perform any services for the company or any of its subsidiaries.

(2) For the purposes of paragraph (1), "remuneration" includes any arrangements in connection with a pension, allowance or gratuity paid, or to be paid, to or in respect of any person who has been a director of the company or any of its subsidiaries, or any predecessor in business of the company or any of its subsidiaries.

20 DIRECTORS' EXPENSES

Subject to the Acts, the company may meet any expenses which the directors properly incur in connection with:

(a) the exercise of their functions; or

(b) the performance of any other duty which they owe to, or service which they perform for, the company or any of its subsidiaries.

SHARES

21 SHARE CERTIFICATES

The company may issue shareholders with one or more certificates for their respective shares in such form as the directors decide.

22 SHARE TRANSFERS

(1) Shares may be transferred by means of an instrument of transfer in a form permitted by law.

(2) Subject to the Acts, the directors may refuse to register the transfer of a share.

DIVIDENDS

23 PROCEDURE FOR DECLARING DIVIDENDS

Subject to the Acts, the directors may decide to declare and pay such dividends to shareholders as:

(a) appear to the directors to be justified by the company's profits; and

(b) are in accordance with shareholders' respective rights.

24 PAYMENT OF DIVIDENDS

(1) Subject to paragraphs (2) and (3), the company shall pay any dividend or other money payable by it in respect of a share by means of:

(a) a transfer to a bank account specified in writing by the holder; or

(b) a cheque sent by post to the registered address of the holder.

(2) If two or more persons hold a share, or are jointly entitled to it by reason of the death or bankruptcy of the holder (or one of two or more joint holders), the company shall pay any dividend or other money payable by it in respect of the share:

(a) by means of a transfer to a bank account specified in writing by the holder who is named first in the register of members, or a cheque sent by post to that holder's registered address; or

(b) (if the death or bankruptcy of the first named holder has resulted in two or more persons becoming jointly entitled to the share), by means of a transfer to a bank account specified in writing by all the persons jointly entitled to it, or a cheque sent by post to an address specified in writing by them.

(3) The company may agree another means of paying such dividend or other money with any person entitled to specify a bank account under this article.

25 RIGHT TO DIVIDEND FORFEITED IF UNCLAIMED FOR TWELVE YEARS

Any dividend which has remained unclaimed for twelve years from the date when it became due for payment shall, if the directors so decide, be forfeited and cease to remain owing by the company.

MISCELLANEOUS

26 COMPANY SEAL

(1) This article applies if the company has a seal (the "common seal").

(2) The common seal shall only be applied to a document if its use on that document has been authorised by a decision of the directors.

(3) If the common seal is applied to a document, the document shall be:

(a) signed by an authorised person; and

(b) countersigned by another authorised person.

(4) For the purposes of this article, an authorised person is:

(a) any director of the company;

(b) the company secretary (if any); or

(c) any person authorised by the directors for the purpose of signing and countersigning documents to which the common seal is applied.

27 INDEMNITY FOR CERTAIN LEGAL EXPENSES

(1) Subject to the Acts, a director shall be indemnified out of the company's assets against any expenses which that director incurs:

(a) in defending civil proceedings (unless judgment is given against the director and the judgment is final);

(b) in defending criminal proceedings (unless the director is convicted and the conviction is final); or

(c) in connection with any application for relief from liability for negligence, default, breach of duty or breach of trust in relation to the affairs of the company (unless the court refuses to grant the director relief, and the refusal is final).

(2) A judgment, conviction or refusal of relief becomes final if:

(a) the period for bringing an appeal (or any further appeal) has ended; and

(b) any appeal brought is determined, abandoned or otherwise ceases to have effect.

(3) This article is without prejudice to any other indemnity to which a director may be entitled.

INDEX OF DEFINED TERMS

In the articles:

"Acts" means the Companies Acts (as defined in section [XX] of the [Company Law Reform] Act 200[X]), in so far as they apply to the company;

"articles" means the company's articles of association;

"director" means a director of the company, and includes any person occupying the position of director, by whatever name called;

"directors' functions" has the meaning given in article 2(1);

"holder" in relation to shares means the member whose name is entered in the register of members as the holder of the shares;

"majority decision" has the meaning given in article 7;

"ordinary resolution" has the meaning given in section [XX] of the [Company Law Reform] Act 200[X];

"shares" means shares in the company;

"shareholder" means a person who is the holder of a share;

"special resolution" has the meaning given in section [XX] of the [Company Law Reform] Act 200[X];

"subsidiary" has the meaning given in [section 736 of the Companies Act 1985 (as amended and in force when the articles became binding on the company)]; and

"unanimous decision" has the meaning given in article 6.

Annex A

Regulatory Impact Assessment

Introduction

This partial Regulatory Impact Assessment (RIA) supports the Company Law Reform Bill, as described elsewhere in this document.

The Bill builds very heavily on the work of the Company Law Review (CLR), which was taken forward by the Government in the White Paper "Modernising Company Law" of July 2002. This RIA therefore largely updates the analysis published in that White Paper at that time, but now reflects in particular:

- comments received on the previous RIA;

- further evidence received in the course of subsequent formal and informal consultations;

- an assessment of the impact of any modifications to those policies which were set out in the previous document; and

- an assessment of the impact of new policies which have been developed subsequent to the last White Paper.

The Government is determined to ensure that the legal and regulatory framework within which British business operates promotes enterprise and growth, and creates the right conditions for investment and employment. This approach underlies the Government's commitment to creating a modern, enabling and robust framework for our companies

Objectives

The Government's overall objective is to produce clearer law, without unnecessary burdens, and which responds to today's business needs and provides flexibility for the future.

The Government's more specific objectives for reform are set out in the Chapter "Setting the Scene" earlier in this document, where they are discussed under the four key headings:

- *Promoting shareholder engagement and a long-term investment culture*

- *Ensuring better regulation, and a "Think Small First" approach to the law*

- *Making it easier to set up and run a company*

- *Providing flexibility for the future*

Risk Assessment

Britain's existing framework of company law is an asset to its international competitiveness. Britain was amongst the first to establish rules for the operation of companies, and our law has been developing ever since. The law has evolved dynamically, taking account of changes in society and the business environment. It has created a product which is, by international standards, flexible, and has generally served the needs of businesses well. Our law has acted as a model for many countries overseas.

But there are also penalties to having been the first nation to establish the rules for corporate business activity. Where a body of law has been in existence for such a long time, it can become outdated. Parts of the law may become redundant or unnecessary. It may present obstacles to the ways companies want and need to do business in today's world.

The primary risk therefore lies in the potential gradual divorce of the legal framework from the real needs of today's businesses – in particular smaller, private businesses, who form a much more important component of the economy now than was the case when the majority of today's company law provisions had their origin.

Unless this process is checked by a reform programme, a number of unwelcome effects risk appearing. For example, entrepreneurship could be stifled as start-up companies find themselves hindered with unnecessary regulation; and Britain could lose out as a location for business in an increasingly globalised economy where companies are more and more able to choose their place of incorporation.

Options

The Government pursues a number of actions, legislative and non-legislative, to achieve its overall goals in the area of company competitiveness and improved standards of corporate governance. Some of these actions are summarised elsewhere in this White Paper. The present Bill, however, is explicitly a *reform* bill, designed to improve and simplify an existing framework of legislation. Of necessity, therefore, the measures included are of a nature that requires legislative implementation, and any analysis of options is essentially concerned with the questions:

- which provisions of the existing law require reform; and

- what form that reform should take.

The fundamental analysis and discussion of these options was undertaken by the CLR itself in its series of reports on individual areas of the law, and in its final report setting out its key recommendations. The Government's approach to taking forward the majority of these recommendations was largely set out in its 2002 White Paper. The present RIA does not attempt to set out again those alternative options which have been considered and rejected in the past.

It is however worth focusing on those key areas where substantive new policies are being introduced which were not considered in the previous White Paper, and which have not been subject to separate consultation with their own RIAs. Essentially these are:

- Deregulatory changes to facilitate e-communications

- Deregulatory changes to "dematerialise" share certificates

- Changes to the position on auditor liability and audit quality

- Implementation of the Transparency Directive

These policies are described in the body of the White Paper text, with costs/benefits briefly summarised in the table to this RIA. Fuller RIAs for each policy are being published separately on the DTI website.

Costs and Benefits

Methodology

It is important to stress that (perhaps unlike some other areas of regulation) there is relatively little in the way of a research base of hard financial information on the costs to business of compliance with existing company law requirements. The quantifications put forward in this impact assessment therefore rely heavily on information provided by consultees, which is necessarily often anecdotal or imprecise. The Government is very grateful to all those who have helped with this exercise, and would welcome any further evidence – however anecdotal – in order to finalise the assessment.

The table which follows sets out the costs and benefits which may apply to the main elements of the Bill. These costs and benefits generally fall under a number of key headings, which are described and summarised below.

Benefits

Direct (regulatory) benefits

Company law is largely facilitative – there is no natural company, it is a product of the nexus of regulation which creates it. It is arguable therefore that company law does not so much impose burdens, as create a product which is, overall, better or less-well designed and fitted to the purposes it is intended to serve. Nonetheless, where elements of this enabling regulatory framework come to serve no useful purpose, they can act as obstacles to optimal economic performance and create compliance costs which are not justified by any benefit they produce. This is a particular danger where, as with companies legislation, the law has developed over a long period.

To the extent that the law can be remodelled to fit today's needs better, as the CLR and the Government intend, then this will act as a reduction in unnecessary regulation, and can produce direct cost-savings for companies in stripping out unnecessary elements of the total compliance cost.

Estimating these direct savings is very difficult. It is often relatively easy to establish from analysis and consultation that a particular regulatory requirement is more or less redundant, and should be amended or removed, but more difficult to establish what the precise impact will be. The table makes estimates, wherever possible based on input from stakeholders, which suggest that the total direct benefits could be of the order of **£250 million** per year.

Dynamic benefits

As noted above, modernisation of company law, by making the company vehicle better fitted to today's business realities, should reduce compliance costs and produce direct cost savings. But equally important is the potential for improved performance across the economy as a whole if the reforms achieve their objective of, for example, encouraging best practice in company decision-making, in transparency of information, and in shareholder engagement.

It is widely accepted that, even in market economies, government intervention is necessary to correct market failures such as the abuse of monopoly power, the effects of externalities and the adverse impact of asymmetric information and the inability of contracting parties to write complete contracts covering all eventualities.

In the case of companies, the problems of asymmetric information and incomplete contracting manifest themselves in a series of agency problems – namely, the potential conflict of interest between directors and shareholders, the potential conflict between majority and minority shareholders and the potential conflict between the company itself and others with whom it establishes contracts such as creditors, employees and customers. Company law has a major role to play in mitigating the first two of these series of conflicts and a lesser role to play in the third.

In the case of the former, company law can place constraints on the actions of agents. Examples of these would be clarification of directors' duties. It can also determine the nature of the affiliation between principals and agents by setting disclosure requirements for agents as well as exit standards for principals. In addition company law can ensure that the rights of principals are protected. Examples of these would be enhancing the rights of proxies and making it easier for companies to enfranchise the indirect owners of shares.

By mitigating potential conflicts such as those mentioned, and aligning better the objectives of principals and agents, company law can partially mitigate the effects of asymmetric and incomplete information which, in turn, helps to reduce the costs associated with contractual arrangements. When the contractual arrangements are between investors and companies that they invest in, a reduction in agency costs should serve to increase the availability and, possibly, cost of capital which should result in more effective and efficient capital markets.

Better regulation and market confidence

A consistent message from consultees has also been that, if the law can be arranged better to fit the realities of modern business life (particularly for smaller firms), then this will increase business confidence in the overall regulatory environment. This confidence may lead to a greater degree of regulatory compliance[2]. It may also, at a more intangible level, lead to companies feeling more comfortable in the market, more willing to participate and to take informed risks, all of which may act to the ultimate benefit of national economic performance.

Costs

Direct (regulatory) costs

There are only a handful of areas where the Bill will introduce new or stricter regulatory requirements, of a sort which might in principle increase compliance costs. These are almost exclusively confined to public/quoted companies, and are detailed in the table. They are estimated to amount in total to approximately **£6m** per year.

Implementation costs

The changes in the law have been designed so that, with very few exceptions, existing companies will not be required to do anything at the point when the new law comes into force or at any particular point thereafter. In some cases, however, companies will need to act if they to take advantage of the benefits of a new reform. For example, if the company wishes to adopt e-communications with its shareholders as the default, it will need shareholder approval to amend its company's constitution. But it will not be obliged to do if it wishes to continue on its current basis.

[2] For quantification purposes, figures in this RIA assume 100% compliance with the existing law – but where current requirements are widely believed to be unnecessary, and enforcement activity may be correspondingly less strict, it is unlikely that compliance levels are in practice so high.

Familiarisation costs

Any change to the law also brings with it the prospect of familiarisation costs, in other words the necessity for those who use it of learning about the new legal requirements. However, a consistent message from business consultees is that companies themselves very rarely consult the law directly at the moment. In most circumstances where companies are conscious of company law requirements impinging on them, they will look to advisors – for example, lawyers or accountants – to advise them. These professional advisors will of course need to become familiar with the new law, but the professions have well-established programmes of continuous professional development which will in due course no doubt cover the changes to company law. While the cost of such training is ultimately passed on to clients as part of the overhead included in fees charged, we (and consultees, including advisors themselves) do not expect any significant increase in fees directly as result of the changes in this document.

Costs to the public sector

There will be costs associated with the enhanced provision of guidance material, but these will generally grow out of the existing activity of, for example, Companies House and genuinely additional costs should be small.

The changes to the functions and operations of the registrar will impose some additional costs on Companies House. It is not easy to separate out those costs arising directly from the changes in the Bill from those which would in any event be incurred as a result of the administrative changes in train at Companies House to facilitate, for example, electronic filing. Nonetheless, there will be some one-off costs of training and familiarisation for staff, and there may be costs associated with informing business of the new facilities for electronic communication. To the extent that these costs are not absorbed by Government, they may be passed on to businesses in the form of increased transactions costs. However, such increases will be more than compensated for by the cost-savings to business of the new arrangements.

Impact on small business

The "Think Small First" approach lies at the heart of the Government's proposals, and measures in the Bill have very largely been designed with small (private) businesses in mind. The vast majority of British businesses are SMEs, and the impact of out of date, badly-designed or excessively complex regulation can be disproportionate on firms who, for example, do not have much in-house resource available to understand and deal with company law compliance issues. The modernisations proposed in the Bill should therefore have a significant beneficial impact, both by removing substantive unnecessary regulation, and (in many areas) by recasting the law to make it more accessible and comprehensible for smaller firms and their advisors. The proposals have been discussed in detail with smaller firm bodies and their members, and reflect their suggestions for improvements to the current regime.

Results of Consultation

The policy development process leading to the measures in this Bill has been extensively participatory, and has involved several formal consultation stages, as well as continuing informal consultation with key stakeholders. The Government's earlier White Paper, and other formal consultation documents, have included RIAs, and responses to these RIAs inform the current assessment. In addition, the Department sent questionnaires setting out what we believe are the most significant proposals to sample public and private companies, both large and small. Focus groups, and other forms of informal consultation, were also held with representatives of small companies. Consultation on likely costs and benefits was held with these organisations and with other business representative bodies, and with individual companies from their memberships who volunteered to discuss the issues with DTI representatives. We are very grateful for their input.

Competition Assessment

We have considered the impact of the proposals on competition between businesses. The draft Bill will affect all companies. It should result in some savings for all companies, though proportionately more for smaller companies, whilst in respect of one or two specific measures larger (quoted) companies will face additional costs. However, the expected savings and costs do not appear to be sufficiently large to affect competition between companies of different sizes. The Bill will not impose different costs on new and existing companies, and as such we cannot identify any grounds for competition concerns. Consultation supports this view.

Devolution

Company law is a reserved matter, and the measures in this Bill will (for the most part) apply to Great Britain only.

Guidance

Plans for guidance are set out in this White Paper. Given the Government's objective that a crucial element of the modernisation of the law should be to make it more accessible and user-friendly, the proposals on guidance should be seen as an integral part of the reform package overall, and not as an addition to it.

Enforcement

Changes of substance to the offences and sanctions regime in the current Act are discussed elsewhere in this White Paper. The aim is to create a coherent and internally consistent scheme of sanctions which supports the requirements to which they relate in a manner which is fair, proportionate and effective.

In introducing greater clarity to questions as to who is liable for a particular breach in a particular set of circumstances, it is hoped that the regime will lead to greater understanding by participants of the requirements they are under, and potentially better levels of compliance. However, the changes are not designed as such to lead to changes in enforcement patterns, and overall it is not expected that prosecution levels will be significantly affected. Enforcement will, as now, rely on a variety of means depending on the nature of the breach (for example, Companies House will be responsible for enforcing penalties for late filing of accounts and similar offences).

Monitoring and evaluation

Any monitoring and evaluation exercise needs to take account of both the regulatory cost savings expected to emerge from adoption of the proposals as well as the longer term, more intangible benefits to shareholder engagement, promotion of a long-term investment culture, ease of setting up and running a company and providing flexibility for the future.

However, we also need to ensure that familiarisation and related implementation costs are, indeed, as low as we expect them to be. With regard to the short term impact it will be necessary to make use of the many, varied stakeholders who have contributed to the Bill's development. Their contributions have been vital in ensuring that the proposals reflect a wide diversity of views. We can make use of these contacts to monitor implementation progress and to evaluate the longer term benefits of the proposals.

In addition we are developing the methodology to establish a comprehensive stakeholder survey which will enable us to determine the impact of both the Bill, as well as other corporate governance measures, across a wide range of market participants including companies and investors. The ongoing nature of this survey will enable us to monitor the extent to which longer term behavioural changes occur which, we believe, will result in enhanced shareholder engagement and the development of a long-term investment culture. The adoption of such a survey will also enable us to assess, in a more timely manner, when there is a need to introduce further improvements to the legislation to take account of changing company dynamics.

Key measure	Costs	Benefits
Shareholder engagement/long term investment culture		
Fostering shareholder engagement by **enhancing the rights of proxies**, and making it easier for companies to **enfranchise the indirect owners of shares** (where shares are held through an intermediary).	Provisions on proxies will introduce a new regulatory requirement, though one which in practice will only bite on companies with large, dispersed shareholdings. Costs may be of the order of **£1.2m** per year (assuming 50 members in each of 1,200 quoted companies appointing additional proxies at an AGM at a cost to the company of £20 per time). For quoted companies, the new ability for members to demand a scrutiny of polls may impose costs. It is difficult to assess, but assuming that one poll at an AGM for each of 1,200 quoted companies is required, at a cost of £1,000, total costs could be **£1.2m**.	Some elements of the new scheme are designed to make it easier for companies to enfranchise their indirect investors without the need for (as at present) complex legal arrangements. We have no evidence sensibly to estimate how many companies this will apply to or what saving it will produce. Overall a key plank in the overall promotion of shareholder engagement. Difficult to quantify the impact but it should help to align more closely, the interests of shareholders and their agents which, in turn, should reduce investment risk and impact favourably on the cost of capital.
Enabling companies to amend their articles, subject to shareholder approval, to default to **electronic communications**.	This is a facilitative measure. It is not anticipated that any costs, other than a small administrative burden to amend company articles, should be incurred.	The e-communications default facilitation is intended to (a) enhance the timeliness of company communications with shareholders, and (b) facilitate significant cost-savings. Sending paper communications, such as the annual report, can cost as much as £100,000-£400,000 per mailing for companies with large numbers of registered members. An industry working group looking into share dematerialisation and investor enfranchisement has suggested annual cost-savings in the region of **£32-55m**, although further analysis should refine the details of the cost benefits.

Key measure	Costs	Benefits
Providing clarity on the **duties of directors**, enshrining the principle of "enlightened shareholder value", and amending provisions on conflicts of interest.	The clarified duties will be for the most part identical with the current legal position, but they will be more accessibly set out. There should therefore be no costs associated with the change.	The previous White Paper suggested that benefits accruing from greater clarity could be of the order of **£65m** per year (assuming 10% of private companies no longer require legal advice of £500). Though this has not been disputed by stakeholders, it may be towards the top end of the range. The figure includes benefits attributable both to the greater clarity and certainty which directors will have as to their existing duties, and greater exploitation by directors of corporate opportunities (commercial opportunities which they become aware of in the course of their company duties, but which the company itself does not propose to take forward), due to the clarified and slightly deregulated new law.
Who can be a director? At least one director must be a natural person, and no director may be under 16.	There are approx 64,000 corporate directors, but most of these boards also have natural persons as directors. The number of those with only corporate directors is small. Some 500 companies have directors under 16, but they will only have to appoint a replacement if the removal of the child director leaves them without the statutory minimum number of directors. Overall, therefore, these measures are likely to affect only a few hundred companies at most (though company formation agents will in future need to appoint a natural person as director for "off the shelf" companies).	Enforcement of legal obligations generally (and therefore compliance) will be improved by ensuring that every company has at least one director who is an adult, natural person.

Key measure	Costs	Benefits
Putting "**derivative actions**" on a statutory footing. These provide a means for shareholders, including minority shareholders, to act for the company in holding to account directors who have breached their duties.	It is possible but unlikely that the change will affect the number of cases brought. There may be some switching from one jurisdiction to another, but total numbers are low and the impact on the courts likely to be negligible.	Although the number of occasions on which these provisions are used, and hence the direct financial benefit of clarifying them, is small, they will provide an important discipline for directors and "back stop protection" for shareholders.
Auditor liability and audit quality.	The Government anticipates that there would be some direct costs, estimated at **£1.8m**, associated with these proposed reforms, primarily arising from legal and administrative compliance. Such costs relate solely to the new disclosure requirements. See separate RIA for further detail.	The Government believes that three key benefits will accrue from its reforms in this area. They are the: • maintenance of a strong and complete audit market, characterised by (at least) existing levels of competition between audit firms; • an anticipated increase in competition between audit firms in key business sectors, as smaller audit firms seek appropriate opportunities for expansion; • further strengthening in the quality of the British audit.

Key measure	Costs	Benefits
Company takeovers – implementation of the Takeovers Directive. The Bill will place takeover regulation and the takeover regulatory authority (the Takeover Panel) within a statutory framework.	Costs are likely to fall only on those companies with shares traded on a regulated market and result from such companies having to include various facts and figures on the control and structure of their shares in their annual reports and making a report to their shareholders at the companies' AGMs. Cost per company in the first year is estimated to be between £400 and £800, total perhaps **£1m** pa. Costs and benefits are set out in the consultative document – Company Law: Implementation of the European Directive on Takeover Bids – published on the website www.dti.gov.uk/cld/current.htm	Principal benefits will result not from the UK's implementation of the Directive but its implementation by other Member States, which should encourage cross-border takeover activity. There are a number of specific provisions in the Directive that should be helpful in freeing up the market and making it more transparent. Such provisions are, for the most part, already included in takeover regulation in the UK.

Better Regulation and a "Think Small First" approach

Simpler law through: **Separate model articles** for private and for public companies, to ensure in particular that smaller companies are not inadvertently encumbered with unnecessarily complex rules. **Restatement** of law in simpler fashion. **Greater accessibility** by providing targeted and tailored advice.	There will be some costs of familiarisation. However, these are likely to fall almost exclusively on company advisors (particularly formation agents) rather than companies themselves.	Simpler law is crucial to shareholder engagement and to reducing agency costs. The point has been made to us very forcefully by SME representatives that simpler law which "fits small business reality" better will greatly increase business confidence in the overall regulatory environment (which should, not least, increase compliance). Based on feedback from SMEs and their representatives, we estimate cost savings of perhaps **£30m** pa. However, final figures are very much dependent on ultimate drafting of the bill and its regulations. The full benefits of simpler law will also depend crucially on the success of parallel non-legislative measures (accessibility and guidance).

Key measure	Costs	Benefits
The law on **meetings and decision-taking** within companies is currently predicated on the model of large (public) companies. The Bill will simplify the regime for smaller companies to bring it into line with their real needs. In particular, it will **abolish the default requirement for Annual General Meetings** for private companies, and make it easier for **decisions to be taken by written resolution** rather than in physical meetings.	There should be no costs arising from the majority of these measures, which are essentially permissive.	Discussions with stakeholders confirm that changes in this area are likely to produce some of the most significant deregulatory benefits, perhaps as much as **£70m** pa, on estimates of he numbers of small firms who may in future avoid the need for unnecessary meetings which they currently hold. Although at first sight this might seem to make it easier for companies to dispense with input from shareholders, in practice more streamlined and efficient mechanisms for taking shareholder views ought to increase effective shareholder engagement.
Dematerialise equities (i.e. removing the requirement for paper share certificates)	This would be a facilitative measure (although there would be implementation costs for those wishing to take advantage).	See separate RIA for further detail.
Abolition of the requirement for private companies to employ a **Company Secretary**.	It can be argued that the requirement to employ a Company Secretary ensures that there is at least one company officer who focuses on legal requirements, thus improving compliance and reducing risk of penalty.	For the majority of smaller companies, it is unlikely that the requirement adds any value to the position that would anyway apply. Analysis in the previous White Paper estimated benefits at **£5m** per year. Although difficult to quantify, this assumes a saving in paperwork of only £10 for 500,000 companies (the number who currently only have one shareholder) who may choose no longer formally to employ a secretary.

Key measure	Costs	Benefits
Changes to the regime on **offences and sanctions**.	Changes are designed to clarify (rather than to widen or narrow) the scope of liability.	Clarification may, at the margin, enhance compliance, and potentially decrease the need for legal advice (in line with other "simpler law" measures).
Deregulation of requirements on maintaining register of members (in particular in respect of past shareholders)	No obvious costs	Commercial sensitivities mean it is difficult to get a feel for how onerous and costly companies find the current requirements. But ICSA suggest that for some large companies, at least, the savings will be very substantial. Direct savings could well be of the order of **£5 – 10m** pa.
Simplification of capital maintenance provisions, including abolition of the "financial assistance" rules for private companies, which currently prevent private companies from assisting with the purchase of their own shares, and clarifications to the rules on intra group transfers of assets.	No obvious costs	Based on estimates provided to the CLR, may save **£20m** pa in transaction costs which are currently incurred.
The registrar (Companies House)	Many of the proposed changes to the operations of the registrar are facilitative, and the detail of (for example) new filing arrangements will take time to implement. The changes will impose some additional costs on Companies House (and possibly on others, such as formation agents, in so far as they need to adapt to new forms etc), but it not easy to separate out costs arising directly from the changes in the Bill from those which will be incurred as a result of administrative changes already in train.	The changes are generally designed to promote swifter and clearer communication between companies, the registrar, and the outside world. In many cases they will facilitate the use of new e-technologies. Again, it is difficult to separate out specifically Bill-related impacts from others, but the general move to more efficient communications should bring great benefits.

Key measure	Costs	Benefits
Changes to the regime on **reporting and accounting**.	Proposals to reduce filing times for private companies from the current 10 months could in principle impose costs. However, consultation responses from small business organisations suggest that the time-limit proposed – 7 months – will not adversely affect current work patterns. There will be new obligations on public quoted companies to publish material on websites. Given that almost all quoted companies will now have effective websites, the incremental costs should be small, perhaps £250 x 1,200 quoted companies = **£300,000** pa.	Changes to the timescale within which small companies produce accounts, and measures to increase transparency, will be of benefit to third-party small company users of those accounts.
Company charges	Policy options not yet clear	Policy options not yet clear
Implementation of major shareholding disclosure provisions in the **Transparency Directive**.	The reduction in scope of the new regime, compared to the existing regime, is expected to reduce compliance costs. See separate RIA for further detail.	Benefits include a measure of deregulation (by excluding non-traded limited companies from the scope of the regime) and greater harmonisation of European disclosure requirements. See separate RIA for further detail.

Key measure	Costs	Benefits
Making it easier to set up and run a company		
Simplifications to the **company formation process** to make it **easier to set up and run a company.** Including the abolition of the requirement to have an initial "authorised share capital", and abolition of the need for statutory declarations (legally attested signatures).	Simpler formation may encourage greater company numbers. This is not automatically a good thing (if it displaces alternative otherwise efficient business vehicles), but it is probable that it will lead to an overall increase in business activity. There have been some suggestions that excessively easy incorporation procedures could encourage the formation of companies for fraudulent purposes.	Savings are difficult to quantify – though even small benefits may produce large savings given the number of formations per annum. Experts have suggested that the potential for savings here is great; but since the majority of incorporations now happen through agents, we are uncertain how much reduction there will actually be in direct costs to companies. The removal of the requirement for statutory declarations should produce some direct savings (perhaps £5 x 100,000 incorporations per year = **£500,000**), but we believe the generally clearer procedures in the new Bill will produce additional savings, perhaps **£2-4m** pa in total.
Simplification of the law on company names.	No obvious costs.	Reduced risk of a company being required to change its newly-adopted name.
Simplification of the law on trading disclosures. Currently, companies are subject to separate regulatory regimes governing their legal name of incorporation, and the names which they choose to use when trading, respectively. The Bill will create a single set of regulation better adapted to the electronic age.	No obvious costs.	Direct savings will largely arise from removal of unnecessary requirements for displaying names in locations to which customers/suppliers have no access, and on the outside of all company premises. Numbers are unknown, but an assumption of a current cost of placing/maintaining names of £10 pa for some 800,000 live companies would produce savings of around **£8m** pa.

Key measure	Costs	Benefits
Reform law on **directors' home addresses** by giving directors the option of filing a service address for the public record (at present it is a requirement for their home address to be public).	No obvious costs.	Direct savings may be around **£400,000** pa (on basis that currently 4,000 directors have sought orders preserving confidentiality for five years at a cost to them of perhaps £500). But more importantly this removes a real disincentive to those considering becoming directors of controversial companies. The current disincentive appears greatest in the biotechnology industry. Its removal may be a significant factor in helping retain and encourage the domestic biotech industry, with the benefits that flow from this.

Flexibility for the Future

Key measure	Costs	Benefits
Power to reform company law in future by means of secondary legislation	No obvious costs.	Although this measure will be cost-neutral in itself, by ensuring that the law can in future be updated more quickly it should unlock significant benefits in future.
Investigations	No obvious costs.	Benefits will depend on if/how power is used, but cost-savings unlikely to be large (and will mostly accrue to Government).

Annex B

Draft Guidance Notes on Model Articles of Association for Private Companies Limited by Shares (the "private company articles")

1   What are articles of association?

Articles of association ("articles") are rules, chosen by the shareholders, which govern a company's internal affairs. The articles form a contract between a company and its shareholders, and between each of the shareholders.

2   Are all companies required to have articles of association?

Yes. A company is required to have articles by law.

3   Why do companies need articles of association?

The shareholders need to agree how things will be done in a given set of circumstances before a company finds itself in those circumstances (for example, the directors of a company may change and the shareholders may find it helpful to agree in advance how new directors can be appointed). The articles help to ensure that a company's business runs as smoothly and efficiently as possible.

4   Are the articles of association the only rules that apply to companies?

No. The articles supplement other sources of company law, for example, the rules set out in the Companies Act 1985 [and the Company Law Reform Act 200X] and case law (rules made by judges when a company law matter is decided in court).

5   What type of rules do the articles of association contain?

The articles cannot contain rules that are against the law. Providing that the shareholders observe this general principle they have complete freedom to choose which rules go into their company's articles.

6   Do the shareholders have to draw up the rules themselves?

No. The shareholders are free to make their own rules if they wish, but the shareholders may find it convenient to use "ready made articles" (see question 7).

If the shareholders decide to draw up their own rules they should consider whether they need to take legal or other professional advice and have "bespoke" or "tailor-made" articles drawn up for their company.

7 Where can I find a set of "ready made articles" of association?

Model articles for public companies and private companies limited by shares are provided by law. For private companies limited by shares formed after the date private company articles come into force, the model articles are set out in the "private company articles" (see questions 11 and 12).

Shareholders can also purchase articles from law/legal stationers and from formation agents.

8 Do the shareholders and directors have to obey the rules set out in articles of association?

Yes! The articles are legally binding on the company and all of its shareholders (even those who did not vote in favour of some or all of the rules set out in the articles, or who have become shareholders after the company was first formed, or after a particular rule was adopted). The directors of a company must also comply with the articles and if they don't they will be in breach of their duties as directors.

9 How are changes made to the articles of association?

Generally speaking, the articles may be changed by special resolution of the shareholders. In very broad terms, this means that 75 per cent of those eligible to vote on a proposed change must vote in favour of it.

10 What are entrenched articles?

The articles can specify that particular provisions in them can only be changed with the support of a higher (but not a lower) majority of shareholders than would be required to pass a special resolution (for example, they may specify that a particular rule can only be changed by unanimous consent of all of the shareholders). This type of rule is sometimes referred to as an "entrenched provision" or an "entrenched article".

Companies House should be given notice of any entrenched provisions and the articles themselves must also make it clear what conditions need to be satisfied in order to change the entrenched provision in question.

11 What are model articles of association?

These are articles provided by law for certain types of company. The shareholders are not obliged to adopt them, but the relevant model articles for a particular type of company will apply, in their entirety, to companies of that type that do not file articles at Companies House (that is, they become such companies' articles by default). Where a company has filed articles at Companies House, the model articles will plug any gaps in these articles (if a company has not made provision for a given set of circumstances for which there is a rule in the model articles, the rule in the model articles will apply by default unless the company's articles make it clear that the default rule should not apply).

12 What are the private company articles?

The private company articles are the model articles provided by law for private companies limited by shares. They replace Companies Act 1985 Table A (the model articles for public companies and private companies limited by shares formed under the Companies Act 1985) for private companies limited by shares formed under the new Act.

Model articles are also provided for public companies (the "public company articles") and private companies limited by guarantee (the "guarantee company articles"). The public company articles replace Companies Act 1985 Table A for public companies formed under the new Act

13 Are the private company articles suitable for all private companies limited by shares?

No. The private company articles are designed with the needs of typical private companies limited by shares in mind. Such companies are likely to be small and may well be owner-managed (that is, the same people may be the shareholders and directors). The private company articles contain the minimum number of rules which it is envisaged that a typical private company limited by shares will need and which the shareholders will want to have.

Some or all of these rules may be suitable for less typical companies, for example, those with a relatively large turnover or a large number of shareholders. If they are not suitable (or become unsuitable as the company's business develops over time), the shareholders can draw up their own rules (see questions 5 and 6), purchase "ready made articles" (see question 7), or change the private company articles to fit their company's needs (see question 16).

14 Which rules apply to companies formed before the date that the private company articles came into force?

The law will not change for companies that were incorporated before the date on which the private company articles come into force ("existing companies"). If an existing company limited by shares has not filed articles at Companies House, the model (default) articles that apply to that company are the articles set out in Table A applicable when the company was formed.

15 Can existing companies adopt the private company articles as their articles of association?

Yes, in so far as they can change their current articles to articles that exactly match the private company articles. This will normally require a special resolution (see question 9).

In these circumstances the company will need to file the "matching articles" at Companies House or, alternatively, notify the Registrar of Companies that it is using the private company articles as its articles. (As the private company articles do not apply by default to existing companies, such companies need to make it clear – in their articles and on the public register – that they are using the private company articles).

16 What if the rules set out in the private company articles are unsuitable for my company?

The shareholders don't have to use the private company articles. If they do decide to use them, they may add to these rules, or exclude or amend any of the rules set out in the private company articles to such an extent as they see fit (so long as any new or amended rules are not against the law).

The model articles for public companies (the "public company articles") contain a fuller set of rules which the shareholders of private companies limited by shares may wish to use as a precedent. There is nothing to stop shareholders from exactly copying a rule from the public company articles, or from previous versions of the model articles (for example, Companies Act 1985 Table A) but they should consider whether the rule in question would work for their company.

17 If a private company limited by shares re-registers as a public company (or other type of company), which model articles of association will apply to it?

If, prior to re-registration, the company was using model articles (for example, Companies Act 1985 Table A or the private company articles), these will continue to apply to the company on re-registration unless they are amended.

Where a company re-registers from one type of company to another (for example, from private limited by shares to public or vice versa), it needs to ensure that its articles are appropriate to its new status and (where necessary) should take legal or other professional advice regarding its articles and re-registration generally.

18 Do articles of association need to be filed at Companies House?

Where a private company limited by shares and formed under the new Act adopts the private company articles without amendment, there is no need for that company to file articles at Companies House.

Where a company limited by shares and formed under an earlier Companies Act has adopted model articles without amendment (in the case of companies formed under the Companies Act 1985, the relevant model articles are the Companies Act 1985 Table A), there is no need for that company to file articles at Companies House.

In all other cases companies are required to file a copy of their articles (and any subsequent amendments to their articles) at Companies House. This includes amendments to the model articles.

19 Other relevant guidance material

Guidance material on linked areas, for example, conflicts of interest and special resolutions, will be available from Companies House.

Annex C

Miscellaneous Repeals

The development of company law over the last 150 years means that there are many provisions in the current legislation which are no longer required. While some examples of these are given elsewhere in the White Paper, there are also a number of other, more miscellaneous provisions which it is planned to repeal.

For example, while it used to be common for companies to convert their shares into stock, this has been much less significant since the entry into force of the Companies Act 1948. The Bill will therefore remove the ability of companies to convert shares into stock, although it will continue the ability for existing stock to be converted back into shares.

The Bill will also abolish the statutory provisions enabling a company to set aside, by special resolution, some element of its uncalled up share capital which could only be called up in the event of the purpose of the company being wound up.

The Companies Act currently lays down how if a director is required by company's articles to hold a specified share qualification the director can acquire that qualification. These provisions are now obsolete, and will be repealed.

Similarly it is planned to repeal the provisions enabling a limited company, if authorised by its articles, to impose unlimited liability on its directors, managers or any managing director.

It is also proposed to remove the statutory provisions limiting the extent to which a director can assign his or her office to another person.

The rules relating to untaxed payments to directors will also be repealed as they now have no practical effect.

The provisions for insurance, deposit provident or benefit societies to make six monthly statements of their share capital, liabilities and assets will be repealed as this has now been superseded by the Financial Services Authority's prudential supervision.

The Government is also considering the possibility of repealing the requirement that the Secretary of State make an annual report on matters within the companies and insolvency legislation to be laid before both Houses of Parliament. Since this provision was originally enacted, both Companies House and the Insolvency Service have become Executive Agencies laying their own full reports and accounts for [Parliament/House of Commons.] In addition, the DTI publishes its own expenditure plans which are laid before Parliament. The Government notes that relatively few copies of the Companies Act Annual Report are now purchased, probably a reflection of the amount of information being provided in other ways. The Government is therefore minded to drop this requirement.

Annex D

Offences – proposed changes of detail

This list covers those offences, under the current Companies Act 1985, where it may be appropriate to include delegates within the frame of liability (D) and/or to remove liability from the company (not-C). It must be stressed that the list is provisional. Individual decisions in this area are frequently finely-balanced, and the views of consultees will be very important in determining the final arrangements.

19(2)	D not-C		233(6)	D	
20(2)	D not-C		234A(4)	D	
54(10)	D		236(4)	D	
88(5)	D		236(4)	D	
97(4)	D		238(5)	D	
111(3)	D		239(3)	D	
111(4)	D		251(6)	D	
122(2)	D		288(4)	D not-C	
123(4)	D		318(8)		not-C
127(5)	D		322B(4)		not-C
128(5)	D		326(2)	D not-C	
129(4)	D		326(3)	D not-C	
156(6)	D		326(4)	D not-C	
169(6)	D		326(5)	D not-C	
169(7)	D not-C		329(3)	D not-C	
169A(4)	D		348(2)	D	
175(7)		not-C	352(5)	D not-C	
176(4)	D		352A(3)	D not-C	
183(6)	D not-C		353(4)	D	
185(5)	D not-C		353(4)	D	
191(4)	D not-C		354(4)	D	
211(10)	D		356(5)	D	
217(7)	D		380(6)		not-C
218(3)	D		382(5)		not-C
219(3)	D		383(4)		not-C
221(5)	D		425(4)	D	
222(4)	D		426(6)	D	
222(6)	D		427(5)	D	
231(7)	D		461(5)	D	

Annex E

Useful background information

Company Law Review (CLR) Final Report
http://www.dti.gov.uk/cld/final_report/index.htm

Company Law Review (CLR) Consultations:
http://www.dti.gov.uk/cld/reviews/condocs.htm

First (2002) White Paper Regulatory Impact Assessment (RIA) and associated documents: **http://www.dti.gov.uk/companiesbill/index.htm**

Company Law & Governance (CLG) Consultations:
http://www.dti.gov.uk/cld/condocs.htm

Trade and Industry Select Committee (House of Commons)
http://www.parliament.uk/parliamentary_committees/trade_and_industry.cfm

Information on the Companies (Audit, Investigations and Community Enterprise) Bill – C(AICE) Bill:
http://www.dti.gov.uk/cld/companies_audit_etc_act/index.htm

Law Commission websites: **www.lawcom.gov.uk** & **www.scotlawcom.gov.uk**

Companies House website: **www.companieshouse.gov.uk**

Annex F

Code of Practice on Consultations

The Consultation Code of Practice Criteria

1 Timing of consultation should be built into the planning process for a policy (including legislation) or service from the start, so that it has the best prospect of improving the proposals concerned, and so that sufficient time is left for it at each stage.

2 It should be clear who is being consulted, about what questions, in what timescale and for what purpose.

3 A consultation document should be as simple and concise as possible. It should include a summary, in two pages at most, of the main questions it seeks views on. It should make it as easy as possible for readers to respond, make contact or complain.

4 Documents should be made widely available, with the fullest use of electronic means (though not to the exclusion of others) and effectively drawn to the attention of all interested groups and individuals.

5 Sufficient time should be allowed for considered responses from all groups with an interest. Twelve weeks should be the standard minimum period for a consultation.

6 Responses should be carefully and open-mindedly analysed, and the results made widely available, with an account of the views expressed, and the reasons for the decisions finally taken.

7 Departments should monitor and evaluate consultations, designating a consultation co-ordinator who will ensure the lessons are disseminated. The complete code is available on the Cabinet Office's web site: www.cabinet-office.gov.uk/servicefirst/index/consultation.htm

Printed in the UK for The Stationery Office Limited
On behalf of the Controller of Her Majesty's Stationery Office
177571   03/05